Alien-Nation and Repatriation

Alien-Nation and Repatriation

Translating Identity in Anglophone Caribbean Literature

Patricia Joan Saunders

LEXINGTON BOOKS

A division of
ROWMAN & LITTLEFIELD PUBLISHERS, INC.
Lanham • Boulder • New York • Toronto • Plymouth, UK

LEXINGTON BOOKS

A division of Rowman & Littlefield Publishers, Inc.
A wholly owned subsidiary of The Rowman & Littlefield Publishing Group, Inc.
4501 Forbes Boulevard, Suite 200
Lanham, MD 20706

Estover Road
Plymouth PL6 7PY
United Kingdom

Copyright © 2007 by Lexington Books

All rights reserved. No part of this publication may be reproduced, stored in a retrieval system, or transmitted in any form or by any means, electronic, mechanical, photocopying, recording, or otherwise, without the prior permission of the publisher.

British Library Cataloguing in Publication Information Available

Library of Congress Cataloging-in-Publication Data

Saunders, Patricia Joan, 1968-
 Alien-nation and repatriation : translating identity in Caribbean literature / Patricia Joan Saunders.
   p. cm. — (Caribbean studies)
 Includes bibliographical references.
 ISBN-13: 978-0-7391-1469-8 (cloth : alk. paper)
 ISBN-10: 0-7391-1469-7 (cloth : alk. paper)
 ISBN-13: 978-0-7391-1470-4 (pbk. : alk. paper)
 ISBN-10: 0-7391-1470-0 (pbk.)
 1. Caribbean literature—20th century—History and criticism. 2. Identity (Philosophical concept) in literature. I. Title.
PN849.C3S28 2007
809'.89729—dc22   2007028975

Printed in the United States of America

∞™ The paper used in this publication meets the minimum requirements of American National Standard for Information Sciences—Permanence of Paper for Printed Library Materials, ANSI/NISO Z39.48–1992.

For the women in my family, whose determination created
the freedom and space to think and dream

Linda Inez Blackman
(1911–1993)

Cynthia Jones
(1933–1993)

Elaine Joan Saunders
(1920–1997)

Contents

Acknowledgments	ix
Foreword	xiii
Introduction: Imagining the Impossible	1
1 The Trinidad Renaissance: Building a Nation, Building a Self	25
2 The Pleasures/Privileges of Exile: Re/covering Race and Sexuality in *The Pleasures of Exile* and *Water with Berries*	57
3 Gender and Genre: The Logic of Language and the Logistics of Identity	87
4 Routes and Roots: Re(in)scribing the Meaning of Home	113
5 Boundaries, Borders, and the Unhoused: Re-Routing Black Identity in North America	131
Conclusion: Mapping Meaning and Identity	153
Bibliography	161
Index	175
About the Author	181

Acknowledgments

This book has been very long in the making and as a result there are quite a few people and places to acknowledge. I would like to thank Adele Newson, who encouraged me to put the world of natural sciences on hold long enough to see if my interest in arts and letters might be more than just something I enjoyed in the spare time between agronomy and botany courses. I am sure conservationists the world over are quietly thanking you also. To Shalini Puri, Nancy Glazener, John Beverley and Susan Andrade, whose care, patience and intellectual energy helped to fuel this project in its earliest stages, my deepest appreciation. As a graduate student, I was of the mind that academic work required solitude, vast quantities of good food (preferably curried) and a good personal library. However, during my time at the University of Maryland, I learned one of the more important lessons in my life as a scholar, teacher and friend: an intrinsic part of a scholarly life is being "in community." For this lesson, your friendship, support and commitment to staying "in community," my deepest thanks to Mary Helen Washington.

There are also friends and colleagues whose intellectual support for this project cannot go unacknowledged: thanks to Majorie Thorpe, Paula Morgan, Glyne Griffith, Kezia Page, Winnifred Brown-Glaude, Donette Francis, Charles Carnegie, Jennifer Rahim, Eintou Pearl Springer and Michelle Rowley whose conversations prodded me to think more critically about this project; your generosity with time, ideas, personal libraries, and hospitality are the reason this project has made it this far. Thanks also to the "grown lady" for whom shoes are a way of life, and to another dear friend whose choicest words come to mind now that this book is done: "yuh see that, yuh see that, we have had another lovely repasssst!" There are friends who you know you can count on for liming, a good film, ole talk, retail therapy and eating chocolate (and did I mention curry?) in vast quantities: particularly Roanna Gopaul, Lynette Brown-Joseph and Ramotse Saunders, thanks for taking the time.

The librarians at West Indiana Collection at the Main Library at the University of the West Indies (U.W.I.), St. Augustine deserve special thanks for their professionalism, their keen interest and enthusiasm about this project, especially Kim Gransaull, Gloria Baptise and Kathleen Helenese-Paul, without whom this project would not have been completed. Also, my heartfelt thanks to the Department of Liberal Arts and the Centre of Gender and Development Studies at the U. W. I., St. Augustine, whose faculty and staff welcomed me into their intellectual community while also creating a space for me to contribute to their thriving academic environment. Your continued support of academics throughout the African diaspora remains an integral part of growing the field of Caribbean Studies nationally and internationally. In this same vein, I want to extend my deepest gratitude to my colleague and friend, Sandra Paquet, whose support of scholars in Caribbean Studies has created a permanent space for critical dialogue, research support and a model for building intellectual communities nationally and internationally. This book would not have been completed without support from several educational institutions and granting agencies. I wish to express my appreciation to the Mellon Foundation, the Porter Fellowship from Bowdoin College, the Ford Foundation's Emerging Voices, New Directions Grant and the Max Orovitz Award from the University of Miami, Coral Gables.

My family has remained a constant source of support, especially those in Trinidad who made coming home to work both productive and enjoyable including my aunts: Ruth Saunders and Marva Benjamin, and my uncle, Ramsey Saunders. To my parents, siblings and extended family, all of whom offered their continued support and encouragement even when they weren't quite sure why this book was taking so long; my gratitude and love to each of you. There are those friends who stand by you, and then sometimes in front of you, as the times, thoughts, and life situations warrant, whose constant and quiet (at times, but not always) persistence, support and faith in me and this book at times exceeded my own: Michelle Rowley, Barbara McCarthy and Joseph C. Razza III, our friendship is such that there is not enough time or space in this lifetime to thank you. To the families of my closest friends, who opened their arms, hearts, and kitchens (especially the ovens) and made your homes a place where I could feel welcomed, you all are responsible for bringing me to a deeper understanding of what "home" really means, and for this I am eternally thankful. There are also those special people in life you meet, lose touch with, and happily reconnect with after many years; G. you must know by now that ours was not a chance encounter and that second chances, though rare, are certainly to be treasured and enjoyed.

And last, but by no means least, there are those in whose loving memory this work is dedicated, knowing that you would expect nothing less than me doing what I put my heart and mind to, keeps me centered and grounded in the assurance that I belong, and have always been, at home in the world.

Foreword

The latest book in the Caribbean Studies Series, Patricia Saunders's *Alien-Nation and Repatriation: Translating Identity in Anglophone Caribbean Literature*, draws on the work of feminist scholars and postcolonial, psychoanalytic, and poststructuralist theorists to explore what she sees as the "limits" of the Calibanesque tradition in Caribbean literature for political subjectivity and social ontology. Saunders explores these limits by examining the possibilities for women in anticolonial narratives written prior to the instantiation of *and restriction to* the normative maternal and domesticated body as the only one that could support the symbolic articulation of a viable nationalism. By focusing on both the imaginative possibilities and the aesthetic closures around the woman's body, Saunders offers a much-needed evaluation not only of the relationship between literature and politics but specifically of that between women's subjectivity and national identity. As the most recent in a new wave of investigation into Trinidadian nationalism, *Alien-Nation and Repatriation* offers a significant addition to the nexus of criticism on Caribbean nationalism, migration, and transnational studies. What distinguishes Saunders's work, however, is what it demands: that the specific epistemological and ontological problems posed for women by either the hegemony of empire or the hegemony of anticolonial and postcolonial cultural nationalism need to be formally read back into the tradition as a significant epistemic flaw with consequences for truly libratory and "alter/native" subject positions. Fundamentally, Saunders suggests that the continued representation of women as "absent present" subjects in literature restricts Caribbean subjectivity by undermining the imaginative ground for figuring politico-cultural identity, and it has resulted in the loss of a critical realism.

In her initial consideration of Trinidadian nationalism, Saunders examines early articulations of a politicized social consciousness and anticolonial aestheticism in the literary magazines, *Trinidad* and the *Beacon* during the 1920s and 1930s. She argues, through her reading of the "barracks-yard fiction" of C. L. R. James and Alfred H. Mendes, that that literature should not be dismissed as realist fiction or a check on the moral aestheticism of Victorian literature. In taking up and configuring a new aestheticism with which to reflect the subjectivity of those whose identities were formed at the limits of formal economy (political, sexual, and material), James's and Mendes's work lay bare the systems of meanings and signifying practices that actually produced those subjects in the burgeoning economic and social categories of early twentieth-century Trinidad. Saunders demonstrates how the protonationalism of this anticolonial aestheticism "engendered a woman-centered national space" that did not reify middle-class sexuality or cultural values as did the later fiction. As the political landscape changed and the elite began to assert their economic dominance and cultural hegemony, the tradition changed, circumscribing this representation of poor female subjects, and in turn this specific sociocritical function of anticolonial literature in which the primacy of race and nation *over* gender had not yet become formative. Through analysis of, among other texts, George Lamming's *Water with Berries*, Saunders argues that while the "exile" of writers like Lamming created an epistemological opening for the male subject, it could not for women. This was not strictly because of the circumstances of women's crossing but because that opening was also one with the early anticolonial modes of representing women's social ontology. The embodiment of the male subject rested upon a reification of the social marginalization of women or their exile at "home."

Saunders, however, is not satisfied with the foreclosure of possibility for female subjectivity and Caribbean subjectivity as a whole. Through a reading of M. NourbeSe Philip's *She Tries Her Tongue, Her Silence Softly Breaks*, Saunders looks at the potential of this kind of literature to create new epistemological possibilities by the imaginative reordering of language and by articulating the relationship of being to meaning as provisional or experimental, rather than fixed. She suggests that the relation between meaning and being is provisional or experimental. This provisionality is not only the new episteme but, in a key link with the early anticolonial aestheticism, is also a recovery of original spaces of possibility. With Philip's work and a reading of Erna Brodber's *Louisiana*, Paule Marshall's *Brown Girl, Brownstones*, and Elizabeth Nunez's *Beyond the Limbo Silence*, Saunders shows the potential of the "demonic ground" (Wynter) of Caliban's absent mother and mate to "repatriate" Caribbean woman's subjectivity and to house the ground of self-creation at the margin of contemporary, post/colonial aestheticism.

S. Jackson, coeditor
Caribbean Studies Series

Introduction:
Imagining the Impossible

> The position from which I write this introduction is a hazardous and difficult one, if only because its fluidity does a disservice to the fixedness implicit in the word "position." It is, however, appropriate that I should be writing this introduction in Tobago, since this is the first and remembered place of exile. Exile—which has come to be the signature and permanent mark of the modern age.
>
> M. NourbeSe Philip,
Frontiers: Essays and Writings on Racism and Culture

EPISTEMOLOGY AND THE PROCESS OF BE(COME)ING WEST INDIAN

My engagement with the concept of re(in)forming fictions and disciplinary discourses begins as a cartographic effort to read and translate the imaginative terrain of Caribbean nationalist narratives. Like most cartographies, this one is based on a few centering discourses about race and identity in the New World and, therefore, I return to some of the prominent texts that provide the "truth claims" upon which colonial expansion was authorized and later institutionalized. This point of departure continues critical considerations of the importance of the imagination for black subjects seeking to make their being-in-the-world intelligible in the face of hundreds of years of scientific research that categorized blacks as "non-human" beings. Like Benedict Anderson, I am interested in the extent to which communities construct their identities through acts of imagination.[1] However, rather than conceiving of the nation as a shared experience imagined by people of a particular community, this book examines how acts of the imagination extend beyond the unconscious, to reshape the relational perspective of historical subjects to their surroundings.

The events of September 11th and the subsequent fallout, along with the recent riots and uprisings by African and Arab immigrants in Paris, France, have made it clear that the extent to which "nations" share common values and ideologies depends largely on questions of economic stability, military strength, and racial, ethnic, and cultural allegiances. These events have initiated a renewed urgency to re-examine what is at stake in constructing national identity. Anne McClintock contextualizes the historical and political stakes in all nationalist projects through an insistence that we conceptualize the nation as a gendered space with specific implications for the sociohistorical practices of communities.[2] Identifying epistemological and ontological violence as interminable aspects of all imagined communities, McClintock asserts that

> All nationalisms are gendered; all are invented; and all are dangerous—dangerous, not in Eric Hobsbawm's sense of having to be opposed but in the sense that they represent relations to political power and to the technologies of violence. As such, nations are not simply phantasmagoria of the mind; as systems of cultural representation whereby people come to imagine a shared experience of identification with an extended community, *they are historical practices through which social difference is both invented and performed.* Nationalism becomes in this way constitutive of people's identities through social contests that are frequently violent and always gendered.[3]

McClintock's effort to reconnect the space of the imagination to historical practices points to the relevance of the politics of the imagination in postcolonial and neocolonial literatures and cultures. Her emphasis on the "invention and performance" of difference suggests that history is, in fact, not opposed to the imagination but depends upon the imagination for its continuous renaissance. By identifying the nation within a context of contested social and gendered spaces, McClintock implicates normative institutional discourses by suggesting that the nation, far from being a coherent, mutually compatible space, is composed of individuals and communities struggling for control of the images, ideas, and discourses that are the foundations of the "nation" (imagined or otherwise).

The difficulty of representing positions and even positionalities is a shared one that frames this book and most debates about identity and belonging. This concern emerges out of an appreciation of the complex nature of being-in-the-world experienced by postcolonial subjects in the Caribbean, particularly within their mindscapes and landscapes. While seemingly cliché, the need to "go back" to a source or originary narrative is of singular importance for understanding the implications and the need for black subjects to reimagine their selves and their being-in-the-world continuously. However, this return is not simply a desire to trace narratives of origin. Rather, it is a critical perspective that acknowledges the countless ruptures of history, time, culture, identity, and Being.[4] The "fixedness," to which Philip refers, marks the ways we, as readers, are disciplined into relationships with words and ideas. The meanings of words like History,[5] language, identity, knowledge, Third World, nation, and Being have as much to do with our "locations" (geographical, political, cultural, social) as they do with the context within which these words are introduced, circulated, revised, and reinvented.

The act of looking back or reflecting is not an effort to return to a romanticized linear narrative of forward progress, but an effort to reverse into Selves that have been buried and silenced within the recesses of institutional discourses on identity and being. This book proposes an examination of the impulse to return through the paths of migration, exile, and repatriation. The overarching concern in this effort is to examine how critical distance from one's geographical, ideological, and national locations invests the acts of departure and return, in their myriad forms, with increasing significance as part of a diasporic practice and performance of identity. Exile, as M. NourbeSe Philip notes, is the signature of the modern age, and arguably the postmodern era as well. The desire to remember the home space is evident, albeit undependable in its uncertainty and inevitable disruptions by the fancy of the imagination. The shifts or unanticipated ruptures in memory can be said to represent intrusions of other faculties upon which the memory depends for its formation. These intrusions offer us a glimpse into the various states of consciousness and the processes involved in the formation of a conscious subject in history.

Carolyn Cooper's notion of "transmigration" articulates the processes of be(come)ing in twentieth-century Caribbean literature. For Cooper, transmigration is a "metaphorical representation of migrating states of consciousness and knowledge."[6] These states, however, are not final points on a continuum of possible ways of being-in-the-world, but are possibilities for thought and be(come)ing for colonial subjects. The problematic of imagining myself, my identity, my "home," bears some resemblance at political and cultural levels to the epistemological and ontological crises under consideration here. When I began writing this book in 2002, the task of identifying difference, once solved by state-sponsored organs such as the census, immigration offices, and other such accounting systems, bore less and less relevance to the ways that citizens imagined themselves and their communities. This reality continues to exert itself on the governmental and national pathways of arrival, belonging, and citizenship to the extent that waves of forced repatriation seem to be the easiest means of repressing the forces that threaten to expose the limitations of nationalism and patriotism on a global scale. With the advent of the "new wars" (against terrorism, fundamentalism, neofacism, etc.) of the millennium comes a rigid reinforcement of the methods and practices deployed by governments and government agencies to identify and police the location and movement of bodies of difference (religious, epistemological, and ontological), as well as "different" bodies (Arab, Latino, black) across international boundaries. Efforts by superpower states to legislate uniform imaginations of the nation-state in order to consolidate a national identity have proven, in their very early stages, to be an important indicator of how the fissures and ruptures in imagination can pose a threat to the collective remembering of histories and lived realities.

McClintock's observations about invention, like Philip's cautions about the situatedness of the Self within constantly changing discourses of difference, offer productive points of entry into examinations of identity and being in Anglophone Caribbean literature. For the last hundred years, Caribbean writers have attempted to move between these two possibilities—of invention and situatedness—in an effort to craft an existential space for their selfhood. Thinking about the nation or national identity in the Caribbean demands that we first understand the social and historical circumstances from which, in Edouard Glissant's words, the Caribbean "irrupts" into modernity.[7] In *Writing in Limbo: Modernism and Caribbean Literature*, Simon Gikandi highlights this distinction between Caribbean modernism and European modernism, characterizing this irruption as a point of engagement and debate within Caribbean and African American cultural studies.[8] For Gikandi, the project of modernity, far from being an alienating force in Caribbean literature and culture, generated a unique response to the imperialist impulses that were an integral component in Anglo-American modernism.

Rather than seeing modernism as antithetical to cultural analyses in the African Diaspora, Gikandi proposes an alternative approach to the binary opposition of modernism and Caribbean literature:

> The long history of colonialism in the Caribbean, and the construction of its cultural landscape under European hegemony, have generated what Glissant aptly calls the region's irruption into modernity as a violent departure from the colonial tradition. Two themes, then, will help us conceptualize this irruption and the narrative and discursive techniques it generates: first, I argue that Caribbean modernity has evolved out of an anxiety toward the colonizing structure in general and its history, language and ideology in particular; second, I examine how this modernism, which is closely related to the process of creolization, develops as a narrative strategy and counter-discourse away from outmoded and conventional modes of representation associated with colonial domination and colonizing cultural structures.[9]

For colonial subjects, constructing a cultural landscape without the immanence of hegemonic structures of colonialism meant first creating a space within their epistemologies to conceptualize an alter/native reality. The possibility of change, of altering discourses of identity in the interest of arriving at an indigenous (or native) articulation of the experience of colonialism, depended largely on embracing their own alienation from their surroundings while also returning to these spaces to discover them anew. The problematic of keeping the nightmare of History at bay while attempting to institute their historical existence as a community of people produces the "anxiety" to which Gikandi refers. I would argue that this "anxiety" proved to be a productive point of engagement that forced Caribbean writers to conceptualize alter/native realities despite the absence of adequate epistemological systems to accommodate these realities.

The epistemological and ontological terrain of the debate commonly characterized as the "Quarrel with History" was initiated by Columbus's 1492 encounter with native peoples in the New World and informed by an imperialist agenda concerned with instituting social and economic structures upon which European national identities could be concretized.[10] One of the first steps in this nation-building project was to build a national literature that would institute a master narrative of History against which all subsequent narratives would have to define and measure themselves. These contestations of imaginative space, because they are concerned with the larger project of articulating national identities, have manifested themselves in very particular forms in Caribbean literature. Generations of Caribbean writers have engaged the problematic of any chronology of the capital "H" history that assumes a narrative of progression beginning with 1492 as the "originary" moment. As Gikandi and Glissant both note, the "irruption" of the Caribbean into modernism meant that modalities for understanding or experiencing reality needed to be drastically altered. The counter-discourses to which Gikandi refers emerge out of a need to express changing realities—one of which is the "lived reality" of modernism—that challenged entrenched colonial structures and ideologies. According to Glissant, the idea of differing from or opposing lived realities speaks to specific impulses that take root in the Caribbean because of the circumstances under which the region was birthed. These circumstances are fertile ground for creating the "counter-discourses" to express the transmigratory subjectivity of Caribbean peoples.[11]

Where Gikandi deploys the concept of "counter-discourses" to describe new forms of representation in Caribbean literature, I employ the phrase "re(in)forming fiction" as a means of challenging the metanarratives that shape the Quarrel with History. The term "re(in)forming" describes how counter-discourses operate epistemologically and ontologically. More than any other term that could be used here, this phrase conceptually facilitates a critical analysis aimed at dislocating the discursive communities that inform the dialogic relationships between constructions of colonial identities and the lived experiences of colonial subjects. Glissant rationalizes the impulse toward counter-discourses in Caribbean literature by asserting that it expresses the relational nature of Caribbean subjects to concepts of time, history, and language in a modernist context:

> The very words and letters of the American novel are entangled in the strands, in the mobile structures of one's own landscape. I do not practice the economy of the meadow, I do not share the serenity of the spring. But what we do have in common is the irruption into modernity. We do not have the time, we are everywhere driven by the daring adventure of modernity. We do not have a literary tradition that has slowly matured: ours was a brutal emergence that I think is an advantage and not a failing. The irruption into modernity, the violent departure from tradition, from literary "continuity," seems to me a specific feature of the American writer when he wishes to give meaning to his environment.[12]

As Glissant notes, the discursive, geographic, and cultural landscapes out of which New World representations emerge reflect the ruptures and fissures in the formation of Caribbean cultures. For Caribbean writers, the march is best described as a lunge into possibility because it was impossible to "escape the anxieties generated by their historical conditions—they were colonial subjects and they had to write for or against colonial modernism."[13]

Read differently, Glissant's insistence (on the relational nature of the surroundings out of which meaning is produced and interpreted) shares an affinity with Gayatri Spivak's contemplative analysis of the condition of the "native informant" of postcolonial literature and philosophy. What Glissant terms the "economy of the meadow" is intricately constructed through particular attention to the discursive frontiers of "Nature" that produced the native informant as located outside of and even beyond this tradition and system of signification and, ultimately, recognition. According to Spivak,

> The possibility of the production of the native informant by way of the colonial/postcolonial route and thus, ultimately, books such as this one, is lodged in the fact that for the real needs of imperialism, the in-choate in-fans ab-original para-subject cannot be theorized as functionally completely frozen in a world where teleology is schematized into geo-graphy (writing the world). This limited access to being-human is the itinerary of the native informant into the postcolonial, which remains unrecognized through the various transformations of the discussions of both ethics and ethnicity.[14]

The implications and affinities between the critical perspectives outlined above require further consideration because of the linkages they share. The most important affinities in this case are the shared axes of culture, representation, and difference in postcolonial literature. Whether this difference is articulated through writing and speech or ethics and aesthetics, Glissant and Spivak are concerned with two things: how we read and interpret cultural difference (discursively) and what these reading practices make possible in the way of knowledge produced about the differentiated subject: the Other or the native informant.

If, as Spivak asserts, "ab-original" subjects are admitted provisionally in a teleology that limits them to their "discovery," we can begin to understand the impulse by Caribbean writers to engage the category of History in order to resolve the contradiction between "what *can* be known and what *must* be thought."[15] The point of engagement for Caribbean writers, the Quarrel with History, far from simply attempting to construct a recognizable version of Caribbean history, is concerned with the way in which the preoccupation with this category functions at the level of discourse. The discursive analysis is important because, as Spivak and Glissant assert elsewhere, the preoccupation with History diverts critical attention from the existence of the subject itself. While the inescapability of History is obvious, the journey of the native informant cannot be determined by the limits of this knowledge. The challenge facing Caribbean writers requires a reconsideration of how History circulates and is represented as an authorizing discourse within Caribbean literary traditions. The task of revising, not only *how* we read History, but to what ends, is the baggage accompanying the "native informant" on her trip into the experience of being-human, without limitations. This latter engagement is what Spivak refers to as "what *must* be thought."[16] If nothing else, the reality of a pre-contact existence prior to the "first encounters" or (at the very least) a post-Prospero/postcolonial existence, created an opening for colonized subjects to begin to reimagine their relationship to an "Elsewhere" (England and, recently, the United States of America) that dominated the imaginations and realities of Caribbean writers. In order to "rethink" their epistemic relationship to Caribbean culture, the first wave of Caribbean writers strove to reinvent and re(in)form their ways of knowing and their interpretative tools for reading and representing themselves in relation to this culture.

Scientific and cultural claims about race were founded on tenets that included the inability of blacks and other "natives" to create art, to reason, and, last but not least, to appreciate beauty and exercise aesthetic judgment. A cursory glance at some of the ideological underpinnings of Enlightenment discourses is necessary here in order to situate the political, cultural, philosophical, and scientific aims of representing identity in the African Diaspora. The authoritative discourses that emerged during the Enlightenment made any ontological existence beyond the "first encounter" of 1492 impossible for colonial subjects. New World "geo-graphy, or writing the world," as Spivak terms it, effectively scripted the colonial Other into the imaginative landscape of Europe as the "raw man" who is "almost human *only by nature*."[17] The task, therefore, of becoming (a Being) depended on inhabiting a new epistemic *vrai*, one not defined by the teleology of the universal project of instituting (European) Man as the purpose of all creation.[18] Once more, this task bears the indelible mark of Empire based on the binary oppositions that have become pillars of the imperialist projects. However, as Spivak rightfully asserts,

> The binary opposition between master and native cannot bear the weight of a mere reversal. Kant "was no crook; indubitably, as he embarked on his great voyages of discovery, he was the great civilizer, a great Prospero of the Enlightenment." Although Shakespeare was great, we cannot merely continue to act out the part of Caliban. One task of deconstruction might be a persistent attempt to displace the reversal, to show the complicity between native hegemony and the axiomatics of imperialism.[19]

Part of the preoccupation with History on the part of Caribbean writers is aimed at loosening Prospero's hold on the New World, particularly in relation to language and representation. However, the task of leaving behind Caliban's inheritance has been a far more difficult process.

In order to relinquish the "supporting role" as Caliban, historically reserved for colonized subjects, Caribbean writers needed first to address their complex relationship to their colonial masters and colonial culture. One of the most effective approaches to representing these complexities was precisely the reversal that Spivak cautions against. This reversal served an important political and cultural function in Caribbean literary traditions. If nothing else, these reversals, or re-visions of Shakespeare's texts and protagonists, provided a paradigm, albeit hegemonic in its own right, for Anglophone Caribbean writers to imagine their relationship as exiled writers in relation to the *British* nation-state. There are, however, other representations of this relationship that engage the "colonizer/native" opposition through alter/native paradigms, many of which address the issue of native hegemony within the context of Caribbean nationalism.

One such instance is the marked disjuncture between the Quarrel with History and contemporary literature by Caribbean women writers. Women's articulations of their historical experiences were marginalized because they did not reflect the agendas of nationalist politics. Moreover, the critical practice of reading Caribbean women's literature through the telos of the Calibanesque tradition limited the kind of knowledge produced about their subjectivity. When this was not the case, their narratives and experiences were spoken and written about (and for) in such a way as to suggest that, as part of the "body politic," they were invested in maintaining the cohesive voice of national politics and identity. To gain entry into this system of signs that informed Caribbean nationalist literature, women writers had to forge a unique relationship to colonial history in order to represent their experiences, while also trying to negotiate the terrain of West Indian nationalism in all its complex manifestations. This effort has taken on several forms, including re(in)forming the scope of our current modes of knowing history, being, and identity. Erna Brodber, in "Oral Sources and the Creation of a Social History of the Caribbean," argues that the history studied by generations of Caribbean writers bears little or no resemblance to their pasts and, as such, limits the nature of the relationship between the subject and her or his surroundings. If we consider the criteria by which history is judged, another problem emerges. Brodber notes that "for the story to be history, it must not only be plausible, but the events of which it consists must have been reported by several persons."[20] When historians are faced with the prospect of constructing histories from their own perspectives, this requirement of "factual support" remains the major pitfall for Caribbean historians. The demand for "evidence" that is supported by factual accounts assures that the experiences represented in most histories of the Caribbean are barred from consideration in the academic annals of History. In response to this demand, generations of Caribbean writers have set out to construct their historical perspectives through fictional accounts culled from oral accounts recorded in historical documents.

However, Brodber poses an important critical question, noting that the relationship of the writer to the "field" or "data" separates these narratives from history proper. She asserts that "What conclusively separates these works from history is the relationship of their writers' 'I' to his data. While the historian, having collected his data, leaves them to move logically to a conclusion, the creative writer can impose his own sense of justice, his own feeling upon the data and guide them to a conclusion which accords with this prejudice."[21] This approach to writing history infuses the narratives with some insight (an eye/I) into the emotional and psychological dimension of historical events in the Caribbean. The creative intervention on the part of the writer, while giving a shape to the skeleton of history that remains in the Caribbean, also confines these narratives to the realm of "fiction." The question that continues to plague Caribbean writers is, "where, if not in the imagination of the creative writers, will we find admissible data on the behavior of people who left no memoirs?"[22] V. S. Naipaul poses the questions in more detail:

How can the history of this West Indian futility be written? What tone shall the historian take? Shall he be as academic as Sir Alan Burns, protesting from time to time at some brutality, and setting West Indian brutality in the context of European brutality? Shall he, like Salvador Madriaga, weigh one set of brutalities against another, and conclude that one had not been described in all its foulness and that this is unfair to Spain? Shall he, like the West Indian historians, who can only now begin to face their history, be icily detached and tell the story of the slave trade as it if were just another aspect of mercantilism?[23]

While none of these options seems viable, there is indeed a need to tackle this dilemma, as it has plagued and continues to plague Caribbean writers for well over a century. This problem is further complicated when we consider the dilemma of representing women's history in the Caribbean.

The problematic outlined above is indeed challenging for Caribbean writers, particularly when neither the subject of history nor the historian is male, as Naipaul's passage assumes she or he will be. Brodber argues that one approach to solving this problem is extending the boundaries of research and "admissible evidence" to include sources such as oral histories given by the children and grandchildren of former slaves.[24] While this strategy is probably the most viable one offered to date, there remains the question of writing Caribbean history based on the assumption that the subject of this inquiry is male. Are we to assume that we can understand the social dilemmas of women during slavery based on these accounts? More importantly, when we consider the project of writing post-emancipation Caribbean histories, how can we represent women's existential and political dilemmas as historical subjects caught between colonialist and nationalist discourses that negate their presence while narrating the nation through their bodies?

Abena Busia describes the constructed absence of black female subjects, asserting that where "the colonized male encounters not himself, but his antithesis; the colonized woman encounters only erasure."[25] I want to suggest, however, that this erasure does not delete the subject without leaving some evidence, some trace of her presence, even if it signifies as absence. This "absence" offers us another means for (re)producing an epistemological and ontological possibility for Be(come)ing. This absence does not appear as a "gap" in colonial narratives, nor does it always represent a "lack" in the system of significations of Otherness. One of the earliest critical studies dedicated solely to West Indian women's writing, Evelyn O'Callaghan's *Woman Version: Critical Approaches to West Indian Fiction by Women*, describes the need to create new interpretative tools for reading this new body of writing. Drawing from African American musical traditions, West Indian musical forms such as "dub," and a long tradition of "master narratives" in Caribbean literature, she argues that the new body of West Indian women's writing is concerned with (re)producing, remixing, writing over, and thus creating its own versions of historical narratives that have, until now, constructed women as silent/absent subjects. O'Callaghan suggests that a useful strategy would

> approach this writing, in light of the above, as a kind of remix or dub version, which utilizes elements from the 'master tape' of Caribbean literary discourse (combining, stretching, modifying them in new ways); announces a gendered perspective; adds individual styles of 'talk over'; enhances or omits tracks depending on desired effect; and generally alters by recontextualization to create a *unique* literary entity.[26]

O'Callaghan's observations are similar to the set of concerns I address in philosophical debates about the *nature* of being for colonial subjects. Her formulation of the "dub version" in West Indian women's writing foregrounds continuities, thematic approaches, and stylistic features in this body of literature while simultaneously engaging the underlying problematic of revising institutional discourses that have constructed women as silent objects of history. In other words, by employing the philosophical discourses of Man that dominated the dialectics of the Enlightenment and imperial expansion, contemporary Caribbean women writers deconstruct frameworks that have foreclosed discussions about the nature of existence for the post-Prospero-and-Caliban Caribbean subject. The impact of systemic oppression on the creative imagination is one site for engaging debates about being and identity. This theoretical approach can provide insights into the relationship between thinking and being, between human being and non-human being.

What is most useful about this intervention is the insistence on engaging these acts of re(in)forming and translating within the institutions and disciplines from which they emerged in colonial contexts. Engaging Enlightenment discourses keeps open space in which we can continuously translate the cultural and philosophical "contact zones" that Caribbean writers deploy to (re)present the processes of Be(come)ing. The impulse toward alterity as the predominant mode for consolidating identity pervades all endeavors to represent national identity during the Enlightenment and continues to impact contemporary discourses on cultural identity. Two texts in particular offer productive instances for exploring this impulse: Immanuel Kant's essay "Observations on the Feeling of the Beautiful and the Sublime" (1764) and his later essay, "On the Different Races of Man" (1775). These were seminal texts for institutionalizing philosophical (and scientific) debates about the classification of Man. Kant's philosophical pontifications on the classes of human beings were particularly consistent in his relegation of Negroes to the lowest rung of humanity. His logic regarding the disparate affiliation of Europeans and Africans is best illustrated by his assertion that "so fundamental [are] the differences between the two races of man, that it appears to be as great in regard to mental capacities as in color."[27]

The rampant imperial expansionism of the Enlightenment foregrounds the way "race" was socially imagined and then converted into immutable "scientific truths." As Paul Gilroy notes in *Against Race: Political Culture Beyond the Color Line*, if we follow the ideological trajectory of Enlightenment discourse we can see that

> It is a short step from appreciating the ways that particular "races" have been historically invented and socially imagined to seeing how modernity catalyzed the distinctive regime of truths, the world of discourse that I call "raciology." In other words, the modern, human sciences, particularly anthropology, geography, and philosophy, undertook elaborate work in order to make the idea of "race" epistemologically correct. This required novel ways of understanding embodied alterity, hierarchy, and temporality. It made human bodies communicate the truths of an irrevocable otherness that were being confirmed by a new science and a new semiotics just as the struggle against Atlantic social slavery was being won.[28]

The discursive interconnectedness between enlightenment, science, and myth emerge most poignantly in travelogues, tales of discovery and conquest, and narratives of "origins," which present "race" as a "philosophical object rather than merely a matter of typology."[29] We cannot, however, lose sight of an integral aspect of Gilroy's commentary on the construction of Otherness: these constructions take root first within the national imagination and then proceed toward a corresponding reality, whether "present" or not. The epistemological force of imperial reason has troubled the waters for Caribbean writers since Columbus's arrival. With the terms and conditions of Otherness so firmly rooted, the project of constructing a postcolonial subjectivity not limited by the events of 1492 had to be waged at the same point of contact from which these discourses of alterity emerged. The possibility for Be(come)ing was diverted through imperialist expansionism and colonial culture, and this divergence occurred at two levels: first, at the level of the social imagination, by creating cultural institutions that construct epistemes of alterity, and thus allowing Europeans to comprehend the barbarism taking place in the New World; and second, through the sociohistorical institutions produced in the Caribbean archipelago that sought to articulate West Indian identity as something different from the British identity, something unique, not identical. This divergence or epistemic appropriation meant that colonial subjects had both to familiarize and alienate themselves from the Other of 1492 (savage natives) in order to accommodate the construction and emergence of an-Other Self.

SUBJECT TO IMPOSSIBILITY: BLACKNESS AND BEING IN THE CARIBBEAN LITERARY IMAGINATION

In the following chapters, I examine a range of texts, all of which challenge us to read against the grain, to move beyond our current modes of interpretation. My goals are to make the absences in our current practice audible and to argue for new interpretative models. The task for Caribbean writers, looking out onto a landscape epistemologically hostile to their lived relationships in their "homelands," is to find a space/place in between the center and the margin. Such a space would necessarily contain elements of both, but would also represent the movements between and across these locations. *Alien-Nation and Repatriation* examines a range of critical approaches to this problematic from a number of different historical, political, and cultural vantage points.

Chapter one, "The Trinidad Renaissance: Building a Nation, Building a Self," considers the cultural and political project undertaken by the writers of *Trinidad* and later the *Beacon*, two early-twentieth-century literary magazines that deployed fiction as a tool to critique the colonial institutions that restricted lived realities and, therefore, the capacities of the imagination. The magazines politicized the imaginary spaces in Trinidad during the 1930s while at the same time politicizing the subjects about whom the narratives were written. These spaces included institutions that had previously been mystified by seemingly private practices in the running of the colony. They included government offices, schools, churches, barrack-yards, oil-fields, dry good stores, gas stations, and other hidden physical and psychological spaces in the national landscape. Legislative decisions, unfair labor practices, and imperialist aggression in Trinidad and abroad, as well as social and cultural events and debates, were among the topics and issues for discussion in the stories, editorials, and essays published in these magazines.

The relationship between experience and existence had to be explicitly stated in order to illuminate effectively the opaque areas of Caribbean culture and society. This illumination, while revealing the more submerged workings of systems of oppression, also exposed the mechanization of these systems, showing them to contain the day-to-day elements that were manipulated at various levels to affect the lived realities of colonial subjects. There were two predominant trends in early Trinidadian literature of the *Beacon* era: 1) representations of labor conditions, including unequal economic compensation for the working classes, and 2) representations of women's lives as a metaphor for the national struggle underway in Trinidad. *Beacon* writers such as Ralph de Boissière, Alfred Mendes, Albert Gomes, and C. L. R. James employed the trope of the barrack-yard woman, with her "wayward" desires for economic, social, and cultural independence, to represent Trinidad's desire for political autonomy. Just as these women sought more self-reliance based on the economic relationships with their "keepers," Trinidad sought a similar reciprocity from its relationship with Britain.

The short fiction published in these literary magazines suggested that collective strategizing was the most effective mode of redistributing resources and controlling labor sources and, through this, the power to demand proper compensation. In other words, these magazines provided a fictional model using tropes that were easily identifiable among the working poor. During the 1940s, the emergence of a powerful labor union movement (which included domestic workers) ushered in a shift in literary representations of the nation and women's relationships to the nationalist movement under way in Trinidad and Tobago. This chapter maps the trajectory of the changes taking place in the political landscape of Trinidad and Tobago while paying particular attention to the extent to which literary representations developed in relation to a newly imagined socially and politically responsible colonial nation-state. I argue that the shifts in literary representations during the Trinidad Renaissance reflected a political agenda that required women to become less visible on the street and more visible in the domestic sphere. However, this task was not easy to achieve, since women were not only on the street but also at the forefront of the labor movement, marching, organizing, and demanding their rights as partners in the labor movement and the nationalist movement for independence.

While tracing this shift in representation, my engagement with *Beacon* writers also considers the impact of the change in the literary form of expression and the increasing importance of migration in these representations. The shift from the short story to the novel brought with it a newly imagined female subject of History, one with markedly different institutional relationships to colonialist discursive terrains. The change in form and representation was part of a corresponding emergence of new value systems within working-class communities that saw to it that the "sons of the nation" ascended to their expected positions as public and political administrators and civil servants. This new value system sent the nation's "sons" abroad to their "homelands" (England and the United States), and these new patterns of migration, or the "brain drain" as it is commonly called, produced a new discursive and metaphysical terrain for colonial subjects. They encountered a new reality: not only were they not "British" in their subjectivity, but the "reality" of their West Indianness had to be negotiated in Britain, not in the Caribbean. Where time and geographical space previously buffered the immediate impact of colonialist expansionism in Britain, the arrival of thousands of "Calibans" proved to be the realization of Prospero's greatest fear. The fear in this instance is not simply that Caliban would people the isle with Calibans, but that Britain would become the new place of residence for his descendants.

Migration and an imagined exile provided Lamming and others with the critical distance needed to reflect on the existential condition of postcolonial subjects in the African Diaspora. However, for some young colonials, the fortunes of migration were realized within the region in the aftermath of the labor riots of 1937 and the subsequent hearing by the Moyne Commission in 1938 and 1939. George Lamming was one such writer, and he would describe his journey to Trinidad in 1946 as one of the most memorable and influential parts of his young life. Commenting on the labor riots in Barbados, Lamming recalls that even in his youth he understood the importance of what was taking place in Barbados and throughout the region. Lamming and his generation of writers were faced with a landscape that demanded they reconceptualize their relationship, not only to the British Empire, but also to other Caribbean countries, and nowhere was this more evident than during his time in Trinidad. The cultural renaissance there included Beryl McBurnie's and Boscoe Holder's dance troupes and the Little Carib Theatre, performances in Woodford Square by Paul Robeson, and the rich company of intellectuals living in Belmont, Port-of-Spain.[30] Lamming's experience reflected not only the cultural and political environment in Trinidad, but also his thinking about how federation occurs in the region at the level of lived experience:

> What I was going to say about the Caribbean shaping of me, in Belmont, which is not only its intellectual center, but among Afro-Trinidadians, every house I went into, whether it was the Braithwaites, or the Ifils, or the Richardsons, the only *Trinidadians* were the children. The parents were not born in Trinidad. In the case of the Braithwaites, the father was from Grenada, the mother was from there, but the grandparents were from Barbados, and then I came to realize that each household was a family of islands. . . . And this was not an exceptional thing. This was right across that Belmont spectrum, and it occurred to me that, certainly within the English-speaking Caribbean, we were already federated by blood; we simply didn't know how to institutionalize that relationship, but that existed there inside the houses.[31]

This interpretation of Caribbean federation—and indeed Caribbean identity shaped by the reality of intra-Caribbean migration—would be a crucial example for Lamming and other writers of his generation. The idea of a Caribbean identity founded on regional migrations would be tested once young colonials like Lamming, Samuel Selvon, and Boscoe Holder left Trinidad for England in 1950. Their journeying to England provided a different context for considering, in political and critical terms, how migration and exile would shape their understanding of West Indian identity.

Chapter two, "The Pleasures/Privileges of Exile: Rereading covering Race and Sexuality," critiques George Lamming's *The Pleasures of Exile* and *Water with Berries*, two texts that are concerned with the phenomena of migration, exile, and identity in the context of England. Lamming's own arrival "elsewhere" (first Trinidad and then England) heavily influenced his development as a writer. *Water with Berries* suggests that, despite Prospero's departure from Caliban's island, the migration of Caribbean artists and intellectuals represents another genealogy of history and national identity, one in which the reality of the "fatherland" (Britain) represents a continuation of the expansionism that landed Prospero on Caliban's island hundreds of years earlier. The significant difference now is that Caliban and the ghosts of several exiled and "disappeared" subjects have taken up residence in Prospero's homeland. Lamming's earlier charge for colonial subjects to "liberate [themselves] into some other kind of being" resonates most profoundly in this context;[32] but where were writers of this generation to begin this journey? Based on the exodus of young men to England and the United States, the answer would seem to be, anywhere but the Caribbean. Lamming puts its best when he poses the following questions:

> How has it come about that a small group of men, different in years and temperament and social origins, should leave the respective islands they know best, even exchange life there for circumstances which are almost wholly foreign to them? Some civilians have been forced by economic necessity to undertake this risk of migration. But what about the West Indian writers who are now resident in Britain? Why have they migrated? And what, if any, are the peculiar pleasures of exile?[33]

Arguably, Lamming sets out to answer these questions in his collection of essays as well as his novels: *The Emigrants* (1954), *Of Age and Innocence* (1958), *Season of Adventure* (1960), and *Water with Berries* (1970). However, Lamming's novels also provide unique opportunities for a gendered analysis of these traditions of migration, nationalism, and imagining home. As the previous chapter demonstrates, the preoccupation with black female subjectivity is integral to the imaginative and national landscapes of pre- and post-independence Caribbean literature. My analysis addresses another set of critical concerns alongside those Lamming poses in the quotation above: where and how do black female subjects figure in the body politic of the emerging Caribbean nationalist consciousness?

Water with Berries (1971) is born out of a moment of speculation in *The Pleasures of Exile* where Lamming questions our ability to "speak with authority" until we have heard from Sycorax and Miranda's mother. The novel takes up the paradigm of *The Tempest* as a point of departure to respond to some of the questions raised in the quotation above. My reading of Lamming highlights the extent to which women's bodies (both black and white) have been discursively silenced, while being made to signify increasingly in narratives about Caribbean national identity. Through an analysis of how the sexual presence of women in *Water with Berries* signifies on the silenced bodies of evidence, I argue that reading strategies need to be reconsidered so that we can begin to interpret these "bodies of evidence," which, although erased, still leave traces of their absence/presence throughout history.

Ultimately, the aim is to engage in a line of inquiry that assumes the possibility that women conceive of "home" and nation differently based on their experiences. Carole Boyce Davies's *Black Women, Writing, and Identity: Migrations of the Subject*, offers an insightful response to these questions through a gendered analysis of migration and subject formation that produces a different set of questions and concerns about these shared experiences. As Michelle Ann Stephens observes,

> Boyce Davies's work has been central for demonstrating that while the woman of color may at first appear invisible in narratives of both nationalism and postcolonialism, it is because "she is somewhere else, doing something else" in less territorial transnational spaces. In Boyce Davies's account, the woman of color becomes the figure for a less triumphalist vision of home, nation, and empire and an often vulnerable mobile subjectivity.[34]

What is important here is Stephens's assertion that the critical concern is not simply whether or not women migrated, but how they interpreted the experiences of migration, exile, home, and nation differently in relation to their male counterparts. In other words, the questions raised by Lamming, while important for women writers, are not the most important for the kind of critical information we are interested in uncovering about these traditions in women's writing. My engagement with Lamming's *Water with Berries* is concerned precisely with the interpretative strategies that have erased and raced these moments of difference in Caribbean literature. I am interested in mapping the political agendas that are a part of the "something else" these writers and their female protagonists are engaged in while the "sons of the nation" are busying themselves with the project of repatriation.

Belinda Edmondson, Brent Edwards, and, most recently, Michelle Ann Stephens have all written about the extent to which masculinity shapes the discursive terrains of black internationalism and Caribbean intellectual traditions. Their texts all suggest, in differing degrees, that formations of black national politics, literature, and identity rest on masculinist discourses of citizenship, belonging, and ownership. I am engaged in a similar project, but my analysis is preoccupied with critical interpretations of the necessary, and yet contradictory, role of black female subjectivity and female sexuality in these articulations. My reading of Edwards and Stephens is tempered by Belinda Edmondson's suggestion that colonial discourses "made men" of colonial subjects, and, in so doing, informed the literary and cultural cartography for the making of Caribbean literary nationalism.[35] A gendered analysis of some these foundational texts on black nationalism, and of the literary and cultural landscapes out of which they emerged, might well provide useful interpretations of reading strategies that mask the ways masculinity, migration, and the desire for repatriation function in the production of imaginary "homelands" embodied through the sign of the black female body.

Chapter three, "Gender and Genre: The Logic of Language and the Logistics of Identity," reconsiders the "pleasures of exile" through the historical and political lens of black female subjectivities and the politics of mobility for women, not simply to highlight the inequitable power relationships that influence all aspects of migration, but to argue for a different interpretation and representation of citizenship in a nationalist context. These modes of representation, far from denying the traditions that preceded them, draw out of these "privileges," offering an-Other way of reading both exile and representations of political and sexual landscapes in Caribbean literature. As Carole Boyce Davies argues, "the re-negotiating of identities is fundamental to migration as it is fundamental to migration as it is fundamental to Black women's writing in cross-cultural contexts. It is the convergence of multiple places and cultures that renegotiates the terms of Black women's experiences at the sites of those convergences."[36]

So vital is the link between identity and migration that women writers have consistently sought to critique the need for a language and a more complex notion of form capable of expressing the lived realities of migrating subjects who are women. Equally important to this debate are the critiques of hegemony and privilege; it is this last point that makes Caribbean women's writing central to critiques of Caribbean nationalist literature. Like Boyce Davies, I explore the points of convergence that emerge as a result of migration in order to highlight the complex imaginings and problematics of translating Caribbean identity in these locations and positionalities. Contemporary Caribbean women writers, including Nalo Hopkinson, Dionne Brand, and Erna Brodber, all critically examine the vexed relationship between content and structure in narratives of national and sexual identity in Caribbean literature and colonial discourses. The range of their writing expands beyond the familiar genres of poetry and fiction to borrow from science fiction and creative non-fiction and prose poetry, suggesting that the emerging narratives of women who have been so long silenced must necessarily be expressed in non-traditional forms that reflect the complex nature of their existence.

Caribbean Canadian writer M. NourbeSe Philip focuses on the discursive and physical silencing of Black women's bodies by remapping geographies of violence in colonialist and nationalist discourses of identity. Her deconstruction of literary form is a discursive performance of the (dis)location experienced by Others and immigrants struggling to exist on the borders of several different histories, nations and identities simultaneously. Her books, including *She Tries Her Tongue, Her Silence Softly Breaks*, *A Genealogy of Resistance*, and *Frontiers: Essays and Writings on Racism and Culture*, address the complex negotiations Africans in the New World make in order to exist and experience the world in languages that are antithetical to their humanity. The alternative to existing in these remarkably cramped spaces, she suggests, is (dis)locating English, wrestling it out of its historical and institutional authority, and pressing it into the service of the realities experienced by African Diaspora subjects. This (dis)location, however, is as much about geography as it is about language, particularly for women, whose relationships to their landscapes are defined and limited by the threat of violence, even in their "internal" spaces. Philip suggests that women have learned to exist and create between spaces of (dis)location, to craft worlds in the spaces "in between." Although the "body" of these texts does not adhere to traditional notions of genre, their structural reconfiguration is a visual manifestation of the physical and discursive contortions black women undergo in the effort to represent their realities.

Chapter four, "Routes and Roots: Re(in)scribing the Meaning of Home" traces the cultural geography of African American and Caribbean political and cultural institutions across the African Diaspora. Erna Brodber's novel *Louisiana* effectively argues for an engagement with African Diaspora politics built on cross-cultural histories and transmigrations at the political and spiritual levels. Where Brodber's project seeks out points of cultural and political intersection, Elizabeth Nunez's novel *Beyond the Limbo Silence*, like Paule Marshall's *Brown Girl, Brownstones*, reflects the coming of age experience through the eyes of young black women in the pre– and post–World War II eras. Both writers are engaged in formulating an imaginative political landscape that complicates the meaning of "blackness" in North America and the Caribbean region. However, the protagonists' vexed relationships to their Caribbean colonial pasts and their interpellation into the racial landscape of the United States suggest that differences among blacks in the Diaspora will prove to be the wall that separates, rather than an occasion for engaging culture and identity.

Far from presenting a picture of cooperation based on race politics that is suggested in Brodber's novel, Nunez's and Marshall's novels represent periods in American history where the fissures, contradictions, gaps, and silences within the communities of the African Diaspora threaten the possibility of political solidarity across racial and economic (or class) lines. Ironically, the imagined distances between West Indian immigrants and African Americans during the Civil Rights era in the United States are not as great as many imagine. However, the notion that acknowledging cultural difference among blacks weakens the political and social power within African Diaspora communities globally has become all the more entrenched since September 11th. My analysis of these texts argues for an understanding that does not see difference as an alterity that needs to be subsumed, dissolved, and interpellated into the prevailing discourses on nationalism in the interest of the "larger good" of being American, British, Trinidadian, Jamaican, and so forth.

This final chapter, "Boundaries, Borders and the Unhoused," examines discursive and political practices that challenge the seemingly fixed, entrenched nationalist discourses that threaten to exile all bodies of difference in the name of originary narratives of nationhood. This closing chapter also addresses the ways immigration and nationalism are creating new terms of engagement within black nationalist discourses, particularly now that "belonging" has taken on such overtly political significance. In order to bring these final considerations into focus, I consider two sites of contestation and engagement: first, women's experience as immigrants who were, in effect, exiled at "home," an integral but unacknowledged aspect of Caribbean women's representations of nation, identity, and belonging; and second, the crucial element of class in discourses of departure and arrival (routes) and home (or roots).

Belinda Edmondson addresses this issue in the final chapter of *Making Men: Gender, Literary Authority, and Women's Writing in Caribbean Narrative*, asserting that women migrated for financial reasons, not necessarily to distance themselves from their ideological "homelands." This, she suggests, necessarily created very different accounts of their relationships to their surroundings because "the *reasons* for traveling to the metropole, then, the conditions of that journey, are by far of more importance than the fact of actually being there, because the capacity in which the West Indian travels to that society will dictate how that society will 'read' her."[37] This argument is not only convincing, but also provides another avenue for interpreting the relationship between class, race, gender, and migration.

Migration to London allowed Caribbean male authors to maintain their relationship to England and their privileged status as "sons of the nation." Explaining why James and other Afro-Caribbean male writers did not "exile" themselves to the United States, Edmondson makes a very important observation: "For [C. L. R.] James to go to the United States would be for James to lose even the class privilege he possesses in the Caribbean by submergence into the underside of the monolithic American racial equation. By contrast England contained a history whereby black middle-class men from the Caribbean and Africa could be granted the privileged status there as gentlemen."[38] This "privilege," though notably different from what I allude to in earlier chapters, is of critical importance for reading contemporary Caribbean immigrant women's writing.

For black subjects, the ideological implications of this "unbelonging" are recognizable in several texts by women writers, but particularly in *Louisiana, Brown Girl, Brownstones,* and *Beyond the Limbo Silence*, all of which are concerned with the experience of immigration rather than exile and the cultural dislocation that results.[39] The final chapter brings the project together with brief speculations on discourses of identity and citizenship alluded to in the earlier texts by James, Mendes, and Lamming. More specifically, chapter five recasts gender constructions and discourses of masculinity and female sexuality through a critique of class and race in America. The emphasis on migration, rather than exile, allows us to reconsider the extent to which class politicizes the social landscape of the United States differently for women who choose (or are forced into) migration for economic reasons. By rethinking the meaning of home through the lens of class and gender, a different set of questions emerge about unbelonging and the unhomeliness of the nation-state for black female subjects.

Coming full circle in my discussion of exile, migration, nationalism, and identity, the conclusion includes a few speculations on the emergence of a new sociopolitical figure in the Caribbean nationalist landscape: the "deportee." Thinking and writing about the "return of the native" to a West Indian mother/land that no longer recognizes or receives her or him with open arms requires new discourses on national identity that figure (un)desirability, mobility, belonging, and citizenship through the lens of forced repatriation. Such a project will necessarily draw on the long history of writing on exile in the region, but also on the technologies of globalization that seek to discipline or disappear black bodies that refuse to be docile or "domesticated." What will the increasingly popular exclusion and banishment from the "body" politic at "home" and "abroad" (however configured) mean for Caribbean immigrants who become doubly dislocated, first from the place they have called "home" for most of their lives, and then by the places of their birth, with which they have little, if any, relationship? If Paule Marshall's representation of the "deportee" in *Brown Girl, Brownstones* is any indication, both the "alien" and the "nation" have yet to come to terms with one another.

NOTES

1. For a more detailed discussion of the role and importance of the imagination in the formation of the nation, see Benedict Anderson, introd. to *Imagined Communities: Reflections on the Origin and Spread of Nationalism* (London and New York: Verso, 1991), 5–7.

2. Anne McClintock, "'No Longer in a Future Heaven': Gender, Race and Nationalism," in *Dangerous Liaisons: Gender, Nation and Post-Colonial Perspectives*, eds. Anne McClintock, Aamir Mufti, and Ella Shohat (Minneapolis and London: University of Minnesota Press, 1997), 89.

3. Emphasis mine. McClintock, "'No Longer in a Future Heaven,'" 89. See Eric Hobsbawm's critique of nationalism in *Nations and Nationalism since 1870* (Cambridge: Cambridge University Press, 1990).

4. The term "Being" is used throughout to represent the nature of existence for black subjects in an ontological context. As such, the phrase "Be(come)ing" is part of this ontological project; it is meant to highlight the ongoing processes that are always under way. Both terms are bound up in the transitional stages of existence that allow subjects to be continuously engaged in producing their Being.

5. My use of the term "History" represents the tradition of interpreting the originary moment of Caribbean existence as beginning with Columbus's discovery. In other words, history (writ large) stands apart from other accounts as the formal, official account of colonial discovery.

6. Carolyn Cooper, "Science and Higher Science: Transmigration in Erna Brodber's *Louisiana*" (paper presented at the 14th Annual West Indian Literature Conference, Antigua State College, March 9–11, 1995.

7. Edouard Glissant, *Caribbean Discourse: Selected Essays*, trans. J. Michael Dash (Charlottesville: University Press of Virginia, 1989).

8. In the introduction to *Writing in Limbo*, Gikandi asserts that limited conceptualizations of modernism have led cultural critics, particularly Michael Thelwell, to argue that emphasizing or engaging with the question of modernism leads to an abandonment of "history and cultural reality." Simon Gikandi, *Writing in Limbo: Modernism and Caribbean Literature* (Ithaca and London: Cornell University Press, 1992), 4–12; Michael Thelwell, "Modernist Fallacies and the Responsibility of the Black Writer," in *Duties, Pleasures, and Conflicts: Essays in Struggle* (Amherst: University of Massachusetts Press, 1987), 221.

9. Gikandi, *Writing in Limbo*, 5.

10. For a more thorough discussion of this tradition in the writings of Wilson Harris, V. S. Naipaul, George Lamming, and Derek Walcott, see Eddie Baugh, "The West Indian Writer and His Quarrel with History," *Tapia* 7, nos. 8–9 (1977).

11. Glissant, *Caribbean Discourse*, 144–50.

12. Glissant, *Caribbean Discourse*, 146.

13. Glissant, *Caribbean Discourse*, 11.

14. Gayatri Spivak, *Critique of Postcolonial Reason* (Cambridge, MA: Harvard University Press, 1999), 30.

15. Spivak, *Critique of Postcolonial Reason*, 30.

16. Spivak, *Critique of Postcolonial Reason*, 30.

17. Spivak, *Critique of Postcolonial Reason*, 33.

18. Sylvia Wynter, "Afterword: Beyond Miranda's Meanings: Un/silencing the 'Demonic Ground' of Caliban's 'Woman,'" in *Out of the Kumbla: Caribbean Women and Literature*, eds. Carole Boyce Davies and Elaine Savory Fido (Trenton, NJ: Africa World Press, 1990), 365. Wynter cites Foucault's use of this term in his discussion of the discursive limitations in various disciplines. In a lecture entitled "The Order of Discourse," delivered in December 1970 and published as an Appendix to the *Archeology of Knowledge*, he notes that Mendel's findings about genetic heredity were not "hearable at first because they were not within the 'vrai' of the discipline at the time." Wynter, "After/word," 369. Like Foucault, Wynter uses this term to highlight the extent to which forms of knowledge are not recognizable when considered within the limited discourses that are available to a given field at a particular historical moment.

19. Spivak, *Critique of Postcolonial Reason*, 37; Spivak is quoting Obeyesekere Ganananth, *The Apotheosis of Captain Cook: European Mythmaking in the Pacific* (Princeton: Princeton University Press, 1992), 24.

20. Erna Brodber, "Oral Sources and the Creation of a Social History of the Caribbean," *Jamaica Journal* 16, no. 4 (November 1983): 4.

21. Brodber, "Oral Sources," 14.

22. Brodber, "Oral Sources," 7.

23. V. S. Naipaul, *The Middle Passage* (Harmondsworth: Penguin, 1969), 28–29.

24. Brodber, "Oral Sources," 7.

25. Abena Busia, "Silencing Sycorax: On Colonial Discourse and the Unvoiced Female," *Cultural Critique*, no. 14 (Winter 1989–90): 95.

26. Evelyn O'Callaghan, *Woman Version: Theoretical Approaches to West Indian Fiction by Women* (London: Macmillan, 1993), 11.

27. Immanuel Kant, "Observations on the Feeling of the Beautiful and the Sublime," in *Race and the Enlightenment: A Reader*, ed. Emmanuel Chukwudi Eze (Oxford, MA: Blackwell Publishers, 1997), 55–56.

28. Paul Gilroy, *Against Race: Imagining Political Culture Beyond the Color Line* (Cambridge, MA: Belknap Press of Harvard University Press, 2000), 57–58.

29. Gilroy, *Against Race*, 60.

30. George Lamming, "The Sovereignty of the Imagination: An Interview with George Lamming," by David Scott, *Small Axe: A Caribbean Journal of Criticism* 12 (September 2002): 87–107.

31. Lamming, "Sovereignty of the Imagination," 99–100.

32. George Lamming, "A Visit to Carriacou," in *Conversations: George Lamming; Essays, Addresses, and Interviews 1953–1990*, eds. Richard Drayton and Andayie (London: Karia Press, 1992), 27.

33. George Lamming, *The Pleasures of Exile* (Ann Arbor: University of Michigan Press, 1992), 23.

34. Michelle Ann Stephens, *Black Empire: The Masculine Global Imaginary of Caribbean Intellectuals in the United States, 1914–1962* (Durham and London: Duke University Press, 2005), 17.

35. Belinda Edmondson, *Making Men: Gender, Literary Authority, and Women's Writing in Caribbean Narrative* (Durham and London: Duke University Press, 1999), 141.

36. Carole Boyce Davies, *Black Women, Writing, and Identity: Migrations of the Subject* (London and New York: Routledge, 1994), 3.

37. Edmondson, *Making Men*, 141.

38. Edmondson, *Making Men*, 152.

39. See also Jamaica Kincaid, *Lucy* (New York: Plume, 1990), and Paule Marshall, *Praisesong for the Widow* (New York: Plume, 1984).

Chapter One

The Trinidad Renaissance: Building a Nation, Building a Self

Stevenson said: "the most influential books and the truest in their influence are works of fiction. They do not pin their readers to dogma, which he must afterwards discover to be inexact; they do not teach a lesson, which he must afterwards unlearn. They repeat, they re-arrange, they clarify the lessons of Life." For these and other reasons which should be obvious, the literature of fiction brings to the doors of people who otherwise would have known little or nothing of these things, the burden of this truth: our social organization is not what it ought to be; it is diseased.

Alfred H. Mendes, "A Commentary," *Trinidad*

RECOVERING FROM HISTORY: LITERARY NATIONALISM AND WEST INDIAN IDENTITY

Despite the numerous historiographies of the Caribbean archipelago and accounts written by travelers and historians alike, critiques of colonialist discourses demonstrate that Columbus's invasion of the New World was not the authorizing moment for the colonial subject's entry into History. Arguably, this historical event provided an occasion for black colonial subjects in the New World to construct their own notions of history and their relationships to Empire. The Trinidad Renaissance is one such instance in Caribbean literary history, in that it began as a literary movement grounded in West Indian cultural expressions that went against the grain of British colonial aesthetics. In the late 1920s, a small group of writers in Trinidad initiated a creative process aimed at constructing a New World historical subjectivity that engaged with and reflected the lived realities of black colonial subjects. Through literary magazines like *Trinidad* and the *Beacon*, readers gained perspectives on historical narratives about Caribbean identity, perspectives that are distinct from subsequently canonized discourses such as the Calibanesque tradition. The cultural and social debates taken up in *Trinidad* and the *Beacon* during the late 1920s and early 1930s served as barometers for the social and political climates of a country coming into its own sense of history. These letters, stories, and articles fueled national debates regarding colonial politics, art, culture, and science. Moreover, these journals provided an important commentary on the potential of a national literature for the largely peasant, ethnically diverse population of Trinidad and Tobago.

Literary magazines were an integral part of pre-independence politics and offered a unique space to express the political and social concerns of disenfranchised black West Indians in colonial Trinidad.[1] The principal questions under consideration about this period of Caribbean literary production are: What do these texts suggest is at stake in defining this Caribbean cultural history? How have these debates challenged traditional constructions of history that were foreclosed, and how have they diverted possibilities for imagining new epistemes between historical subjects and their surroundings? Finally, to what extent are nationalisms always already invested in suppressing alter/native narratives of history and identity that challenge overarching discourses of "community" and national identity? These questions provide a primary lens through which we can view the literary renaissance under way in Trinidad and understand its development in relation to the other literary movements taking place elsewhere in the Anglophone Caribbean during the political upheaval of the late 1930s and 1940s. In an interview with David Scott, George Lamming puts the literary tradition emerging in the region into a more pan–(Anglophone) Caribbean context:

DS: I want to come to that. I think you've said this yourself. The emergence of *Bim*, or what *Bim* becomes with Collymore, is part of the quickening of the tempo of colonial life in the 1940s, as in one sense *Focus* was in Jamaica with Edna Manley, and *Kyke-over-Al* with A. J. Seymour in Guyana.

GL: Yes. The thing that is interesting here is the *difference*, the profound difference, in both the temperament and intentions of the editors [of these magazines]. For example, when you are dealing with *Focus*, you are dealing with a very conscious expression of nationalist affirmation. And when you are dealing with Seymour in *Kyke-over-Al* there is in a Guyanese kind of way (but a Guyanese extending into the Caribbean) that consciousness of creating something out of this colonial world.... Collymore's relationship to *Bim* is, "let us encourage and collect what is the finest literary talent here." It is not, as I recall, connected to a Barbadian nationalism, or a Caribbean nationalism, or any of that. It is going in fact to become that, in spite of him.[2]

While Lamming's characterization of *Bim* as "apolitical" in its earliest configurations is open for debate, what is more important here is the realization that the literary renaissance taking place in Trinidad had a broader context in the Anglophone Caribbean, in much the same way that the political unrest of the period did. The significance of this shared literary history will become more evident in our discussion of the next generation of Caribbean intellectuals who build on the national sentiment and artistic expression of this period.

The creative objectives of the *Beacon* group were based on developing artistic images that had not been represented in the cultural landscape or social value systems in Trinidad during the 1930s. The manifesto for these literary magazines included defining a "uniquely" West Indian literature that saw itself as going against the grain of colonial culture. In order to implement new images and new ways of reading effectively, *Beacon* writers constructed new yardsticks for defining aesthetics and politics in Trinidad. The dominant social value systems maintained that aesthetic and political discernment were reserved for those trained in the "finer" aspects of life. However, these young writers played a significant role in formulating aesthetic standards that would be the map for their reading audiences to traverse the contested and hierarchical landscapes of "taste" that defined modes of cultural expression and production in British colonies in the 1930s.

The 1930s saw the emergence of the colored middle class in Trinidad, many of whom were the children of laborers who recognized that opportunities for their children lay in the colonial education system. The rigorous tradition of colonial education that emerged in Trinidad during this period produced several important intellectuals, nationally and internationally. Young men like Ernest Carr, Cyril Lionel Robert James, Malcolm Nurse, Eric Williams, Rudranath Capildeo, and Adrian Cola Rienzi, having completed their secondary education in schools like Queen's Royal College, were eager to put their minds to work on developing their society.[3] These young men found themselves with only their civil service training and colonial education as vehicles for exercising their talents and earning money. Another group of young Trinidadians, Albert Gomes, Alfred Mendes, and Ralph Mentor, all members of the "middle minority," found themselves in similar positions, though with more social and financial resources and connections at their disposal. James, Nurse, and Williams were members of the black West Indian middle class and Capildeo was of East Indian descent; education and/or employment abroad was their only hope for advancing up the social ladder in the Caribbean since the sociocultural landscape of Trinidad severely limited possibilities available to Afro- and Indo-Trinidadians.

Because of the demographics, class structures, and racial separation in Trinidad, one may wonder how these young men came into contact with one another.⁴ Although work places and social gatherings followed these social conventions, a love of arts and letters brought together some of the country's most prominent minds for informal meetings. What began as gatherings at Mendes's house to discuss literature and art eventually evolved into a literary magazine titled *Trinidad*. Founded by Albert Mended in 1929, *Trinidad* became a conduit for a young generation of colonials to articulate their political and cultural perspectives. *Trinidad* was the first magazine of its sort ever to be published in an Anglophone Caribbean country. Stories that appeared in the magazine, such as "Triumph" and "Her Chinaman's Way," would later become signature pieces for C. L. R. James and Alfred Mendes. Their short fiction marked the beginning of a literary tradition that turned to the cultural environment of Trinidad for its source of inspiration. Although the magazine lasted only one year, the members of this group would continue to write and publish in the *Beacon* after *Trinidad* went out of circulation.

Many of the writers and readers of *Trinidad* were guided by the disillusionment of those who had fought to protect the British Empire, only to return to their colonies and be treated as second-class citizens. Mendes, in particular, saw firsthand the contradictions between what he had fought to protect in the war and the manifestations of these ideals for colonial subjects in their day-to-day existence. He discerned a growing sense of the necessity for articulating a uniquely West Indian perspective in all areas of culture. Many of the articles in the literary magazines pointed to an increasing dissatisfaction regarding the state of national affairs at the local level. More importantly, however, the aim of the writers in magazines like *Trinidad* was to "afford our fellow men and women an opportunity for self-expression and expansion, and if the assistance required is forthcoming, to touch life at all available points. Again, there is an abundant activity in the West Indies, a well-conceived record of which would add to the literature of these islands. Everyone's experience in art, or literature, or life itself is extremely important; the attempt to make it interesting should be made."⁵ This desire was echoed later by writers associated with the *Beacon*, who sponsored contests to encourage contributors to submit stories that reflected life in Trinidad in all its variations. Their main concern was to express a uniquely West Indian identity.

Charting the emergence of literary traditions in Trinidad and Tobago, Reinhard Sander maps the political and cultural development of the literary renaissance that took place. The Caribbean writers formulating literary and political traditions out of the necessity produced by the social circumstances in this crown colony were largely concerned with the political battles raging in the colonial government during the period. The 1930s were filled with intense political change around the globe, and black subjects of the Empire felt the effects of these changes regardless of their geographic and cultural distances from the metropoles.⁶ Sander's account of the complex racial and political dynamics at work in this literary tradition and the social milieu out of which these young artists wrote is my point of departure for considering the long-term impacts of the Trinidad Renaissance on the next generation of writers and texts produced in the Caribbean and in England during the pre-independence period. The articles and short stories that appear in *Trinidad* and the *Beacon* are invaluable vehicles for considering the possibilities of national literature as an active medium for challenging the very idea of a national identity within the nation-state.

Alter/native narratives, including "Triumph" and "Her Chinaman's Way," appropriated women's sexuality as a trope for national resistance. However, there was a subsequent shift in the representations of women in Trinidadian literature as the drive for self-government took center stage. Novels such as *Crown Jewel, Rum and Coca Cola*, and *Black Fauns* reflected the transitions taking place politically during this period, and these transitions were captured in literary representations of women's experiences. These representations are of singular importance because they functioned as the framework for an emerging consciousness in the national imagination of Trinidad and Tobago.

These narratives constructed what Edouard Glissant refers to as a "forced relationship"⁷ with other imagined communities in the archipelago, Africa, the United States, and Europe. These relationships are "forced" because black colonial subjects had very little historical and cultural relationships to these places beyond the exercises of legislation. The cultural, social, and political environment from that these literary magazines emerged and the larger implications of this project provide a crucial vantage point for interpreting the nation's shifting ideological understanding of itself and its citizens. Pre-independence representations of gender and identity in nationalist literature of the Caribbean changed the relationships between cultural expression and the subject. The most significant change in this relationship was a revision in the way political and cultural agency was conceptualized in Trinidad. The *Beacon* writers were engaged in negotiating the terms of this agency. The project of constructing the literary and political presence of the underclass in colonial Trinidad was a necessary first step toward transforming the cultural landscape.

The epistemological shifts represented in the literary production of the Trinidad Renaissance chronicle these "acts of fiction" that challenged the rigorous institutionalization of identity through British social and political landscapes. The conditions of production for writers in the Trinidad Renaissance were such that there were no models, except for the Other of imperialism, for conceptualizing this "unique" West Indianness. However, the emergence of an-Other alter/native subject provided a moment of "productive" engagement (or possibility) for the imagination to entertain itself in the creation of an identity. In other words, these "acts of fiction" proved to be the impetus for political and cultural agency for this generation of writers.[8] The shifting national formations represented in early barrack-yard short fiction, and then later in the more socially and politically "responsible" novel, have been read as a natural linear progression of the national (British) fiction of History. However, a closer examination of the political and cultural developments taking place reveals efforts to reimagine the structure and function of colonial narratives in sociohistorical institutions in Trinidad. The difficulty in carrying out this examination lies in charting the complex negotiations under way in the political and cultural landscape of Trinidad.

These "acts of fiction" were a means through which alienated black colonial subjects began to interact with the terms and conditions of their existence. Through art, the subject's relationship to the "real" begins to take on meaning through processes and interactions that, in turn, make the systems of their environment accessible. According to Adorno, "Art does not become knowledge with reference to mere immediate reality, i.e. by doing justice to a reality which veils its own essence and suppresses its truth in favour of a merely classificatory order. Art and reality can only converge if art crystallizes out of its own formal laws, not by passively accepting objects as they come."[9] The power of art, as Adorno notes, lies not in its reproduction of the "real" but in its efforts to produce an-Other image or "look" at the systems, markers, and signs that inform our aesthetics and ethics. Literary magazines mediated the interactions between Caribbean subjects and the colonial systems that shaped their lived realities. Through the public debates launched in these magazines and others that were taking shape on the political front throughout the region, Caribbean people began to formulate their own systems, or other "looks," and through this process sought to redefine the meaning of their existence and their Be(come)ing. The Trinidad Renaissance would provide the basis of "formal laws" (of aesthetics and ethics) for black Caribbean subjects to fashion their national identities and nationalist politics.

UNRULY BARRACK-YARD WOMEN: THE POLITICAL ECONOMY OF GENDER AND SEXUALITY IN TRINIDADIAN LITERATURE

C. L. R. James's "Triumph" (1929) appeared in the magazine's first issue and explores colonial exploitation in its most extreme forms. The short story describes a community of barrack-yard women struggling to survive in the face of poverty and discrimination. The protagonists, Mamitz, Celestine, Bertha,

Josephine, and Irene, and a small cast of marginal male figures are engaged in a fierce struggle to keep food in their pots and a roof over their heads. Without steady work, Mamitz and the other women in the yard have to rely on being "kept" by men in order to feed themselves and their families. Mamitz's apparent "fall from grace" is the source of concern in the yard because she has always been the most prosperous among the women and therefore has held a higher status in the hierarchy of the yard. What is worthy of note here, however, are the qualifications that have kept Mamitz atop the social hierarchy of the barrack-yard:

> She was a black woman, too black to be pure negro, probably with some Madrasi East Indian blood in her, a suspicion which was made a certainty by the long thick plaits of her plentiful hair. She was shortish and fat, voluptuously developed, tremendously developed, and as a creole loves development in a woman more than any other extraneous allure, Mamitz (like the rest of her sex in all stations of life) saw to it when she moved that you missed none of her charms.[10]

James parallels the beauty of Mamitz's color and her ethnic lineage, her physical beauty and economic development, and her capacity to manage her "assets" in relation to the market of keepers who are attracted to her.

The central action in the story takes place when Mamitz, after a short spell without a job or a keeper, is aided by Celestine (the resident obeah woman)[11] in finding not one, but two, keepers: Popo des Vignes, a young entrepreneur (loan shark and con man), and Nicholas (a butcher). Mamitz's windfall draws the jealous attention of another woman in the yard, Irene, who sets out to bring about her downfall. When Irene tells Nicholas that Mamitz is entertaining another man in the room he is paying rent for, Nicholas arrives unannounced and threatens to kill Mamitz. However, everyone in the yard sides with Mamitz, assuring Nicholas of her "fidelity"; in the end, he has a change of heart, turns up to beg Mamitz's forgiveness, and leaves her his entire paycheck. Mamitz and her supporting cast later laud this "triumph" over Irene, who is completely undone by their blatant gloating.

James's use of local idioms and the physical and cultural specificities of barrack-yards in Trinidad drew harsh criticism from readers.[12] "Triumph" opens with a very detailed description of the yard and its inhabitants that sets the tenor of the interactions between the spaces and the people who occupy them. In fact, the complexities of James's characters and the corresponding smallness of their physical spaces emphasize the need for relief, as well as the degree of creativity necessary to survive. James begins by suggesting that differences that attend the emergence of these urban spaces and that the intersectionality of race and poverty reach far beyond the boundaries of "First

World" and "Third World." Drawing on the shared historical and social contexts of poor blacks across the Diaspora, James opens his story with a passage that lessens the geographical distance:

> Where people in England and America say slums, Trinidadians say barrack-yards. Every street in Port-of-Spain proper can show you numerous examples of the type: a narrow gateway leading into a fairly big yard, on either side of which run long low buildings, consisting of anything from four to eighteen rooms, each about twelve feet square. In these live, and have always lived, the porters, prostitutes, carter men, washerwomen, and domestic servants of the city. On a Sunday morning in one of the rooms of a barrack in Abercromby Street sat Mamitz. Accustomed as is squalid adversity to reign unchallenged in these quarters, yet in this room it was unusually triumphant, sitting as it were, high on a throne of royal state, so depressed was the woman and so depressed her surroundings.[13]

James's juxtaposition of the "slums" and "barrack-yards" against the "royal state" brings his comparison between the dilemma of black citizens and the trappings of imperialist expansionism to the fore despite the growing sense of the differences created by geographical boundaries. The textual proximity between slums/barrack-yards and the "throne of royal state" effectively reduces the geographical distance between these two conditions by drawing the historical circumstances of both positions into an immediate spatial relationship to one another.

James's emphasis on the limitations of physical space in the barrack-yard and the "triumph" of squalor in this space is later challenged when we see the characters transcend this cramped physical space through humor and social strategizing. His story is one of the few in which obeah, picong, and other counter-cultural epistemologies appear in the sociohistorical fabric of Caribbean society.[14] In fact, I would suggest that James's use of Trinidadian counter-cultural knowledge opposes the tight physical spaces that threaten to stifle life and creativity in the barrack-yards. The popular perception of this social class as "non-productive" is challenged by Celestine's and Mamitz's imaginative capacities for weathering the storms and claiming "triumph" over their surroundings. Obeah thus functions as an alternative system of order within existing sociohistorical institutions at work in their communities.

Mamitz's suspicions about her ill fate are placed squarely in relation to the jealousy and spite of other women in the yard, women who are versed in the "higher sciences." This knowledge serves as both a weapon and shield for the community of women in the barrack-yard: ". . . Irene they knew would do them mischief, and on mornings when Mamitz got up, on Celestine's advice, she looked carefully before the door lest she should unwittingly step on some church-yard bones, deadly powders, or other satanic agencies guaranteed to make the victim go mad, and steal or commit those breaches of good conduct punishable by law."[15] The juxtaposition between "higher science," or obeah, and the possibility for invoking violations of social laws and institutions in the yard suggests that there is a code of ethics that can easily be overturned by "outside forces." Mamitz's obvious respect for Celestine's knowledge suggests that she understands that there are different orders of knowledge operating within the yard and that not all of them are equal. Mamitz does not attribute her loss of social status simply to "bad luck"; she realizes there are various forces conspiring against her in the barrack-yard. Irene, in contrast, is taken aback because Mamitz's status is not reduced in light of her recent "fall from grace."

As Sander notes, James employs a technique "associated with the writer Henry Fielding of ironically distancing himself from both his subjects and his audience and making use of the epic devices to ennoble his humble protagonists."[16] Sander's critique, however, offers little commentary on Mamitz's abuse and exploitation, and the parallels between these (as common experiences for kept women) and the conditions of existence for the women whose welfare is the topic of discussion in the *Beacon*'s editorials. The irony of James's title, "Triumph," is not lost on the reader as we are introduced to a scenario that makes the notion of triumph over such oppressive conditions difficult to conceive. The story opens with the main character, Mamitz, "in derricks"[17] after losing her "keeper," a loss that has serious implications in this setting:

> First of all the tram conductor who used to keep Mamitz (seven dollars every Saturday night, out of which Mamitz usually got three) had accused her of infidelity and beaten her. Neither the accusation nor the beating had worried Mamitz. To her and her type those were minor incidents of existence from their knowledge of life and men, the kept woman's inevitable fate. But after a temporary reconciliation he had beaten her once more, very badly indeed, and left her. Even this was not an irremediable catastrophe.[18]

Her condition reaches epic proportions when her main source of income, her attractiveness and sexual desirability, fail to attract another keeper. With all of these things working against her, Mamitz tries to find work as a washer or cook, but is unable to do so. James's representations, far from implying a social narrative of correlation between his protagonists and working women in Trinidad, create a critical distance that provides his audience with a space to critique the relationships of power at work in the barrack-yard — and in the larger society. For instance, James's characterization of Mamitz's beatings as "minor" suggests that, in a cost-benefit analysis, Mamitz understands this as an expected risk in her line of "work." The political economy of the barrack-yard reflects many of the power relationships, market demands, and economic systems at work in the relationship between Britain and Trinidad. The allegation of "infidelity" is of singular importance here since the barrack-yard is clearly presented as an oppositional space in relation to the institution of marriage. In fact, when read as a companion text in relation to the debate raging in Trinidad at the time over the Divorce Bill, "Triumph" suggests that the relationship between the colonies and the British Empire is an exploitative one that should allow some opportunity for creative alternatives for how the colonies (the women) imagine their relationships with their "patrons." The barrack-yard inhabitants' persistent struggle for consistent financial support reflects the poor compensation for domestic, industrial, and agricultural laborers in Trinidad at the time.[19]

According to her friend Celestine, Mamitz's "blight" is the result of her neighbor, Irene, whose jealousy stems from her dissatisfaction about her place in the hierarchy of the yard. Whereas Celestine's and Mamitz's men keep them so well they do not need to work, Irene's keeper, described as a "stinkin so'-foot man," is married, with a wife and children to support. This means that Irene has to work to supplement his contributions. Celestine and Mamitz, she notes with disgust, "merely cooked and washed clothes for their men."[20] It is clear that Irene considers her additional labor more valuable in the economy of the yard than that of Mamitz and Celestine. However, in the eyes of the other women, the fact that she has to take work from "outside" to make ends meet moves her to a lower-class status within the barrack-yard system. Moreover, in the political economy of the yard, sex serves a very utilitarian purpose. Sex is exchanged for capital, which, in turn, is used for their "productive" gain. The "investments" of the keepers produce opportunity, something of which inhabitants of the barrack-yard have little experience. In exchange for payments (of food, money, or clothing), the women provide their keepers with sex, a hot meal, and clean clothing. It is no coincidence that the services rendered by these women are the same as those of women employed as domestic workers in Trinidad, many of whom could not, after being paid their salaries, afford to pay rent or buy food.

Eventually, Mamitz catches the eyes of Popo and Nicholas. Mamitz prefers Popo, but when his visits—and payments—begin to decrease in frequency, she decides to take Nicholas as her keeper, as he makes far more money than Popo and lavishes her with gifts of pints of stout and nice cuts of beef. After all, the narrator remarks, "a pound of beef was a pound of beef."[21] The provider of these commodities is insignificant and, in fact, easily exchangeable. One Easter morning when Popo arrives to spend the day with Mamitz, the yard is filled with a tense energy. Mamitz and Celestine plan a big spree (or party), sending to Nicholas for pork and beef to celebrate with Popo. Irene, however, goes down to the butcher shop to tell Nicholas that Mamitz is entertaining another man in the room for which he is paying rent.

Fortunately, Celestine observes Irene's departure from the yard and advises Popo to leave and come back another day. When Nicholas shows up, the other inhabitants of the yard swear that Irene is lying; he leaves, promising to return later in the evening to beat Mamitz for her deception. By the end of his workday, however, Nicholas's resolve changes:

> At about half past ten he found his resolution never to look at her again wavering. "Damn it," he said to himself. "That woman Irene is a liar. She see how I am treatin' Mamitz well and she want to break up the livin'." His reason inclined him to believe that Mamitz had been entertaining des Vignes for the whole day in the room he was paying rent for; while he, the fool, was working hard for money to carry her. But stronger powers than reason were fighting for Mamitz, and eleven o'clock found him in the yard knocking at the door.[22]

By the end of the story, Nicholas returns to Mamitz, begging her forgiveness for threatening to kill her. After sufficiently "cussin" him, his mother, sister, aunt, and wife (though he isn't married), Mamitz agrees to give him a second chance as her keeper.[23] The next morning, Mamitz parades fresh pieces of mutton *and* pork, now cooking in her new coal pot, all sent to her by Nicholas. The kind of meat cooked here is of great significance since it is commonly understood in the yard that cooking a meal without meat on a Sunday is a source of great shame for the poor soul reduced to such a menial situation. That Mamitz can parade both mutton and pork, however, is a notable mark of her wealth and the exceptional level of investment being contributed by her keeper.

While Mamitz remains in her room, Celestine assists her by putting three coal pots on the fire to cook, a feat unknown to most inhabitants of this or any yard. The source of Mamitz's "triumph" in these adverse conditions is suddenly revealed in the final events of the story. To have food to cook in one coal pot was, at times, impossible—but three pots on the fire at once, with two different types of meat! Irene is irate at this flaunting of good fortune. By this point, she is also skeptical about Mamitz's absence in the yard. However, soon after, Mamitz and Celestine throw the door of Mamitz's room open, and the events of the morning are made clear:

> Both halves (of the door) were plastered with notes, green five-dollar notes, red two-dollar notes, and blue dollar-notes, with a pin at the corner of each note to keep it firm. Irene was so flabbergasted that for a second or two she stood with her mouth open. Nicholas had come back and begged pardon, and given her all his money. There must be forty, no, fifty dollars, more spread out on the door.

Mamitz and Bertha's sister were sinking with laughing, and the joke was spreading, for other people were coming up to see what the disturbance was about. Tears of rage and mortification rushed into Irene's eyes.[24]

The image of the money pinned, each note individually, to Mamitz's front door captures the "worth" and value at work in the barrack-yard. Her particular form of triumph has a remarkable impact not only on Irene, but also on the "market" of the yard: it reinserts her as a formidable force. In this instance, it is not just the money that assures her this position, but her willingness to laugh aloud, blatantly, at Irene and her efforts. This laughter, though at Irene's expense, assures the community who rallied around Mamitz of their piece of this triumph, as it belongs to each one of them on this glorious morning.

James's "Triumph" is one of the few barrack-yard narratives with a humorous slant. Most end with some form of tragedy or distress. James's deployment of ironic humor in this short story effectively creates a moment of humanity in an otherwise demoralizing social atmosphere. That these women are not only able, but determined, to find their own source of fulfillment and even satisfaction, in spite of their exclusion from social and economic opportunities, attests to the sense of "triumph" from which James draws his title. In this respect, the barrack-yard narratives go far to shape new perspectives on sociohistorical institutions by creating systems for existence in spite of popular prejudices. James's story is also significant because it pays particular attention to the divisive effects of power structures among the poor and working classes. Within the barrack-yard, daily necessities become the markers of social value. James's deployment of the barrack-yard as a site where hierarchal structures parallel those of the working and middle classes reveals the stark contradictions at work within these communities. Where "mutton and pork" serve as markers of upward mobility in the barrack-yard, skin color and education are means of establishing social value among the working and middle classes in Trinidad. That sexual intercourse is the main currency (the exchangeable commodity) in the story is a significant commentary on the exploitative nature of labor practices in Trinidad.

In "Triumph," sexual intercourse is constructed as "productive." In this context, the absence of children in the barrack-yard is significant because it recasts the value of sexual activity for women beyond producing children, which would have been the "socially responsible" form of "productive labor" acceptable to the social value system. James portrays these women as "workers" who, like any laborer, seek security, good wages (or food and shelter), and fair treatment from their employers. In so doing, he ties these expectations to their rights as citizens, regardless of their trade or position within the hierarchy of a closed economy such as the barrack-yards. Sylvia Wynter discusses James's effort to engage the "multiple modes of domination" at work in economies such as those represented in his barrack-yard stories. According to Wynter,

> The fictional systems in both *Minty Alley* and "Triumph" constitute the site of the yard, that is, a tenement house, overcrowded, its life spilling out into the yard where people jostle each other, and most are jobless or underemployed in a world ruled by chance and instability. These are people whose societies are reserve societies drawn into the system when the profits of single crops boom, and expelled when single crop booms burst. The identity of labor is not the norm. In the value code of the hegemonic system, most of the dwellers of the yard are condemned like Bondsman to accept their incalculated zero value of identity, their own nothingness.[25]

The open neglect of and unconcern for popular values and mores shown by the characters in "Triumph" are more than a reflection of the squalid state of their lives. These attitudes also defiantly affirm another conception of value and utility for women's work in a system of labor that traditionally constructs women's work as unproductive. The colonial government considers labor productive if, and only if, it develops or contributes to the economy of the Empire. However, James's model for the working poor suggests that the well-being of the nation, represented through the yard, is communal, as the occupants of the yard share in the "wealth" of various members of the community. Thus, the other women share in the benefits of Mamitz's newfound wealth of keepers, just as they contribute to and share in Irene's disgrace.

By redefining sex as a form of capital through which freedom and goods can be acquired, James challenges what Wynter refers to as the "cultural law of value."[26] Through his refiguring of "utility," the value of these "unemployed" (by middle-class definitions) people is no longer dependent on production, but is now defined in relation to the (sexual and domestic) energy expended to be "kept." Hence, "people and the condition they represent" are brought into a different relationship, beyond mere "utility." The characters in "Triumph," apart from being a vehicle for challenging middle-class sentiments of decency and the sanctity of social institutions such as marriage and "productive" labor, also seek to restore cultural value to the masses of unidentified laborers in the country. James uses physical appearance as a means for drawing connections between growth, well-being, and the availability of labor when Mamitz's voluptuousness suddenly attracts the men who paid her no attention when there were no outward signs of wealth. Her size, as she literally grows more amply voluptuous, and her status as a "kept" woman, are juxtaposed with the uneven power relations between colony and Empire experienced by James and other working-class blacks of his generation in

Trinidad. Mamitz's prosperity and size by the end of the story are distinctly different from her condition in the beginning. However, her "fatness" is accomplished largely through her own improvisation, wit, and street smarts because her keepers (like the British Empire) are only interested in her immediate value as a labor source (one who provides sex, meals, and clean laundry). What is of importance here is the sense that Mamitz, like other laborers, is awakening to her power as the engine that moves the larger vehicle of the colony. More importantly, the solidarity that emerges between Mamitz and the other inhabitants of the yard foreshadows the future of the labor movement in Trinidad and other parts of the region.

This reading of James's story refigures the language of political economy such that gender and sexuality take on an overt market value, one that was always already a part of the colonial economy in Trinidad. This refiguring, however, resists the institutional appropriations of gender and sexuality in the service of overarching narratives of the nation and Empire. In other words, as Wynter suggests, the new market structure defines its rewards by a different, though related, system of value, and it was precisely the revaluation of this system that prompted a full-scale condemnation of the magazine and its content. One of the most notable cultural critics of the time, James Belmont, expressed his "disgust" at the presentation of these "types of people" as Trinidadian society and Trinidadian "art." What is most interesting about his objections is the contradiction between his desire to maintain freedom of speech and his need to question who is "worthy" of representation. His cold reception of *Trinidad* is couched in discourses of taste and aesthetics. The suggestion that imagination and creativity are governed by an unspoken set of laws serves to buttress the role of art in exercising and teaching social responsibility. Foremost among the tenets of social responsibility is the ability to distinguish "art" from what Belmont sees as "pornography": "From the first time I started to think for myself I've always agreed with the doctrine that an author should write of life in all its circumstances not only with a view to revelation of character but also, and I hold chiefly, although I know there are many who will not agree with me, for the creation of artistic pleasures in the mind of a reader. What produces these pleasures in one type of mind may not do so in another."[27] As Belmont's critique makes clear, the particularities of having discerning "taste" derive from good judgment. Belmont's concern is aimed at reminding the readers, and indeed the writers, of the fine line between those who have access to colonial education, which produces this kind of genius, and "certain types of people in which vice is an accepted accommodation of life."[28]

These "depraved" people, as Belmont calls them,[29] represent a condition that can only evoke sympathetic pity in the readers, but serves no purpose where the "true doctrine" of the social responsibilities of literature is concerned. The discourse Belmont employs throughout the article is in keeping with debates taking place in Europe and the Americas about the ability of blacks to aspire to and achieve Art and "higher things," a phrase that Belmont uses repeatedly in his article. Belmont's didacticism is directed specifically at black West Indian middle-class readers who, with the benefit of colonial education, have their sights set on brighter futures. The "doctrine" to which Belmont refers is more than an ideological goal for national literature; it is a guide for social and political etiquette for the emerging "genius" he sees in the editors of *Trinidad*. His critique of the magazine questions the editor's judgment and lack of aesthetic consideration.

Another critic, Elizabeth Peabody, submitted a provocative essay to the *Beacon*, seemingly in response to the condemnation of the barrack-yard stories.[30] In her essay, "Defence of Modern Realism in Fiction," Peabody takes the unprecedented (in the context of the *Beacon*) position of charging readers with being "immature" and "indiscriminate" in their responses to issues such as sexual education, pornographic magazines, and literature. In making her case for socially responsible literature, Peabody draws from vast literary traditions to assert that artistic literature should expose the workings beneath the surface of society. She notes that texts such as *Passionate Virgin*, *Monte Carlo's Mistress*, and Eugene O'Neill's *Strange Interludes* all have value for what they contribute to the broader narrative of life. Peabody makes a passionate plea for readers to consider the social and political value of literature when she comments that "It is both unfair and lacking in discernment to class with these charlatans, posing as realists, the serious artist who in his attempt to paint life as it is, must, of necessity bring in phases that many of us choose to ignore as existing. I am no Freudian, nor a disciple of Jung or Alder, but I recognize the vitality of sex in our lives and realize that in order to portray real human beings this life force cannot be discounted."[31] This charge seems to be a direct response to Belmont's earlier criticism of the stories that appeared in *Trinidad*; but her juxtaposing of realist and serious artists is particularly bold in light of the debates taking place in the 1930s about realist art in Europe, and she is clearly aware of and engaged with these debates throughout her essay.

Peabody's claim situates the realist narrative emerging in Trinidad as more than a record of the emergence of a new social tradition. She suggests that the realist tradition emerging in Caribbean literature offers an instance for cultural expression to work in the service of the subject by creating itself (through fiction) in order to maintain itself. In other words, the true object of the realist tradition in Trinidadian literature was not solely realism itself, or pure reflectionism, but the emergence of new modes of expression and intervention that had not existed prior to the Trinidad Renaissance. Although she asserts that literature can indeed capture life "as it is," she stops short of defining this as "authentic realism." Peabody cites Katherine Mansfield, Elizabeth Arnim, and Anton Chekhov on the emerging debate about realism and artistic literature. The texts she selects all buttress her final analysis of the role of literature in society, which, she argues, is not to entertain or to pass on dogmatic perspectives.

Her closing comments cut right to the heart of what is at stake in the ongoing struggle in Trinidad to define a nationalist literature:

> We presume to criticize those authors who try to penetrate beneath the surface of mankind, who probe for the real personality, who portray people as they are in an attempt—perhaps vain—to discover what life is like, to understand the reasons that motivate people's actions, and the circumstances that make them what they are. And if the author in his probing, finds that we are not all gods in miniature, but that we still have much of the beast in us—what of that? Is it not better to face it, rather than ignore it and allow ourselves to become more of an unthinking animal? By acknowledging our weaknesses, we have already started on the road of progress, and at least raise the possibility of becoming—better beasts.[32]

In this passage, Peabody asserts that the philosophical intervention of creative expression is a matter not only of aesthetics, but also of cultural ethics. She insists that the work of art has a greater political and cultural charge, to provide the impetus for thought and understanding the subject's existence in the world, and to "raise the possibility of becoming," as she asserts, "better beasts." It is important, however, to note that her image of this "better beast" is not founded on any notions of improving the "civility" of middle-class society because civility, she argues, is founded on social prejudices. Her defense of modern fiction is nothing short of a manifesto on the value of thought, not simply the social value of morals and upward mobility. These two points are of singular importance because the Trinidad Renaissance writers would eventually be pushed to develop both strains of this debate through a national literature that was at once founded on the lived experiences of Caribbean subjects, but also critical of these experiences and the institutions that informed them.

SHIFTING NATIONALIST TERRAINS: ETHNIC CURRENCY AND THE DOMESTICATION OF WOMEN AND POLITICS IN TRINIDADIAN LITERATURE

The mid-1930s marked a significant shift in the organization of women's labor in Trinidad and Tobago. Trade workers, market-women, domestics, and clerical workers began to gain support for their labor concerns from local unions. Elma Francois, Christina King, and Daisy Crick were the vanguard of the labor union movement in Trinidad. King and Francois, who founded the Negro Welfare Social and Cultural Association (NWSCA), were central figures in the mobilization of workers across the country around issues of poor working conditions and salary inequity. Apart from their contributions as labor organizers, these women launched an important grassroots movement on platform issues similar to those debated in *Trinidad* and the *Beacon*. These issues included equal pay and job opportunities for local workers, better working conditions and pay for agricultural, industrial, railroad, and dock workers across Trinidad and Tobago, and self-government in the political arena.

One of the most significant aspects of the NWSCA was its effort to address nationalist politics through the cultural and social development of laborers. Daisy Crick and other women took the lead, seeing the emphasis on cultural and social politics as an opening to bring working-class women into public debates. The Garveyite Movement was also a major force for politicizing working-class women in Trinidad. As Rhoda Reddock points out, Amy Garvey's visit to Trinidad during the early 1930s brought national attention to the already prominent Garvey Movement in Trinidad. The United Negro Improvement Association's (UNIA) newspaper, the *Negro World*, was in circulation in Trinidad as early as 1919. By 1927, there were more than thirty UNIA branches in Trinidad; only Cuba had more branches than Trinidad.[33] Several of the leading figures of the women's labor movement were members of the UNIA and had ties to members of the British Communist Party. The literary representations of changes taking place reflected the complex cultural and political milieu in Trinidad. Some of these social developments included depictions of an emerging working-class labor movement that was articulate in its insistence on self-government. There was also another emerging class of "middle minority merchants," who played a significant role in changing the cultural and social landscape of the country.

This class of small business and storefront shop owners presented important employment opportunities for women aspiring to improve their situations by means of personal relationships and liaisons. Small storefront businesses increased the need for cashiers, typists, and secretaries. As Mendes's short story, "Her Chinaman's Way" (1929), suggests, the status of the newly emerging "working woman" was vastly different from that of her literary predecessors in the barrack-yards. "Her Chinaman's Way" foreshadows another aspect of the changing situations for the working classes in Trinidad. Mendes's story features a young woman who, like her literary foremothers in James's "Triumph," depends on a "keeper" for financial support. In spite of the clear inequities in the relationship, the social position of Maria, the protagonist in

Mendes's story, is significantly different from that of the women described in "Triumph."

Maria's dwellings are not those of the barrack-yard, although we are told early in the story that she had previously resided in one, and her lover is not a mere "keeper" as is the case in the barrack-yard stories. "Her Chinaman's Way" draws its imaginative perspective from the productive forces (economic and physical) of different ethnic groups in Trinidad. The shift from the barrack-yard to the storefront business and from the predominantly black barrack-yard dwellers to the "middle minority" (Chinese Creoles, Portuguese Creoles, Syrians, and Spanish Creoles) stresses the relationship between ethnicity and social stratification in Trinidad. We are introduced to Maria through her physical features, all of which signify that she is not "fully" African or black, but is a mixture of those cultures or "races" that commingled in this part of the New World:

> Sitting now on a soiled soap-box—relic of the shop—her brown face handsome in an exotic way with its full lips, large nose, and small eyes told you there was Chinese blood in her veins, she looked a strange queen. Her *voluptuous figure*, inherited from her half-breed Venezuelan mother, had always been *sought after by men in town*. Before she met Hong Wing, *many men had owned her for periods ranging from three months to one year*; but these were men of her own class—foremen-stevedores and porters, head messengers of the large firms in Port-of-Spain, cabmen, and once a Portuguese barber to whom she had been more than willing to be faithful, for his being white gave her prestige, but he had so ill treated her during his frequent bouts of drunkenness, she had been forced to leave him.[34]

The barber's ethnic identity moves him higher up the social and economic ladder in Trinidad. In the same vein, the protagonist is identified as a having desirable "assets"; her fortune is represented in terms of her "inheritance" of phenotypical characteristics that identify her as not "fully" African. What is more interesting, however, is that her "voluptuous figure" is attributed to her "half-breed" Venezuelan mother. We are left to speculate about the relationship between the "full lips and large nose" and her "half-breed" mother; the "other half" is presumably visible in the phenotypical descriptors. In the genealogical trajectory being mapped here, naming Maria's blackness would disrupt the social and economic hierarchy under construction.

Despite having keepers with better incomes than those in James's story, Maria knows it is more advantageous to be kept by a "white" barber since his skin color would inevitably increase her "market value." The value of "non-blackness" in this story cannot be understated. The outward physical markers of Maria's hybrid ethnic identity ensure that her proximity to African ancestry and, therefore, poverty cannot be directly traced. This fact makes her the object of desire for middle-class and working-class men alike. The evidence of "Chinese blood in her veins" suggests that her liaison with Hong Wing does not cross ethnic boundaries, a concern slowly beginning to emerge among middle minorities in Trinidad. The narrator's description of her past relationships as men who had "owned" her is particularly insightful because it situates the sexual economy of urban spaces like Port-of-Spain in the context of colonial systems of exploitation.

Maria's relationship with Hong Wing, therefore, makes her social position very desirable since he owns his own business and has an earning potential far greater than anything she could have achieved with men "of her own class." The growing middle-class and bourgeois fear of miscegenation was being subverted in a most peculiar way in Trinidad. Liaisons between working-class people reflected the same pragmatic desires for upward mobility as the British and West Indian bourgeoisie. Nowhere are these desires as evident as in the acquisition of that which was so scarce or virtually absent in barrack-yard narratives, space and children:

> At one time she and Hong Wing—that was before their baby arrived—lived on the premises of the shop like all other Chinese shop-keepers in Port of Spain, but Maria had persuaded him to take a couple of rooms in Charlotte Street. Maria liked to think that she was more respectable than those other women of her acquaintance who were kept by Chinese shopkeepers: they all lived without one exception that she could think of, in rooms at the back of the shops where the various scents of pork, hogs' head, salt fish and ham boiled weeks before the retail pervaded the atmosphere.[35]

This passage makes clear the fact that there is a growing community of women for whom these liaisons were a means of upward mobility. New communities emerged out of an increasing population of "middle minority" businessmen for whom urban businesses also meant adopting urban lifestyles and becoming part of the neighborhoods in Port-of-Spain. These communities were primarily black poor and working-class people, the same people to whom these shopkeepers sold their goods and merchandise. The measure of "respectability" here needs to read as part of the reward system to which Maria belongs. Her fairness in complexion assures her a measure of privilege, and unlike other female acquaintances, she would not remain in the back room with the pork, salt fish, and other goods to be sold. It is worth noting that the list of foods mentioned here (hog's head, salt fish, ham) are all those commonly associated with Afro-Trinidadian working-class communities.

Despite the fine line (or, in this case, the extra rooms) that separates Maria from other black women who are "kept" by shopkeepers, the differences between the black characters and Maria are marked in stark terms, physically and linguistically. Philogen, who lived in the same yard with Maria prior to her good fortune, is described as "gaunt, ugly and black."[36] We are reminded of her physical appearance several times in the story, particularly in comparison to Maria's beauty. Moreover, where Maria's dialogue is written in Trinidadian patois, Philogen's speech is represented through a series of mispronunciations meant, one can assume, to indicate her position at the bottom of the social hierarchy of the yard. However, like the protagonist in "Triumph," her knowledge of obeah makes her an important asset to those in the yard because she can assist in times of distress:

> [O]ne night, as twelve o'clock sounded from a distant church steeple, Philogen bathed Maria in water prepared from rare herbs and roots, at the same time enjoining upon her the necessity for saying a prayer every night and morning. It was after that that Hong Wing had appeared on the scene. Philogen had said, "Gerl, you take it from me, dat is de praise you offer up to de Almighty to shake of dis debil work on you, wit' dat bat. You ain't going to refuse Hong Wing?" And she [Maria] answered, "I don' know." "Buh you mus' know gerl. Dese Chinks likes women like you—half paniol. Don' make a blarsted fool o' yourself gerl."[37]

Maria's good fortune, then, is the work of "higher science," and she is able to move from the yard into Charlotte Street in Port-of-Spain. While this is by no means a great leap in terms of dwellings, it marks a significant improvement from her former state. It is important to note, however, that despite Philogen's knowledge of obeah, she remains in the barrack-yard and can only visit Maria in her newfound comfort. Philogen is an adroit reader of the ethnic landscape of Trinidad, as she reminds Maria that her "half painol" status is highly sought after, particularly by Chinese men, whom she derogatively calls "Chinks." This latter terminology is particularly telling because it is indicative of an increasing tension between black Trinidadians and the business-owning "middle minority" classes in Port-of-Spain, a tension that, more often than not, manifested itself in contestations over the availability and accessibility of black (or mixed) women.

Mendes's story takes a rather unexpected turn, however, when Maria meets and falls in love with Adolphus, a "lithe black carter man."[38] When Maria meets Adolphus, she realizes that her life with Hong Wing is uninteresting and annoying because she "had never been able to understand him."[39] As the narrator tells us, Maria had been used to dictating and controlling her men, but with Hong Wing she finds herself having to beg timidly for the things she wants. Maria decides to leave Hong Wing for Adolphus, and, once again with the help of Philogen, she sets about planning Hong Wing's downfall. Maria decides to inform the police of Hong Wing's trafficking in and use of opium. She believes this is the only way to get out of the relationship and keep her child, since she has no job and no means to sustain herself and her son; Hong Wing, despite his immense dislike for the child because, as he puts it, "He too much expense, give too much trouble," has the money and institutional support to force her to give up her child.[40]

Maria gives the police information about the place and time of an arranged drug deal between Hong Wing and one of his associates. However, the plan goes completely awry, a young man is killed, and Hong Wing escapes. He returns home suspecting Maria's involvement in his misfortune but does not play his hand immediately. Instead, he treats her warmly and asks for a cup of coffee since the rain outdoors has given him a chill. Maria returns, fearful that he knows of her part in the night's events. She begins to think about how she might escape when he finally confronts her:

"Who tell police I go las' nig' for op'um, ehn?" he hissed at her through the two rows of black mouse-like teeth. She heard the empty cup smash against the partition, and then his voice thin, steady. "I no vex love. You give me op'um. I go give flien' some," and he limped out of the room into the windy street. Maria gazed at the closed door, wondering what he had gone out to get. To await his return would be folly. She would go straightaway to Philogen. She could walk the distance quite comfortably with her baby. Going up to it, she withdrew the shawl. She couldn't believe her eyes. Her new dress was on the baby, around its neck, drawn tight-tight. . . .[41]

This conclusion, and indeed the entire story, is fraught with ambiguous significations regarding the changing cultural and social landscape in Trinidad and Tobago. Maria's decision to leave is marred, not by an absence of wit, but by the presence of her child because, as the streetwise Philogen notes, having a child does not make it easy for her to move at her own pace and fancy. In most of the barrack-yard fiction, there are no children, nor any mention of women's desire to have and raise them. Still, Maria is depicted as a very loving mother who shows a serious concern for Hong Wing's jealousy of the bond between her and her child. Where Maria had the freedom to "cuss off" and dispense with her last keeper, the chance for a clean and dignified break is complicated by her new responsibilities as a mother.

This new development is one of the first steps toward a more socially responsible narrative of resistance in Trinidadian literature that emerged as the nationalist movement toward self-government gained strength. Literary representations of the political changes taking place in Trinidad after 1935 featured women who were far more invested in socially responsible relationships. The romance plot, featuring fiancés, marriage, and common-law arrangements, was now a prominent part of the literary landscape, although emphases on race and class politics in Trinidad were still central to depictions of the nationalist landscape; yet the newest element in this social arrangement was the prominence of maternity in the newly emerging nationalist narrative of resistance. This shift marks the beginning of the domestication of women's political roles and visibility in the literary landscape of the Caribbean. Alison Donnell suggests that this change was a response to the way the new Caribbean nationalism took up the European cult of domesticity, beginning in the mid-1930s and intensifying through the 1940s:

> It could be argued that for women writers this crossing between colony and nation . . . was harder to make because of the social pressures attendant to the relentless promotion of the European cult of femininity. Both black and white middle class women were the targets of a strenuous socialization programme, which admonished them to perceive marriage, maternity, or alternatively chastity and charity as suitable paths of feminine development, and many literary depictions both reflected and consolidated these female destinies. What I am trying to suggest here, then, is that pre-1970 Caribbean women's writing has to some extent been a casualty of the need to articulate and narrate an emergent nationalist history and culture in the Caribbean. It was a bend in the river which could not usefully be navigated in that crucial crossing between colony and nation.[42]

Donnell astutely identifies the inherent contradictions that needed to be negotiated as Caribbean literature moved closer to articulating a nationalist narrative of unity and social responsibility. Her analysis of the excision of Caribbean women's writing from literary histories of the region can easily be extended to include the literary representations of women's historical experiences. The possibility of an emergent nationalist movement that recognized the liminal spaces of the "hinterlands" that have always been central to Caribbean anti-colonial resistance was sacrificed in favor of a unified, seamless narrative of national unity.

The nation, in order to be independent, had to be imagined through the lens of institutionally sanctioned discourses of paternity, sovereignty, and charismatic leadership. As Donnell points out in her critique of V. S. Naipaul's *Bend in the River*, once the boats left Caribbean nation-states, and expatriation and exile became the models for constructing postcolonial Caribbean identities, all citizens "in between" were left at sea. Caribbean literature and politics had reached a significant historical juncture that demanded that the literary landscape be regendered and, indeed, reinvented through the performance of femininity, maternity, and domesticity. Donnell's observation about Caribbean women's writing reflects the reconfiguration of colonial subjectivity and the nation-state as first and foremost male. The bend in the river, as she suggests, could only be maneuvered with the weight of the "body politic" distributed evenly among the "sons of the nation." However, the literature of the period maintained a nationalist discourse that attempted to be inclusive, paying marginal attention to women and East Indians although each made up a significant portion of the labor force. The "sons of the nation," poised to receive their inheritance, when threatened with an increasingly diverse "body politic" placed women below deck but never off the boat, since the strength of this constituency as a literary trope and political force had been tested and not found wanting.

If barrack-yard women are a trope for the nation, their waywardness is a radical positioning in terms of labor, culture, and economics for a colony intent on becoming a nation. This same brash waywardness proved to be the case put forth by colonial officials for retaining control of the colonies and exercising the benevolent patronage that profited Britain tremendously. The Colonial Office responded to the growing sentiment toward self-government with sheer contempt, suggesting that black West Indians were incapable of appreciating the full meaning of self-government. In a letter from the Colonial Office, Governor G. Grindle commented to his colleague "the vivid imagination of the negro tends to hypnotize him with words that he uses without understanding their meaning. I suggest, therefore, the dispatch should explain what 'self-government' means and tell them plainly that they are not going to have it."[43] This sentiment, shared by most governors in the Colonial Office in Trinidad, was made public on several occasions when appeals were made for local representation in the governing body, particularly for the largely dissatisfied working classes.

When these appeals continued to fall on deaf ears, local agitators such as Arthur Andrew Cipriani, Elma Francois, Jim Barrette, Tubal Uriah Butler, Daisy Crick, and Adrian Cola Rienzi (to name a few) began a concerted labor unionization movement. The effect of this movement would be felt across the Caribbean as it culminated in the Labor Riots of 1937, which virtually shut down the industrial and agricultural sectors of Trinidad. The impact of the island-wide strikes was felt most deeply in the sugar and oil industries that were Britain's largest sources of income in the country. The changing social and political climate of the region was reflected in the shift in the literary landscape as well. The short story form gave way to the emergence of the novel and the literature of the post-riot period focused on forging national alliances between middle-class men and working-class women. Novels such as Ralph de Boissière's *Crown Jewel* (1952) and *Rum and Coca-Cola* (1954) examine the changes under way in Trinidad in the late 1930s and offer some insight into the new relationships across classes. Both novels are set during the labor movements of 1937 but feature the newly politically astute middle-class sons of the nation, who are committed to struggling against colonial exploitation. *Crown Jewel* features a young woman named Cassie, who is raised by both of her parents who, we are told, were employed even in the hardest times. This point is of great significance because it is an implicit means of distinguishing this generation of black working-class women from the poorer and (in the traditional sense) unemployed women represented in the barrack-yard narratives. The newly emergent novel was not so much a break from the writing that began in *Trinidad* and the *Beacon* as it was a gradual transformation that reflected the changing social and political landscape.

The prominence of the nuclear family in the new West Indian novel of the 1940s coincides with other British and European paradigms of social responsibility. The twist in de Boissière's novel occurs when Cassie becomes involved in the trade union movement alongside her husband. In a scene indicative of the turbulence of the period, Cassie is arrested, taken to the station, and beaten by Sergeant Duke in the presence of her "keeper" and soon-to-be husband:

> Popito saw Duke's enormous black, smooth, perspiring neck bulging over his collar. He felt he was going to hit Cassie again and he shouted: "I was at home!"
> And at that moment Duke punched her in the belly forcing her to breathe out in a grunt. "She expecting a baby and you lettin' this animal beat her?" Popito shouted, quivering. After attempting to frighten Cassie with a severe warning he released her from custody.
> That evening she lost the child. The doctor he had rushed to call ordered her to hospital.[44]

The presence or possibility of maternity is a casualty of the mobility and political efficacy of de Boissière's female protagonist. The implication that Cassie mourns her role as wife and not necessarily as mother is significant for her political development in the novel. She becomes even more involved in the trade union movement after the loss of her child. Halfway through the novel, Popito is killed, and this becomes the definitive moment in Cassie's labor activism. She emerges as a fervent leader, speaking on labor platforms across Trinidad. Because she no longer has anything to lose, having lost child and husband, she is able to pursue her political career. Cassie emerges as the only woman in the novel whose political consciousness is not defined through her domestic or maternal responsibilities. Naturally, she is not the "leader" of the movement; this role is preserved for a middle-class black man named Le Maître, who helps to shape Cassie into a well-schooled comrade. However, gender constructions of the period made it inconceivable that a woman like Cassie could become the political voice of the movement. Like her political extra-literary predecessors, Daisy Crick, Christina King, and Elma Francois, Cassie's role in the political movement is curbed by the rise of black nationalist discourses in the Caribbean.[45]

The emergence of middle-class romance novels represented the shifts taking place in the political landscape. More importantly, this kind of novel introduced a new, "responsible" national subject, the politically conscious but socially conforming woman of the nation. In Cassie's case, there are explicit consequences for crossing the boundaries of these socially acceptable roles. This transgression costs her the newly valued identity as "woman" as she is slowly stripped of all the markers that allow her entry into this order of signification. She is neither mother nor wife and can, therefore, pursue a role as a foot-soldier in the movement from colony to nation. *Crown Jewel* and its sequel *Rum and Coca-Cola* make it clear that there is no option for both in the march from colony to nation in the Caribbean.

Rhonda Cobham comments on the reversal of the centrality of female characters in the works written after the periods of unrest in Trinidad. Cobham observes that the changes taking place in the political arena are reflected in the new novels of resistance and independence:

> Before 1937 the women of the lower classes had been the major bread-winners for their families. Their men were often unemployed or absent working overseas. After the post-war reforms the women continued to work and to push their sons toward the newly attainable goal of middle-class respectability. But where an earlier generation of writers had concentrated on the struggles of the working class seen in the lives of women, it was the newly arrived middle-class man whose problems of identity absorbed the writers of the 1950s, themselves the products of a new social mobility.[46]

In the literature before 1937, the struggles of the working classes in Trinidad had been embodied in the struggles of women so that their "world view is allowed to permeate the reader's responses to all issues, from religious belief to sexual preferences."[47] The women in these pre-1937 stories do not simply represent or perform male functions, nor do they represent an effeminate maleness. In fact, I would argue that the fiction published in *Trinidad* and the *Beacon* effectively engendered a literary tradition that centered women's experiences within the context of national spaces in colonial Trinidad. In her introduction to Alfred Mendes's novel, *Black Fauns*, Cobham acknowledges this shift and discusses its implications. As she points out,

> *Black Fauns* is dominated by important female characters—a feature the work shares with most of the novels written by West Indians whose formative years

pre-date the events of 1937–38. Among the next generation of West Indian writers; Selvon, Lamming, Walcott, Brathwaite, Harris, Hearne, Naipaul, and Dawes—the pattern is completely reversed. Though many of these writers present female characters sensitively in their works the woman's role is usually defined in terms of a central male protagonist.[48]

The trope of the economically exploited, morally corrupt (in conventional terms), and sexually and socially wayward woman in early Caribbean fiction challenged the Victorian sentiments that pervaded Trinidadian colonial culture. The response to the stories that appeared in *Trinidad* and the *Beacon* put the conditions of poor peasant and working-class Trinidadians in the limelight, even if the stories were later castigated as lacking aesthetic value and social acumen. It was enough that the ruling elite were offended by the conditions represented in these stories because they highlighted the dehumanizing realities of the workers in the country. However, the march toward independence necessitated the marginalization of these women in order to construct the image of a colonial subject more conventionally and institutionally suited for the responsibilities that self-government and national independence would bring.

The interpolation of creative expression and interpretations of colonial rule in Trinidad into a coherent, "unified" Caribbean nationalist narrative ushered in a new age of consciousness among West Indian writers and a new relationship to the British Empire. This mass movement began to have less and less to do with the nation's citizens and much more to do with the objective of nationalism itself. Therefore, the erasure of these "unruly" subjects effectively created an instance in which the productive capacities of the imagination (or as Heidegger refers to it, "the look" of the imagination) were reduced to a "reproductive" representation of colonial institutions, only modified to express the realities of colonial subjects.

The polemics of women's welfare was a productive allegory for an emerging nationalist movement. Prevailing discourses of ethnicity and definitions of womanhood were deployed in order to shed light on the political and philosophical agendas from within the marginalized spaces they occupied. The shifts in literary representations that I have outlined here, for example, need to be read, to borrow a phrase from Paul Gilroy, as an "expressive counter-culture" that refuses prevailing discourses on the separation of ethics and aesthetics and culture and politics. According to Gilroy, this separation has, for too long, divided authorized knowledges from other social and cultural institutions when, in fact, they are intricately connected to and dependent on one another for their continued relevance. As Gilroy asserts, we need to

Reread and rethink this expressive counter-culture not simply as a succession of literary tropes and genres but as a philosophical discourse, which refuses the modern, occidental separation of ethics and aesthetics, culture and politics. This tradition maintained the idea that good life for the individual and the problem of the best social and political order for the collectivity could be discerned by rational means. Not perceiving its residual condition, blacks in the west eavesdropped on and then took over a fundamental question from the intellectual obsessions of their enlightened rulers. Their progress from the status of slaves to the status of citizens led them to inquire into what the best possible forms of social and political existence might be.[49]

The literature of the Trinidad Renaissance is an instance of such a critical inquiry, as "fiction" provided the opportunity to experiment with the possible forms of social and political existence under colonial rule.[50] The counter-cultural expression of these possibilities sets larger questions in motion regarding the colonial subject's relationship to history and thought beyond the British Empire.

The short fiction published in these literary magazines provided desperately needed imaginings of working-class landscapes, struggles, and epistemological reference points for colonial subjects to reconceptualize their social and political existence. As the landscape evolved, so too did the art form, moving from short fiction to the more middle-class genre of the novel, and from this shift emerged a more responsible model of nationalist literature, one that strove to work within the colonial structure to change and strengthen the working-class foundational structures within Trinidad and Tobago. However, as Lamming's comments earlier in this chapter suggest, a consciousness of creating something new out of the colonial spaces within the larger Caribbean artistic and political landscape was slowly emerging in the region. By 1946, when a young George Lamming arrived in Trinidad, the arts scene in the country had grown in every conceivable facet: dance, literature, and theatre. Equally important was the fact that the art emerged as part of a growing social and political consciousness that could not be contained within the confining institutional spaces available to young, black, educated men in the colonies. The political and social interest of this new generation of Caribbean writers (George Lamming, Wilson Harris, Derek Walcott, and C. L. R. James) saw the growth in the region as an integral part of a larger set of philosophical questions that had yet to be sufficiently addressed in the arts movement in the Caribbean. In an effort to comprehend the "residual conditions" of their existence, colonial subjects exiled themselves to the seat of the Empire in order to eavesdrop. The geographical and social distance provided a new critical landscape to engage and express their Selves and their surroundings.

NOTES

1. The phrase "black West Indians" is used here to indicate West Indians of African descent. While there are large populations of West Indians of East Indian descent in Trinidad, the magazine's writers and readers were largely (though not exclusively) either black West Indians or members of other "ethnic minorities" in Trinidad (e.g., Portuguese, Syrian, white). This is not to suggest, however, that the magazine did not address issues and concerns that pertained to Indo-Trinidadian communities. One particular issue with implications for Trinidadians across ethnic and class lines was the Government Divorce Bill of 1930, which *Trinidad* and the *Beacon* opposed.

2. George Lamming, "The Sovereignty of the Imagination: An Interview with George Lamming," by David Scott, *Small Axe: A Caribbean Journal of Criticism*, no. 12 (September 2002): 86.

3. For a more comprehensive discussion of the emergence of black intellectuals and nationalism in Trinidad and Tobago, see Ivar Oxaal, *Black Intellectuals Come to Power: The Rise of Creole Nationalism in Trinidad and Tobago* (Cambridge: Schenkman Publishing, 1968). Several members of this group gained political prominence as the country moved toward independence. Adrian Cola Rienzi, a young Indian writer at the time, later became a leading figure in the trade union movement after the social disturbances in 1937. Albert Gomes, a Portugese Creole (and thus a member of the "middle minority"), was elected to the Legislative Council as a candidate of the Socialist United Front after holding several national portfolios. He later headed the Party of Political Progress group, which was soundly defeated by the newly popular People's National Movement and Eric Williams. Ernest Carr, also a member of the group, was an important contributor to Williams's political platform, while C. L. R. James went abroad to continue his education and became a leading left-wing intellectual and a staunch supporter of the labor union movement.

4. The social structure in Trinidad at the time made this kind of ethnic mixing unlikely. Schools were largely divided along class lines, which meant that very few black Trinidadians would have had the opportunity to attend the "prestige" schools. Additionally, a distinct split between urban and rural cultures emerged as a primary dividing force between East Indians, Afro-Trinidadians, and the white elite. The small business-owning class, which consisted primarily of Syrian and Chinese immigrants, took solace in their businesses and had very little interaction with the major institutions of the country. The end result of these internal divisions was an ethnic division of labor. Afro-Trinidadians made up the civil servants of the country, the white elites controlled and managed the nation's business sectors, East Indians were the primary agricultural support, and the Syrian and Chinese immigrants provided the small business support, running dry goods shops, fabric stores, and laundry services.

5. *Trinidad*, Editorial, 1, no. 2 (Easter 1930): 57–58.

6. Reinhard Sander, *The Trinidad Awakening* (New York: Greenwood Press, 1988).

7. Edouard Glissant, *Caribbean Discourse: Selected Essays*, trans. J. Michael Dash (Charlottesville: University Press of Virginia, 1989), 120.

8. I appropriate Kant's notion of fiction as an "actual fantasy" in order to reimagine the role of fiction in the Trinidad Renaissance. Kant's definition of fiction provides a context through which we can read and comprehend the contradictions between the social realist narratives in *Trinidad* and the *Beacon*, and the cultural and social landscapes they are said to represent. Kant defines fiction as the "actual fantasies with which the mind entertains itself as it is continually being aroused by the diversity that strikes the eye"; Immanuel Kant, *A Critique of Judgment*, trans. Werner S. Pluhar (Indianapolis, IN: Hackett Publishing, 1987), 94. Kant's conceptualization of the term "fiction" offers us another lens through which to appreciate the function of cultural expression in the formation of the subject. There is a metacritical element implicit in both Kant's use of the term and my own deployment of the concept as a tool for reading the literary genre.

9. Theodor Adorno, "Reconciliation under Duress," in *Aesthetics and Politics* (London and New York: Verso Press, 1997), 159–60.

10. C. L. R. James, "Triumph," *Trinidad* 1, no. 1 (December 1929): 32.

11. The term "obeah" is used to describe a spiritual order of knowledge founded on the belief that through necromancy or witchcraft one can affect or predict the future.

12. See, for example, James Belmont, "James Belmont Condemns Local Magazine, Shocked Readers Write to the *Guardian*," *Trinidad Guardian*, December 22, 1929, 4, 10, for further commentary on the stories that appeared in *Trinidad*.

13. James, "Triumph," 15.

14. "Picong" is a term used to describe a form of verbal banter that utilizes double entendre, irony, and satire, all of which are employed and operate within a tension of provocation and jest. This tension is significant primarily because it allows the initiator of the provocation to resort to the lightness of banter (e.g., "I was only joking") if and when antagonisms intensify.

15. James, "Triumph," 37.

16. Sander, *Trinidad Awakening*, 58.

17. This term was often used to describe a condition of hopelessness, near destitution, and despair. In James's story, Celestine, another tenant in the yard, uses this phrase to describe Mamitz's condition. James, "Triumph," 32.

18. James, "Triumph," 34.

19. Several letters to the editor of the *Beacon* highlight discrepancies in wage compensation for women and working-class laborers. See, for example, Alfred Mendes, "Shop Girls," *Beacon* 1, no. 6 (September 1931): 11. The editorial note raises the issue of compensation for young women working in the shops downtown in Port-of-Spain, arguing that their working conditions are in no way sufficient in relation to the work they are expected to do and the manner in which they are expected to carry out their duties. Mendes notes that "They have a 'breakfast hour' which they must spend off the premises; and that perhaps is just as well. They are on their feet all day. There is no where to sit down for a moment. They may not sit down. They must be patient and polite. They go home at 4 o'clock: to Belmont or San Juan, or St. James. Some have bicycles: but what right has a girl to a bicycle

on $2.50 a week? Some take the tram—but by what system of economics can such a girl afford a tram? Some walk—but by what system of morality can such a girl be expected to walk home at 4 o'clock in the afternoon—at the end of the day's unrest? The problem is more difficult for the girls than for those who have the means of tackling it." Other editorials addressed the specific details of barrack-yard fiction and the responses by the public to the appearance of these stories in literary magazines like the *Beacon*. The editorial "What the Planter Plants," by James Cummings, author of the story "Barrack Rooms," takes one particular reader to task for his comments on the content of his story: "He feels that one should write only about the squanderous lives of the aristocrats and that the working classes must be left in their miserable plight.... They would believe that the lives of the labouring classes is one continuous heaven while in truth and fact it is a positive hell. The time has come when the working class is demanding its rights, not only as human beings, but as the pillars of the colony's progress and soon more evidence of this will be seen"; James Cummings, "What the Planter Plants," *Beacon* 1, no. 8 (November 1931): 22.

20. James, "Triumph," 33.
21. James, "Triumph," 37.
22. James, "Triumph," 40.
23. James uses this instance as one example of the role of picong as weapon for holding power in the barrack-yard. When Nicholas calls Mamitz a dog, Mamitz responds with one of "Celestine's most brilliant pieces of repartee," saying, "You' mother, you' sister, you' aunt, you' wife was the dog." Since Nicholas isn't yet married, she is cursing his future as well as his current family. Adding insult to injury, Celestine chimes in to add what was, at the time, the harshest of insults: "Its the wo'se when you meddle with them common low island people," referring to the fact that Nicholas was from St. Vincent, which (along with Grenada and the smaller islands) was an island "looked down upon by the Trinidad negro as low-island people"; James, "Triumph," 38.
24. James, "Triumph,"40.
25. Sylvia Wynter, "The Counter Doctrine of Jamesian Poesis," in *C. L. R. James' Caribbean*, eds. Paget Henry and Paul Buhle (Durham: Duke University Press, 1992), 75. In her discussion of what she calls a "Jamesian Poeisis," Wynter describes the tensions between "fine and non-fine arts," which help to legitimate an aesthetic of differential value. According to Wynter, an aesthetic of differential value "Stabilizes and legitimates, the differential value empirically expressed between the life value of the middle class and the life value of the popular forces. This differential value is then validly expressed in the differential rewards, that is, of the differential between the consumption ratio of the middle classes and the consumption ratio of the popular forces"; Wynter, "Counter Doctrine," 73. Such a cultural law of value works to instill in the masses a sense of inferiority while concretizing the implicit value of "utility" in a capitalist system of social organization. Moreover, as Wynter asserts, the value of education and of social and cultural etiquette is increased and becomes a seemingly natural part of the teleology of class hierarchies.

26. Wynter, "Counter Doctrine," 75.

27. James Belmont, "James Belmont Condemns," 4. In this lengthy condemnation, Belmont characterizes the short story as "utter nastiness": "I've just finished reading *Trinidad*, a yellow bound volume of short stories, articles and poems written by a half dozen talented men who live in Port-of-Spain. I picked it up in pleasant anticipation, I set it down disgusted. In *Trinidad*, there are many quite admirable things. In fact everyone is agreed the book is unique not merely as the first collection of local short stories by local authors ever published but as an example of inspiration of those who are aware of the sittings of an awakening genius in our own sons. I would feign [*sic*] say in our daughters as well. But how many thousand pities is it that the artistic and the obscene are disproportionately mixed in these creative efforts. Life and those who live it are made cheap without the compensating hint of higher things. Read what Mr. Mendes writes about the three men conversing in front of the provisions store in South Quay. It is one of the most revolting things I have ever come across. Its truth is no excuse for its utter nastiness. Mr. Mendes knows as well better than many of us what idle men at South Quay or anywhere else talk and think about, but he might have spared us the disgusting chronicle"; Belmont, "James Belmont Condemns," 4.

28. Belmont, "James Belmont Condemns," 4.

29. Belmont, "James Belmont Condemns," 4.

30. In the byline of her essay, an asterisk appears next to Peabody's name. The footnote that corresponds to this asterisk reads, "Miss Elizabeth Peabody, who lives in Brockton, has done book reviewing for several American newspapers, and is a graduate of Tuft's College, Boston"; Peabody, "Defence of Modern Realism in Fiction," *Beacon* 2, no. 6 (October/November 1932): 5. This announcement of Peabody's credentials as a writer clearly situates her as an "authority," or at least a person with credentials outside the region on literary matters. The note is also significant because it highlights the extent to which women's contributions were limited by their access to education and inclusion in these literary circles.

31. Peabody, "Defence of Modern Realism," 6.

32. Peabody, "Defence of Modern Realism," 8.

33. For a more detailed discussion of the impact of the Garveyite Movement in Trinidad, see Rhoda Reddock, "The Politics of Race and Class," in *Women, Labour, and Politics in Trinidad and Tobago* (Kingston, Jamaica: Ian Randle Publishers, 1994), 99–120.

34. Alfred Mendes, "Her Chinaman's Way," *Trinidad* 1, no. 2 (December 1929): 15 (emphasis mine).

35. Mendes, "Her Chinaman's Way," 15.

36. Mendes, "Her Chinaman's Way," 16.

37. Mendes, "Her Chinaman's Way," 14.

38. Mendes, "Her Chinaman's Way," 16.

39. Mendes, "Her Chinaman's Way," 16.

40. Mendes, "Her Chinaman's Way," 21.

41. Mendes, "Her Chinaman's Way," 18.

42. Alison Donnell, "Difficult Subjects: Women's Writing in the Caribbean Pre-1970" (paper presented at the Sixth International Conference of Caribbean Women Writers and Scholars Conference, Grenada, 1998), 4.

43. The letter, written by G. Grindle in Hollis (Governor) to Passfield on December 18, 1930, is reproduced in Brinsley Samaroo, "The Trinidad Disturbances of 1917–20: Precursor to 1937," *The Trinidad Labour Riots of 1937: Perspectives 50 Years Later*, ed. Roy Thomas (St. Augustine, Trinidad: The University of the West Indies Press, 1987), 45.

44. Ralph de Boissière, *Crown Jewel* (London: Pan, 1981), 151–52.

45. I am not suggesting that women were being written out of the labor movement completely. Instead, there was a concerted effort to redirect women's political involvement toward organizations and unions in the social welfare sector, effectively distancing them from the centralized struggles taking place in the industrial sectors. For a more detailed account of the shift in trade unionism and the woman worker, see Rhoda Reddock, "Responsible Trade Unionism and the Woman Worker," in *Women, Labour, and Politics in Trinidad and Tobago*, 245–87.

46. Rhonda Cobham, introduction to *Black Fauns*, by Alfred Mendes (London and Port-of Spain: New Beacon Books, 1984), viii.

47. Cobham, introduction to *Black Fauns*, ix.

48. Cobham, introduction to *Black Fauns*, vi.

49. Paul Gilroy, *The Black Atlantic: Modernity and Double Consciousness* (Cambridge, MA: Harvard University Press, 1993), 39.

50. Again, the term "fiction" is being used in a double sense to refer to the genre of artistic expression and also to Kant's notions of fiction as a mode of entertainment deployed by the mind in response to the different encounters of the eyes. Kant's definition of fiction is important here because, as we will see later, it becomes one of the contexts from which the possibility of a national imagination emerges when Caribbean intellectuals migrate to the place that has captured their imaginations for so long, England.

Chapter Two

The Pleasures/Privileges of Exile: Re/covering Race and Sexuality in *The Pleasures of Exile* and *Water with Berries*

> Caliban cannot be revealed in any relation to himself; for he has no self which is not a reaction to circumstances imposed upon his life. He is not seen as a possibility of spirit, which might fertilise and extend the resources of any human vision. In all his encounters with his neighbours—whether they be Kings or drunken clowns—Caliban is never accorded the power to see. Caliban is the excluded, that which is eternally below possibility, and always beyond reach.
>
> George Lamming, *The Pleasures of Exile*

CALIBANS IN THE (M)OTHERLAND: IDENTITY AND THE PROBLEM OF BLACK BEING(S)

From the inception, Caliban's role as a sociopolitical figure in Anglophone Caribbean literature was meant to represent a struggle for liberation between native peoples in the Caribbean and European colonial expansionism. The themes of exile and repatriation made *The Tempest* a seemingly appropriate colonial narrative for colonial writers to engage because it so aptly reflected their own struggles through Shakespeare's Caliban. Although the comparisons between the play and historical circumstances are straightforward, the complexities of the New World and its post-Prospero existence could not be contained by this colonial narrative for several reasons. The shape, form, and content of the idea of History was shifting daily as formerly colonized peoples began to transform their relationships to the institution of history writ large.

As new conceptions of history emerged, various imagined communities, formerly subsumed under the sign of Empire, sought to position their narratives on the grand stage of History. Various literary traditions of revision suggest that historical accounts are based on inclusions and exclusions, none of which emerge out of situations of equal power. The rise of Caliban as a sociopolitical figure in Caribbean literature and politics was no different. The ascendance of literary and political figures such as Eric Williams, C. L. R. James, Derek Walcott, Aimé Césaire, and Stokeley Carmichael was paralleled by the emergence of Caliban's career as a literary representation of colonialist oppression. His transformation from a symbol of American consumerism to a symbol of Caribbean resistance marked a new perspective on history, one that signaled an increased awareness about the stakes in the debate commonly characterized as the "Quarrel with History."

Although a tradition of resistance emerged through appropriations of Caliban as a trope for oppressed peoples in the Caribbean, there was no equivalent historical paradigm for women writers to draw upon to articulate their historical perspectives. The fact that *The Tempest* was an institutionalized "master narrative" served to situate the appropriations of this text into an already existing tradition of debate on Caribbean identity. *The Pleasures of Exile* is, therefore, an important text to consider because it is one of few texts that take a critical pause over the assumption of this trope as a central mode of representation in Caribbean literature. In *The Pleasures of Exile*, Lamming speculates on the absence of Sycorax (Caliban's mother) and of Miranda's mother. He asserts that "we cannot speak with authority until we have heard from Sycorax and Miranda's mother in *The Tempest*. They are both dead; and so our knowledge must be postponed until some arrangement comparable to the Haitian Ceremony of Souls returns them to tell us what we should and ought to know."[1]

Lamming uses this assertion as a point of departure for his creative examinations of the nature of existence for Caribbean people in the African Diaspora. Lamming's later engagements with Shakespeare's text, as a result, do not continue in the same trajectory as the Calibanesque tradition. Despite critical interpretations of *The Pleasures of Exile* and *Water with Berries* as significant parts of the Calibanesque tradition, I want to suggest that these texts, when read against the grain, point to the limitations of the Calibanesque tradition, not to its liberative capacities as some have suggested.[2] Lamming's early speculations on the absences and silences in this tradition of appropriation and revision provide the critical insight for several of his post-Prospero engagements with Shakespeare's text. Moreover, his insistence on the "incomplete" nature of any "knowledge" produced in the presence of these silences opens a space for readers to imagine and experiment with alter/native modes of narration and representation of images.

If Caribbean identity depends on the subject's ability to create and comprehend her or his relationship to the their surroundings, then another renaissance in Caribbean literature was necessary in order for postcolonial subjects to reacquaint their Selves with the social and political landscape of their homelands, the intimate spaces of their own Being. This renaissance, however, would not come from the production of new literary traditions per se, but rather from the critical dialogues and interpretations of nationalist narratives of liberation. In other words, the challenge for both writers and readers of Caribbean literature was no longer one of creating a connection between the subjects and experiences; it was now a matter of interpreting these relationships and the implications they would have for the *nature* of Being made possible through these experiences. The changing social and cultural landscape required new analytical tools to comprehend the epistemological shifts taking place. This was most evident in nationalist narratives written by young colonials who had exiled themselves to England in order to come to terms with the meaning of their West Indianness.

The experience of migration offered young men, educated under the colonial education system, a new "reality" from which they would continue to reflect on their positionalities. There is much to be said about the conditions of their migration and the impact it would have on their worldview and their writings;[3] yet, to understand the changes taking place in West Indian literature, we cannot simply focus on the "genius" of the generation of writers that migrated to London and the United States. We must, as Lamming suggests, understand the migration, the works produced, and the intellectual development of this generation of writers as a reaction to a set of circumstances imposed upon their lives. Not only were they visitors in a strange land, but they had to come to terms with what their West Indianness meant in a British context. Between 1950 and 1960, more than 80 percent of the books written by Caribbean writers were published by presses in Britain and the United States.[4] Moreover, the texts produced seemed consciously directed at reflecting upon the nature of the relationship produced in colonized nations between black colonial subjects and the British Empire, but now with the added reality that the "prodigal sons" were returning home—home to Britain, not Africa. The shift, then, from the African motherland to the fatherlands of the West produced a peculiar set of problems for young colonials. Departure from their respective homelands meant liberation to many of these writers, but at what cost? What were they liberating themselves into? Besides financial gain, what would this new space, this foreign space, offer them that they could not attain in their "homelands"?

The Pleasures of Exile is one of Lamming's responses to these questions. Moreover, these same questions serve as the foundation for his investigation into the nature of existence for his generation of writers and what this trend of migration would mean for the literature of the region. Holding firmly to his belief that the "West Indian's relation to the *idea* of England" creates a particular kind of shortsightedness, Lamming argues that Anglophone West Indian students should not be sent to study in England.[5] The fact that West Indian students have such a profound connection to the idea of England makes it extremely difficult for them to distance themselves from the alienation they have experienced to see the reality of their non-existence prior to arriving in England.

England offered these writers the opportunity to liberate themselves from oppressive colonial systems that limited their advancement at home. However, the idea of liberation was far more complicated than geographic distance from home and increased opportunity in their respective countries. Moreover, they were yet to understand the complexity of what lay ahead of them. Years later, Lamming would assert that the possibility for liberation lies primarily in the subject's ability and desire to free her- or himself—a very honorable aim. However, the question of what lies beyond the abyss would prove to be a more pressing concern for postcolonial subjects.

Addressing an audience in Grenada, Lamming emphasizes this understanding of liberation and instituting identity:

> I said it [liberation] is a word which suggests process. It is a process of trying to free self and society from various forms of imprisonment. The imprisonment of social injustice, the imprisonment of intellectual backwardness, the imprisonment of disfigured spirits. We liberate ourselves from a condition that is undesirable or intolerable but there is an implication in this word that we have to liberate ourselves into some other kind of being.[6]

For Lamming, the truly political nature of the idea of liberation lies in the subject's ability to move into another state of being. His approach ties the necessity for liberation to the metaphysical condition of colonial subjects in a politicized manner. That is, Lamming's charge here, of "liberating ourselves into some other kind of being," situates the call for liberation in relation to the knowing subject and its ontological condition or "being in the world." This relationship is political insofar as the exchanges between these two positionalities (the knowing subject and her or his ontological condition) depend upon a process of struggle, resistance, and negotiation for this movement toward this "other kind of being."

Further, Lamming's critical approach marks a new epistemological paradigm based upon the alienation of the colonial subject from her or his surroundings. This shift, from understanding Being as fixed within a limited set of possibilities to thinking about Being as predicated upon a continuous set of processes, would have a lasting impact on how identity and difference were critiqued in the Caribbean region. The idea that being and identity are linked to the subject's imaginative capacities and agency created a new political relationship between these seemingly opposed modes of existence. Moreover, this critical approach provided a context within which Caribbean writers could begin to reconceptualize their relationships to their landscapes and mindscapes. While the Trinidad Renaissance writers deployed female sexuality as a trope to articulate nationalist politics, Lamming raises similar concerns in a transnational context. What is interesting, however, is the extent to which his analysis of female sexuality and nationalism in *Pleasures of Exile* and *Water with Berries* is entangled in colonialist discourses of gender and identity, despite his political commitment to freeing black subjects from colonial imprisonment.

The project of creating a literature that represented an existence that, for all intents and purposes, was written out of history would depend largely upon the newly emerging relationship between colonial subjects migrating to the metropoles. In *The Pleasures of Exile*, Lamming raises several key questions regarding the nature of existence for Caribbean peoples, noting that their existence has historically been based on a set of circumstances entirely beyond their control. This "condition," according to Lamming, is one that has haunted Caribbean peoples since 1492. Thus, Lamming's project in *The Pleasures of Exile* articulates an existence not governed solely by those forces that forged Caliban's identity. The appeal of Prospero's gift of Language draws Lamming to consider the ambiguities implicit in this moment as a means of fruitful resistance. Moreover, the historical and political erasure (or silencing) of both Miranda's and Caliban's mothers begs the question as to the possibility of "liberation" within Caribbean nationalisms, given the hegemonic discourses at work in nationalist narratives.

The Pleasures of Exile begins with Lamming's consideration of the predicament that led a generation of West Indian writers to leave their islands to travel to the London metropolis. Drawing comparisons between the conditions of existence of blacks in the United States of America and blacks in the West Indies, Lamming highlights some of the specific peculiarities that brought him to these concerns. He argues that, whereas blacks in America have had to live with the cultural reality of being a minority, West Indian blacks have never had to cope with such an experience. This, he claims, is one of the most perplexing problems facing West Indians. According to Lamming, the overwhelming comfort of West Indians in the presence of their white counterparts has led to a growing sense of complacency with regard to attaining national sovereignty. Though Lamming is aware of the complexities of the West Indian situation, he offers very little commentary on the extent to which these complexities might disrupt the nationalist project in which he is so invested.

Lamming's observations on the cosmopolitan nature of West Indian people are based on demographics and the multiethnic communities that were an end result of the colonial plantation economy. He appropriates the ethnic diversity of the early stages of Caribbean nationalist politics to build an ideological platform of West Indian "unity" for his writing. For the newly exiled writer, this "unity" was a willful act of the imagination initiated at the moment of contact with the metropole. For the colonial subject, her or his West Indianness is based on their status as non-British, non-white. This "reality" effectively reduces the possibility of existence for colonial subjects to that of an unyielding reflection of "lack" in the mirror of the Empire. Any recognition of the self is experienced as nothing more than a defective imitation since the colonial subject is neither British nor white. The extent to which such an existence constitutes "being" for the colonized subject is the subject of much debate in the Quarrel with History.

The project of constructing an identity during the 1930s is central to deconstructing the legacy of non-Being founded on the precarious nature of Caliban's borrowed existence. In *The Pleasures of Exile*, Lamming suggests "Caliban cannot be revealed in any relation to himself; for he has no self that is not a reaction to circumstances imposed upon his life. He is seen as an occasion, a state of existence which can be appropriated and exploited for the purposes of another's own development."[7] Caliban's "lack" of the possibility of Being was a major trope in European travel writing and dramas of the colonial period. The project of colonialism itself was predicated upon the need to expand an empire and to construct and define Britain as a nation. Hence, *The Tempest* is seemingly the most appropriate drama to characterize the complexities at work in colonial history, particularly the necessity to imagine an Other against which to institutionalize and solidify Empire and its expansion.

While several postcolonial writers have appropriated *The Tempest* as a means for articulating the complex relationships between former colonies and colonial Empires, Lamming's rendition is unique in its creative engagement with the underlying implications of *The Tempest* in a postcolonial context.[8] The "encounter" between England and colonial subjects produced immediate crises in the nature of existence for colonial subjects. In the context of England, their blackness took on new significations they had not been faced with in the Caribbean. The reality of a faltering Empire also meant the power of "whiteness" no longer carried the unquestioned reverence it did at the height of imperial conquest. In essence, then, both colonizer and colonized had to come to terms with their postcolonial existences. Lamming sets the scene for these epistemological and ontological queries by returning to the "fatherlands," as colonial subjects "discover/invade" England. This discovery/invasion, however, was filled with obstacles and institutional powers that sought to stem the tides of West Indian immigrants into Britain. Moreover, this reversal of colonization was neither as devastating to the native population nor as rewarding for formerly colonized subjects as it had been for Columbus and his cohorts. Although the *Water with Berries* is set in London, far away from Shakespeare's fictitious island, the novel recasts the problematic of repatriation for both Prospero's descendants and Caliban's as well.

WATER WITHOUT BERRIES: RACE, SEXUALITY, AND ABSENT (M)OTHERS IN THE CALIBANESQUE TRADITION

Lamming's *Water with Berries* is a "cusp" text that is situated between two important historical junctures in Caribbean literary history. The first is the appearance of the exiled writer as a trope for an emerging national consciousness, founded on writers' experiences as expatriates or as the newly emerging "sons of the nation" groomed under the Union Jack. The second significant point in this literary history is a rapidly changing landscape within the Caribbean, one that featured a growing politicized body that was overtly gendered and highly sexualized, though not in the same way as was represented in the barrack-yard fiction of the Trinidad Renaissance. Where sexuality in the barrack-yard was understood as a form of capital exchanged in the interest of individual desire and pleasure, post-independence fiction emphasized the sexual body as the purview of the nation-state. Productive citizens and their output were harnessed in the service of the state; this included the sexual productivity as well as labor. This configuration had particularly problematic implications for women who, while certainly citizens, were not afforded the same rights, protections, or privileges as men. The newly forged relationship to nation and state meant an increased emphasis on the distribution of national resources, rights, and privileges to the citizens of Trinidad and Tobago. However, as Anne McClintock reminds us,

> No nation in the world grants men and women the same access to the rights and resources of the nation-state. Not only are the needs of the nation typically identified with the frustrations and aspirations of men, but the representation of male national power depends on the prior construction of *gender* difference. All too often in male nationalisms, gender difference between women and men serves to symbolically define the limits of national difference and power between *men*.[9]

The second important juncture is intimately connected to the first, and is expressed in McClintock's observation about the relationship between masculinist authority and power in the nation-state and its dependence on clearly marked gender differences. What McClintock defines as the "limits of national difference" finds its most pronounced manifestations in the legislative structures of the nation-state: rights and protection under the law, labor and compensation, and social and cultural expression, all of which are the yardsticks for defining citizenship. Obviously, citizenship in the legislative sense assumes that the subject of the nation-state (the civic subject) is male and, more often than not, white. The Law of the Father authorizes those who are recognizable in the system of signs; Others are displaced to the realm of the untranslatable.

Difference is, more often than not, marked and defined through a more rigidly enforced containment of the gendered body politic in landscapes that are visibly and discursively hostile to black women's bodies and sexualities. The "silent spaces" in *Water with Berries* are extremely important as they speak to the gender politics of the Caribbean nationalisms and the refusal to adopt Caliban as a paradigm for colonial resistance by many Caribbean women writers. Although Caliban never actually appears in *Water with Berries*, the struggles of the three West Indian artists are constructed to remind us of those encountered by him. Like Caliban, they struggle to find a means of holding on to their individual modes of expression in the face of a landscape that alienates them from their Selves. They exist in a land that is theirs as "British subjects," but foreign to them as black subjects in post-independence England; they are aliens in a nation/fatherland that has expelled them after raising them as the "children of Empire." Their expatriation produces a peculiar artistic crisis as they seem further distanced from their "mother tongues," so much so that they struggle to find their own voices throughout the novel. Teeton, an Afro-Caribbean painter, is secretly engaged in plans to return to San Cristobal (a fictional Caribbean island) and the revolution in progress. The other two artists, Roger, a musician of East Indian descent, and Derek, an actor, are engaged in struggles to keep their past histories at bay in order to succeed as artists in exile. Miranda is resurrected both as Myra, a white prostitute whom Teeton meets on the heath (and later discovers is the Old Dowager's daughter), and Randa, a black West Indian woman who is Teeton's wife and comrade in the revolution of San Cristobal. Randa remains in San Cristobal after many of her comrades flee for their own safety. The one character who seems to inhabit an existence beyond Prospero's postcolonial reach in this narrative is Nicole, Roger's wife, who commits suicide after learning of her husband's accusation of infidelity. Her ethnic identity is left open to the reader's interpretation although it is suggested that she is simply American; her national identity seems to take precedence over her ethnic identity.

As a nationalist narrative, *Water with Berries* opens on the heels of a revolution on the plantations of San Cristobal, suggesting that the entire text is indeed preoccupied with the "unfinished business" of resistance and change. At the same time, however, Lamming's narrative is concerned with writing the obvious wrongs of Shakespeare's *The Tempest*. The most prominent aspect of this effort is Lamming's construction of mother figures in the novel. Lamming engages the absence of mothers in Shakespeare's text by creating the "mother of all mothers" in the Old Dowager, a British matriarch endowed with the magical power of Language and insight. Lamming finds in this character a vehicle for expressing what might have been possible had we heard from the woman who is only referred to as "a piece of virtue" in Shakespeare's play. When the play is read closely, one is left to wonder about the nervous suggestion that Prospero's paternity is only assumed based on what Miranda's mother says.[10] In like fashion, Lamming's scrutiny calls the "virtue" of all mothers into question in both *The Tempest* and *Water with Berries*. However, he also cross-fertilizes the gender difference of the nation-state through the figure of the Old Dowager, who has the same "magical" power of words that Prospero holds. This power baffles Teeton, as its source and function seem just beyond his path of vision and just out of his reach much in the same manner as Prospero's books are for Caliban in Shakespeare's play:

> [Teeton] had often tried to explore her silence that night. Now he reflected on the value of negative statement; for it wasn't a silence which he had witnessed, nor was it a form of refusal, but rather the positive and disciplined act of not speaking. What then was the name for such an exercise in concealment? That concealment that continues to work when everything is known; remains transparent to all. Her behavior, like its meaning, had become invisible. He couldn't see what she was doing although it was happening under his eyes.[11]

The Old Dowager transforms her access to Language into a "mastery" of silence that keeps Teeton under her spell, in much the same manner as Prospero's spells work against Caliban. Access to Language remains the privilege of Prospero's descendants as the Old Dowager's silence suggests that Language is hers to give and hers to withhold. The use of "silence" in the novel is a different strategy for exercising power by withholding knowledge, a strategy that is effectively disempowering for Teeton.

The title of Lamming's novel hints at the relationship between Prospero and Caliban, emphasizing the bittersweet exchange that would frame the relationships between the British Empire and its colonies. The curse of the "gift" of Language in *The Tempest* and a "home" in Prospero's Britain is one that follows Caliban's descendants well into post-emancipation in the Caribbean and post-independence in their newfound "motherlands."[12] The Calibanesque figures in Lamming's narrative soon begin to realize their precarious existence in relation to their newfound "home," in much the same manner as their predecessor in Shakespeare's play. However, unlike their literary forefather, who transformed Language into a weapon to resist Prospero's rule, they had no relationship to the social, cultural, or geographical landscapes and, therefore, no means through which to articulate their resistance. Caliban reminds us of this when he bemoans his generosity in his initial encounters with Prospero:

> When thou cam'st first,
>   Thou strok'st me and made much of me, wouldst give me
>   Water with berries in't, and teach me how
>   To name the bigger light, and how the less,
>   That burn by day and night; and then I lov'd thee
>   And show'd thee all the qualities o' th'isle,
>   The fresh springs, brine pits, barren places and fertile.
>   Curs'd be I that did so! All the charms
>   Of Sycorax, toads, beetles, bats, light on you![13]

Caliban's position in his relationship to Prospero mirrors that of Lamming's protagonist, Teeton. Caliban curses Prospero's deception as well as himself for investing so much faith in Prospero's promises. This scene is paralleled near the end of Lamming's narrative when Teeton is unable to break his attachment to the Old Dowager in order to return to San Cristobal and the revolution in progress. Like Caliban, Teeton is engaged in the same struggle to free the Self from Prospero's colonial legacy, but the consequences of his failure in Lamming's narrative leave the possibility of resistance shipwrecked by a tempestuous storm of murder.

In her essay, "*Water with Berries*: Caliban in Albion," Sandra Pouchet Paquet suggests that Lamming's novel is an attempt to engage the postmodern implications of Prospero's colonialist project for the British colonial and the West Indian in exile. Her critique suggests that there are implications for both the oppressor and the oppressed in the aftermath of colonial expansionism in the New World; but the cost of this experiment is most noticeable if we read the texts of violence and the silent bodies of evidence littered throughout Caribbean nationalist narratives. While Lamming draws important critical parallels between the social and historical connectedness of British and West Indian subjects, the violence enacted on the bodies of women in his narrative points to the continuity of imperial patriarchal control in postcolonial and nationalist narratives. Paquet asserts that Lamming's engagement with Shakespeare's play opens a space for (re)presenting the colonial heritage of rupture and disembodiment within the "reality" of Prospero's home. She notes that

"In *Water with Berries*, Teeton and Myra share a common history of lost innocence, displacement, dispossession, and alienation. [Myra] is the white West Indian in exile first in San Cristobal, and later in the land of her parents as well. Like the Caliban figures in the novel, she is one of the homeless, placeless victims of Prospero's colonial experiment."[14] As Paquet argues, the scope of Lamming's inquiry reaches beyond the newly independent nations to consider the impact of Prospero's colonial experiment, as neither time nor geographical space separates Prospero's and Caliban's descendants from its effects. Teeton's reflection is not directed at his own way of seeing or knowing; rather it is directed at the *fact* of his own lack of insight, language, and presence in relation to the Old Dowager and his surroundings. The significance of Teeton's description of the implicit power of the Old Dowager's use of language should be underscored because it offers us a critical perspective for reading the absence/silence of Other (read black) women's experiences in Lamming's narrative. Teeton's interpretation of the Old Dowager's reserve through silence is understood as a "positive and disciplined act of not speaking."[15] Her positionality, however, is not marred by the possibility of being read/understood as absent.

If we reflect on the missing inhabitants of Shakespeare's tempestuous island, here refigured as England, we realize that black women are "absent from the drama on the stage and are identifiable only by their relationship to the males present, 'Prospero's Wife' and 'Caliban's Mother,'" or in the case of Lamming's narrative, Teeton's wife, Roger's wife, or Fernando's daughter.[16] Sycorax's absence leaves us with only the knowledge that her pregnancy is the "one thing" that spared her life.[17] Abena Busia draws a connection between Sycorax's voicelessness and a colonialist discourse in which "sexuality and access to language together form part of the discourse of access to power."[18] However, as Busia suggests, the Old Dowager's claims to legitimacy (as a knowing subject) have already been instituted through her continued access to language, but her sexuality is held in abeyance until the end of the novel. The representations of the Old Dowager as "undesirable" in the eyes of her tenant (except as a sentimental hyper-matriarch) are significant in this context. Her desexualization allows the novel to suspend the possibility of miscegenation, which, if we recall, is Prospero's greatest fear: that Caliban might be sexually attracted to Miranda.

Teeton's relationship to Myra, however, is remarkably similar to the relationship between Caliban and Miranda in Shakespeare's play. As the narrative plot thickens, we learn that Myra is the Old Dowager's daughter. The sexual tension between Myra and Teeton provides an interesting contrast to the contradictory space Teeton inhabits in his relationship with his wife. The Old Dowager's sexual undesirability and her whiteness secure her access to language. The one thing we know of Miranda's mother in Shakespeare's play is that she was a "piece of virtue" and, as such, is not to be heard from again. Shakespeare's Miranda shares a similar space by virtue of her "innocence" concerning matters of men, except for Caliban's alleged advances.

The contrast in Lamming's re-imaging of this play is powerful as he juxtaposes the two Miranda figures in relation to the same problematic, sexuality and access to language. This decision is significant because it brings with it a critique of race (more specifically whiteness) and the privilege of claiming ownership of one's sexualized body (through language or other forms of signification). Historically, this has not been an option for women of color in colonial texts. Therefore, the juxtaposing of these two literary figures through a different racial and historical lens makes the power inequity more visible to the reader. Busia asserts that imperialist narratives such as *The Tempest* are "choreographed to keep darker women and *all* women subject."[19] She suggests that Miranda's future is dependent upon her entrance into the symbolic order of Language that is the source of Prospero's privilege:

> Like the colonized country itself, the women, both African and European, become representative objects of desire, and their conditions are to some extent parallel. Nonetheless, it is the singular and significant exception of their continued access to language in these works, which clearly distinguishes the European woman from the African woman no matter what the similarities.[20]

The women in *Water with Berries* primarily occupy the text as objects of desire. Beyond this function, their relationship to the events unfolding in this narrative is minimal. However, this is not necessarily produced through the construction of the narrative: it is also a function of the reception and interpretation of women's presence within certain systems of signification.

This analysis extends Paquet's and Busia's critique of Lamming's novel by examining the Old Dowager's privilege of continued access to language, and thus opening a space for examining how Prospero's privilege has manifested in the white, female, matriarchal body in Lamming's text. It is as if the "magic" conjured by Ariel in Shakespeare's play, still has a hold on Teeton in neocolonial Britain and on a generation of readers alike. Teeton's relationship to the Old Dowager and to language is continually read by critics as a "given" in the narrative, in much the same manner as is Randa's "absence." Another reading of Lamming's positioning of the Old Dowager might consider her "silences" as a kind of "strategic positionality" that engenders a radically different subjectivity, one beyond those historically designed for black and native women in colonial narratives. In other words, the "silent" white female body is positioned in a strategically more powerful position than that of black women whose physical presence is still not sufficient to render them intelligible.

If we assume that signifying within discursive systems must occur through Language, then, as Busia notes, women of color are destined to be constructed, read, and subjected to the realm of permanent silence. However, *Water with Berries* offers us an occasion for taking up the challenge the novel places before its audience: expanding our expectations and understandings of how and where women's articulations of historical and narrative presence and identity emerge. Gayatri Spivak, some twenty years later, challenges canonical constructions of nationalist culture on the same ground in "Can the Subaltern Speak?" While Spivak's essay offers an elaborate critique of Western critical traditions and traditions of cultural and political activism, I am interested primarily in her reading of *sati* and its relationship to institutionalized representations of the act within Indian culture and British imperialist history.

Tracing the emergence and dissemination of the term *sati* from Hindu mythology to its contemporary evocation in historiographies as a possible model of intervention against British imperialism, Spivak asserts that this practice, like the women within it, is caught between two powerful, opposing systems of representation and interpretation:

Within the effaced itinerary of the subaltern subject, the track of sexual difference is doubly effaced. The question is not of female participation in insurgency, or the ground rules of sexual division of labor, for both of which there is "evidence." It is, rather, that, both as object of colonialist historiography and as subject of insurgency, the ideological construction of gender keeps the male dominant. If, in the context of colonial production, the subaltern has no history and cannot speak, the subaltern female is even more deeply in shadow.[21]

The precarious "positionality" Spivak describes throughout her essay is indicative of the problematics of "representation" and the unequal power relations at work in aesthetic and political meanings of this term. Spivak suggests that "giving voice," like efforts to "speak for" and "on the behalf of" subaltern subjects, are all examples of "imperialist effects" of Western intellectuals and colonial officials alike. These effects, in the end, silence subaltern subjects, leaving them without a space or place to express their positionalities in their own modalities. Where Spivak asserts, "the subaltern cannot speak," the "empty" spaces of Lamming's novel are shown to be voids that resonate at variable frequencies, shedding light on these seemingly inaudible moments (of enunciation).[22] The fictionality of Randa's "absence" is exposed when Teeton is confronted with the news of her suicide. Myra also attempts to bring Teeton to a deeper understanding of his past by telling him about her dispossession and sexual abuse at the hands of several of his comrades. However, Teeton's reaction to Myra's rape suggests that it is disconnected, in his mind, from his own participation in the revolution/uprising; to assume some responsibility here would perhaps require him to accept Randa's own act of sexual transgression.

Rereading Lamming's narrative in a national context, which is the primary aim of this critique, provides a revealing analysis of the privilege of location for white female subjects. After hearing Myra's account of being raped by her father's servants and dogs in San Cristobal, Teeton is drawn even closer to her:

> He judged it would be wrong to touch her now; to convert this sudden liberty of speech into some crude abuse of privilege. It was her privilege to stay as she was; to choose whether this was the moment she would make her body known. Would she have taken him in the dark? Taken him in all intimacy into her sex before they had ever seen each other? But knowing was a kind of seeing, Teeton thought. He wanted to diminish the special authority of his eyes; to reduce his claims of sight.[23]

Lamming's emphasis on sight and blindness shifts the grounds of the debate from the silence/speech motif that frames the novel. The shroud of darkness serves as a cloak to protect both Myra and Teeton from the drama that unfolds that very night. Lamming's analogy, however, is of great critical import because rather than implying "absence," it draws our attention to the constructed nature of "darkness" by slowly revealing the content of this seemingly inaccessible space. This process of revelation is fraught with historical tensions that have to be negotiated in this new historical and geographical context. As Myra recounts the events of the revolution on the island and her rape on the night of the coup, Teeton's (in)sight into the events that led up to his escape/release is sharpened. His refusal, however, to expose himself (sexually and politically) to the darkness and the implications of his own involvement in the coup and its aftermath suggest that he is unwilling to face the consequences of this knowing or "sight." To do this could mean exposing himself and revealing his helplessness and complicity in systemic violence and sexual abuses visited upon both Myra and Randa.

The question of "rights of possession" (physical bodies, spaces, language, and being) is clearer once race and gender are recognized as central to nationalist narratives of independence. The grand narrative of belonging, rights, and ownership (upon which so much of colonial literature depends) begins to take on a different meaning when the intertwined histories of black and white women are shown to undergird the construction of colonial and postcolonial nation-states. Near the end of the novel, we learn that the Old Dowager, more than being Prospero's mirror image in postcolonial Britain, is actually Myra's mother (and, we could imagine, Miranda's missing mother in Shakespeare's text). She is separated from her daughter through the plotting of her husband, who discovers that his brother Fernando (read Ferdinand) is Myra's biological father. Teeton and the Old Dowager are stranded on an island with Fernando, and the complications of the interconnectedness of race and sexuality begin to rear their heads in myriad ways. The intertwined myths of sexual innocence, national resistance, and racial constructions conspire to reveal the centrality of gender and sexuality in neocolonial and postcolonial nationalist narratives. *Water with Berries* stages the confrontation that readers of Shakespeare's play cannot envisage, if only out of their fear that the order Prospero sought so desperately to maintain would be thrown irrevocably out of control.

Shakespearean scholars, most notably Stephen Orgel, have commented on the absence of mothers in Shakespeare's works. His interpretation of Shakespeare's play is particularly insightful when read in relation to Lamming's post-Prospero revision of *The Tempest*. Commenting on the "missing wife" in Shakespeare's play, Orgel asserts that

> She is missing as a character, but Prospero, several times explicitly, presents himself as Incorporating her, acting as both father and mother to Miranda, and in one extraordinary passage describes the voyage to the island as a birth fantasy:
>
>> When I have decked the sea with drops full salt,
>> Under my burden groaned, which raised in me
>> An undergoing stomach, to bear up
>> Against what should ensue. (1.2.155-58)
>
> To come to the island is to start life over again—both his own and Miranda's—with himself as sole parent, but also with himself as favorite child. This too has the shape of a Freudian fantasy; the younger child is the usurper in the family, and the kingdom he usurps is the mother.[24]

The most intriguing aspect of Orgel's reading for my critique is precisely the relational positioning of women's bodies in the play. Although absent, both Miranda's mother (Prospero's wife) and Caliban's mother (Sycorax) are evoked by Prospero in order to institute his own authority as the ultimate patriarch of all families and, of course, of the nation-state. The symbolic birth fantasy is particularly relevant because it affirms the desire to relieve the anxiety of patriarchal structures of Victorian England, while at the same time claiming the female body's "labor" (in this case the heirs to the throne) for itself and its aims. Miranda's newly found interest in the men who arrive on the island must be seized upon and directed, lest the order of things be turned upside down completely as is threatened earlier in the play when Caliban is accused of attempting to rape Miranda. In *The Tempest*, as

Orgel argues, "family structures and sexual relationships become political structures . . ., and these are relevant to the political structures of Jacobean England."[25]

What are the implications of these family structures and sexual relationships in postcolonial England, where both Prospero's and Caliban's descendants are now free to roam from the colony to the fatherland? Lamming's novel highlights a concern similar to that expressed by Shakespearean scholars where are the mothers and what are the implications of their absence, especially for black women who are doubly erased? Though Lamming's novel does not offer us an explicit response to this question, the structure of his narrative suggests that the response to these questions is also implicitly available to readers of Shakespeare's text—but that the answers require us to read against the grain. As in Shakespeare's play, when the central actors of Lamming's novel assemble on a small island outside the metropolis of London, the question of absent mothers, paternity, and usurped powers offers a scandalous interpretation of Prospero's wife's absence. In *Water with Berries*, the lasting effects of a mismanaged state return to haunt Myra's father in the form of a revolt in San Cristobal, and his brother Fernando challenges his authority as ruler, father and husband:

> "I wanted to marry [the Old Dowager]," [Fernando] said. "After my brother went away I would have brought our daughter back. He knew she was our daughter. He knew it. Just as he knew the woman he called his wife [the Old Dowager] was really mine, *my own kingdom*. Mine. She was mine. . . . But he took our daughter. Out of spite."
>
> . . . .
>
> "Her only child," he cried, "hardly old enough to know her name. Myra was barely three when he took her to that forsaken hell of an island. To live on estates he had never seen. Knew nothing about although they were his own. He carried this infant off like a common slave. Carried the infant off to bring her up among a tribe of monstrous butchers. Living with brutes."[26]

The seemingly disparate histories collide to produce this unexpected turn of history and representation in which Prospero (or Fernando's brother) is not only absent, but murdered by his own brother in revenge for his theft of Fernando's child. Lamming's "tempestuous island" gives birth to a resoundingly different outcome in some respects, and a somewhat predictable result in others, in that Randa, the sole black female subject in Lamming's novel, like Sycorax remains absent from his narrative. However, more important than this meeting is the "off-stage" action that takes place. The obvious parallels between Fernando's description of Myra's "theft" and the plight of "common slaves" cannot be overlooked, nor for that matter can the discourse of sovereignty and ownership of land, nations, and rights through the "ownership" of women. Prospero's attempt to reconsolidate his power through his "property," or his daughter (Miranda), is mirrored in this post-Prospero context as Fernando himself sees the Old Dowager and his daughter as parts of his "kingdom."

One of the most damning aspects of Fernando's recounting of these events is not necessarily the ills done him by his brother, but his inability to see these violations a part of the systemic oppression that brought Africans to the shores of the Caribbean and later to Britain. Fernando's accusations, in his rage, are remarkably similar to those of his literary predecessor in Shakespeare's play. When Fernando discovers that Teeton is the boarder in the Old Dowager's house, he accuses him of "undoing" Myra with his sexual advances. Once again, Lamming draws us back to Shakespeare's narrative, but this time with a rather interesting reconfiguration of gender and sexual roles. Here, it is supposedly Teeton's "black magic" (since they have never seen each other in the light, only in the darkness) that poses the threat to the white female body and, ultimately, to the authority of the patriarch. However, we cannot forget the centrality of the black female body in the systemic negotiations for power taking place between these two authoritative narratives, lest we perpetuate the myth of her silence in our reading of the text.

As McClintock reminds us, the imaginings and ultimately the manifestations of the nation are conceptually masculine and are meant to consolidate male authority at every level. She also reminds us of Fanon's famous representation of the relationship between the "settler" and the "colonized man" in *The Wretched of the Earth*. Fanon writes, "The look that the native turns on the settler town is a look of lust...to sit at the settler's table, to sleep in the settler's bed, with this wife if possible. The colonized man is an envious man."[27] As if to bring us face to face with this formulation of the masculinist national terrain, Lamming, in San Cristobal, represents this urge with a particularly poignant twist, one that implicates both black and white men in staging nationalist violence upon women's bodies (both black and white) in the name of "resistance" and "conquest." In a bizarre reimagining of Prospero's own complicity in creating what he, in the play, refers to as "this thing of darkness," Lamming transforms this "darkness" into physical manifestations of brutal violence and violation. In *Water with Berries*, what is done in the darkness in Shakespeare's play is brought to light and, in true Fanonian fashion, is reproduced through the territorialization and violation of (black and white) female bodies:

> "The monsters," he cried out, hoping to revile Teeton with the habits of his kind, "I should have saved her before that black breed of scorpions seized the

chance to crawl over her. God, God, the monsters. How they took her body, like cannibals feeding on some carcass they had never hoped, never dreamed they might ever taste. God, how they brutalised her beauty. For she was that: absolute beauty until they set the hounds upon her. Can you imagine that? Or perhaps you can, you can. Perhaps you can imagine how they made the hounds violate her sex. The animals. Just as they had seen their master do with some of them. His own field servants. Oh, yes, my brother, come from the same blessed loins, the same ancestry of privilege and blood; my brother had made this devil's crime a common sport upon his servants. Male and female alike. Trained his hounds to mount a human sex. That monster. I should have killed him before; could have taken her away before the monsters got at her."[28]

The ambiguous references to "the monsters" that opens and closes this lengthy passage is worthy of note since it is indicative of the doubling of historical and political narratives in which Lamming is engaged. The vile acts for which Teeton's comrades are responsible are revealed as a reproduction of the "sport" practiced by the Old Dowager's husband, acts of violence and rape visited upon the servants who in turn mimic these acts when the opportunity presents itself. What Fanon imagines as "envy" for what the settler has, Lamming represents as "revenge" for what has been "taken" and the realization of Prospero's worst fear, the violation of his woman, or his "property," his land, and his country.

Fernando's reference to the "monsters" needs to be read within a cultural and historical context that assumes equal modalities of interpretation and audibility for all utterances. That is to say, the racist discourses that inform Fernando's assertion that he should have saved Myra before "that black breed of scorpion seized the chance to crawl over her," have, at their crux, a history of sexual violence against Africans in the New World that produces the venom expelled during the San Cristobal revolution. However, such a reading is only possible if the audience is prepared to adopt an interpretive lens that considers the "unsaid" or unspoken narratives that undergird the novel. Fernando's recounting of Myra's rape is one such instance. Although Fernando's lament opens with his expression of disgust for the sexual perversion exercised by his brother, by the end of his account the hounds are indistinguishable from the field servants. He describes them as part of a "breed of animals" trained to desire "human" sex. Although this language is used to refer specifically to the hounds, both the third-person narration and the first-person account work effectively to equate the actions of the hounds and those of the field servants in a kind of bestial, unnatural desire for "human" (read white) flesh.

The equation of Myra's rape with "cannibalism" is Fernando's final effort to come to terms with the terror of colonialism, a terror he sees as having no significant impact on the black population of San Cristobal, either in relation to the immediate violence enacted upon their physical bodies or on the subsequent economic and social body of the country. Moreover, Fernando's final pronouncement is an important revisioning of the "curse" that Caliban calls down on himself first and then upon Prospero in Shakespeare's text. The curse is realized in this post-Prospero, postcolonial narrative. According to Fernando, Teeton's appearance, in his sole place of refuge from the consequences of the colonialist experiment gone awry, is proof positive of the wretched curse that is a result of the failed "experiment in ruling over your kind."[29] The doubling effect of these historical narratives cannot be overlooked because it sheds light on the contradictions, bringing the reader out of the "darkness" of the heath to the burning "lights" of the fires that burn both in San Cristobal and later in Britain.[30]

The "thing of darkness" that Prospero claims in Shakespeare's play is revealed to be the hatred and violence produced not only in Caliban, but also in Fernando's brother's acts of inhumanity. Moreover, once Prospero's authority as father (his "paternity") is called into question, the stability of the nation is compromised, and it falls into the hands of revolutionaries. Fernando, who appears as a Father in name (and not in Law, since he is not married to the Old Dowager when Myra is conceived), fails to perform his duty by not being able to protect his child from the "natives" and to claim his (kin and) kingdom in the Old Dowager; he is now faced with the possibility of having his physical and paternal space violated once again, this time by Teeton. By tracing the systems of representation and signification here, I want to highlight, as McClintock does, how gender difference and power differentials effectively discipline women's physical, sexual, and political bodies into silence.

If Myra's fate is sealed within the hermeneutic logos of the Father, what are we to make of her literary and historical counterpart, Randa? How, and where, does the latter figure within this system of signification and negotiation? We need, first, to consider Randa's relationship, not to the narrative of male national power that we are given through out the novel, but to her own political power as an agent in the San Cristobal revolution. Sylvia Wynter ponders exactly this question in Shakespeare's text and other nationalist discourses:

> And here, we begin to pose in this context a new question, the question not of the absence of Caliban's legitimate father as posed by Aimé Césaire and commented on by Clarisse Zimra in her essay on Francophone Caribbean women writers, nor even the question posed by Zimra herself, that of the "silent presence of a mother not yet fully understood," which carries with it the implicit project of "discarding the Logos of the Father," and of replacing it instead with "the Silent Song of the Mother," but the new question related to a new project. This question is that of the most significant absence of all, that of Caliban's Woman, of Caliban's physiognomically complimentary mate.[31]

Lamming's protagonist, Randa, is his post-Prospero response to the symbolic and discursive absence of what Wynter terms "Caliban's physiognomically complimentary mate." However, in *Water with Berries*, physiognomic similarities do not necessarily translate into political compatibility. Teeton, unlike his literary predecessor, is indeed afforded what Wynter argues Caliban is denied, Randa, a black "Woman"; but, as my reading of Lamming's novel suggests, her mere presence in the novel, like that of Miranda's mother in Shakespeare's play, is too much of a threat to the order of things in the San Cristobal revolution.

Randa's erasure from the narrative of resistance circulating among Teeton's comrades in the Gathering is reminiscent of Sycorax's own erasure and silencing in Shakespeare's text. Like her literary predecessor, the "one thing" Randa does that causes her to be banished is also sexual in nature. It is Sycorax's pregnancy that saves her life; but, in Lamming's novel, Randa's banishment comes in Teeton's refusal to accept her bodily offering as an act that assures his own escape. In other words, her sexuality offers him freedom, while imprisoning her, not in a tree as Sycorax is imprisoned, but certainly in the island/nation where the revolution takes place.[32] Lamming, through Randa, achieves an earlier desire expressed in *The Pleasures of Exile*. Although Lamming's rendition of the Ceremony of Souls is slightly different from the ritual in Haitian culture, his evocation of this tradition is an attempt to recuperate the traces of presence that have been covered over in nationalist discourses.[33] The implications of Randa's suicide, the murder of the Old Dowager and Nicole, and the rape of the young woman on stage at the conclusion of the novel all signify the price of the ticket for entry into the system of signs in nationalist politics, in both San Cristobal and London. What is only hinted at in Shakespeare's text is fully articulated in *Water with Berries*: the erasure of women's (especially black women's) bodies constitutes exile for what Lamming represents as acts of sexual transgression.

ALIEN/NATIONS AND EMIGRANTS: READING THE BODIES OF EVIDENCE

Teeton's safe arrival and indeed his "presence" in the novel can only be understood through Randa's sexuality, which is politicized and deployed in the interest of the nation. The difference, however, is that Randa's sudden appearance as a political force late in the novel clearly marks her as an agent for political change and, therefore, situates her as a stakeholder in the struggle for power among men. We find out through Jeremy, an old San Cristobal acquaintance of Teeton's, that Randa is responsible for Teeton's safe departure from San Cristobal. Prodded by Jeremy, Teeton reproduces his narrative about Randa's "infidelity":

> "Yes I know. By now everyone must know," said Teeton. "Randa slept with the American ambassador; fornicated with him every night of my internment. I know that. Offered to become his mistress if it were possible to get me off the island. And of course anything was possible for the American. He made Judge Rivera destroy the evidence of the security officers. Made them drop every charge. Randa kept her end of the bargain. And so did the ambassador."[34]

We never hear from Randa herself; she is, as Busia suggests, *constructed* as silent, and therefore, read as "absent" from the narrative. Moreover, her own act of liberation, exchanging sexual favors with the American ambassador for Teeton's safe passage from the island, here seems at odds with the nationalist project of San Cristobal, at least in Teeton's eyes.

As Wynter suggests, the variable of "race" shifts Randa from sharing the space claimed by Myra (that of gender) to another space in the current system of meanings (beyond gender). Teeton's double erasure of Randa is as much a racial erasure as it is a gendered one because when gender and sexuality are contested they have historically been understood and read as struggles for power and recognition between men *over* women's bodies. Busia speaks directly to these constructions of silence or *silencing* in the portrayal of black women in neocolonial literature by asserting that "the unvoicing of the black woman is literal, and her essence projected only as a void. In the colonial novel, the colonized male encounters not himself but his antithesis; the colonized woman encounters only erasure. She hears her own voice in silent space."[35] However, when the news of Randa's death by suicide reaches Teeton, he, like the reader, must account for her absence up until this point. This act of self-possession, while it can be read as a kind of victimization because of the unequal power relations at work between Randa and the U.S. ambassador, demands a broader consideration, one that understands it in opposition to the power structures of colonialism and nationalism. Randa's actions, therefore, need to be read against the grain of both of these discourses in order to rescue their political efficacy as an articulation of resistance and presence.

It is indeed significant that Randa's body emerges at a critical point in the novel, when all the threads begin to unravel, threatening to prevent Teeton from returning to San Cristobal. Seven years after his escape from the island, he feels that he deserted his comrades. We never hear, however, of the circumstances of his departure. At the same time that he confronts Fernando, who holds him at gunpoint, the other two Caliban figures in the novel are also embroiled in their own dramas. Roger, a failed musician and undercover pyromaniac, has begun a rampage throughout the city in search of his missing wife, Nicole, who, unbeknownst to him has committed suicide. When the Old Dowager finds the body, she and Teeton decide to bury Nicole under an old tree trunk in the yard, the same tree trunk that Teeton has kept in his room for the last year or so. Nicole emerges as the Ariel figure, imprisoned in the tree once again, this time never to be freed. As Roger sets about burning down all of the places they frequented in the hope that he can burn the memory of her from his mind, Derek, an actor who constantly plays the part of a corpse, rapes a woman on stage during a performance of *A Summer's Error in Albion*. The frustration that has threatened to overtake him throughout the novel finally rears its head in this act of violence, as he attempts to show to the audience that he is indeed alive and carries within him the power of contempt.

When Teeton hears the news of Randa's suicide from an old nemesis who he feels has sold out to the American and German ambassadors during the revolution, he is stunned into the realization that he has failed to hide from his own past. In an instant, all of his doubts about deserting his comrades are suddenly shifted to the reality of what Jeremy's news means, something he could never have accepted. Back on the heath, he begins to reflect on his silence of the last seven years; he hasn't written, hasn't even tried to contact her, and Jeremy's unspoken accusations haunt him:

> He couldn't resist the dangers now lurking in any charge which might relate him to the cause of Randa's suicide. There was a feeling of dread before his lack of foresight. His hatred of Jeremy couldn't obscure what he had already known. Did you really know how much she loved you? Randa had not, in any important sense, betrayed her love for you. He was lingering on this knowledge; hoping it seemed, to bring some skeptical intelligence to his aid. You will think well of Randa now that she is dead. He had to preserve some confidence in his judgment. Her suicide had made San Cristobal more than a place of birth. The island was a nerve his exile could not kill.[36]

Finally we are made privy to the source of Teeton's anxiety throughout the novel. Although his wife's selflessness is unacknowledged, he realizes that it is the thing he fears more than anything else, the thing that separates him from his *natio*, or place of birth, and the place from which he is exiled. He knows he can never return "home" to Randa, but her death now seals his fate because it is indeed impossible for him to reclaim her body, and therefore his country, as belonging to him.

It is not without significance that Randa's death occurs in Teeton's seventh year of exile. As he recalls the first time they met, at the Ceremony of Souls in San Cristobal, he realizes that he too will be made to answer all of the questions that Randa would have surely taken to her grave with her. As he lies in the darkness on the heath, he meets Myra once again, for the last time, and begins to recount to her the traditions of the Ceremony of Souls:

> "The relatives gather," said Teeton. "Every eight years or so according to custom. In one place. And when the Priest has found his powers, the dead come forward. You don't see them; but they will be there, and you can hear them. They speak about all of the things that had never been said when they were alive. They are now free to accuse, and free to pardon. And the living must reply. Always through the Priest. Sometimes they argue all through the night. For hours. The living and the dead. The end of all complaint from the dead; the end of all retribution of the living. The dead depart, and the relatives are free at last to go home."[37]

We are left to speculate about Teeton's return to the island and the impending revolution being planned by the men in the Secret Gathering. One thing is certain, however: the "pleasures of exile" must be weighed against the promise of repatriation, and both are not without complex negotiations between imagined homelands and the reality of race and gender differences that define the structure of these imagined spaces.

The silencing of black women in *Water with Berries* is both a physical and discursive violence that "covers over" Randa's body. Despite the clear similarities between the historical dispossession and violence that attend all women in Lamming's novel, it is Randa's race that relegates her to an space of exile as black/woman/Other: as Busia argues, "in a discourse in which sexuality and access to language together form part of the discourse of power, her position is overdetermined, since current readings of her racial coding place her beyond sexuality and beyond gender."[38] Her agency is subordinated to the needs of the nation. Belinda Edmonson observes that, while nationalisms rely heavily on narratives of exile and repatriation as a means of conferring "authority," the symbolic return to the "motherland" needs to be read through the "matria" or the mother's body. Thus, the black woman's body is necessarily the referent for exile and ultimately for return:

> If exile . . . is predicated on the banishment of the writer by patriarchal authority, the place "he" is banished *from*, the native land, the "*matria*," is maternalized. Similarly, Freud equates exile from one's native land with exile from the mother: the nostalgia for the home country is in actuality a nostalgia for the mother's body. The land-as-mother plays the "object" to the exile's "subject" status. A return of the exile to the "motherland" is then a reappropriation of it. The *matria* is the "internal exclusion" of *patria*, "the other by and through which patria is defined." Its exclusion or "exile" therefore is the very condition of patriarchy's existence since "*matria* is always ex*patriated*."[39]

If we consider this an example of the angst of alienation endured by Lamming's three Caliban figures and read the novel's conclusion in violent matricide, then we can only conclude that the idea of England can no longer sustain their expectations, imagined or lived. Teeton murders and burns the body of the Old Dowager in a final attempt to escape the prison house that has entrapped him for the last seven years in England. However, if Edmondson's engagement with Shari Benstock's notion of "symbolic matricide" is indeed correct, as I believe it to be, then how are we to configure the landscape of Caribbean nationalisms? Based on the conclusion of the novel, we can only imagine a landscape in which "bodies of evidence" lie buried under the surface, awaiting their summons to be heard.

Sylvia Wynter asserts that these "silences" represent the possibility for new interpretative models for reading and decoding these silenced spaces. Wynter's assertion underscores a salient moment in critical approaches to nationalist narratives in Caribbean literature, the need for another epistemic frame for engaging gender, sexuality, and race in postcolonial nationalist terrains. However, such a critical intervention, she warns us, cannot serve simply to give "voice" to the silenced spaces in nationalist narratives:

> In effect, rather than only voicing the "native" woman's hitherto silenced voice we shall ask: What is the systemic function of her own silencing, both as women and, more totally, as "native" women? Of what mode of speech is that absence of speech both as women (masculinist discourse) and as 'native' women (feminist discourse) as imperative function?[40]

The task, then, is not simply to raise the bodies and voices from the dead to hear their grievances, but also to understand how "bodies of evidence" could assist us in understanding how these silences govern our interpretations or race and gender. The ground, therefore, of Caliban's "woman/native/Other" is also the location of a new epistemic relationship that lies just beyond our current modes of knowing:

> [If] we are to understand the necessity for such an *other* term as a term which, whilst developing a fully articulated theoretical/interpretative reading model of its own, nevertheless, serves, diacritically to draw attention to the insufficiency of all theoretically interpretative models, both to "voice" the hitherto silenced ground of the experience of "native" Caribbean women and Black American women as the ground of Caliban's woman, and to decode the system of meanings of that other discourse . . . which has imposed this mode of silence of some five centuries, as well as to make thinkable the possibility of a new "model" projected from a new "native" standpoint, we shall need to translate the variable race . . . out of the epistemic 'vrai' of our present order of "positive knowledge," its consolidated field of meanings and order-replicating meanings.[41]

Wynter's critique is part of the "authoritative" beginnings initiated by the Calibanesque tradition in Caribbean literature. Like Prospero, the Old Dowager's centrality in *Water with Berries* would mark the "beginning" of all Caribbean histories, and leave "native" women beyond the reach of both history and gender. If Shakespeare's text is the mirror within which the colonial subjects view themselves, the Old Dowager is the only figure that can be fully "recognized" in this new system of signification. However, rereadings of nationalist narratives like *Water with Berries* may well provide us with the critical tools needed to uncover the bodies of evidence that have been read (rather than written) out of existence. Written more than thirty-five years ago, Lamming's novel offers us another lens through which to read and consider what is at stake in the political structures of Jacobean England. More important, however, are the continuities between the struggles for power in Shakespeare's plays and those same struggles in postcolonial nation-states. The consistent erasure of black women's bodies then, as now, suggests that no matter the historical context, nationalist narratives that describe the pathways to power depend on reading with (not against) the grain as another strategy for consolidating existing meanings and interpretations rather than producing new ones. Randa's silenced body has always been present for interpretation. However, for several decades, *Water with Berries* has received scant attention in comparison when compared to Lamming's other novels. As critics, we must be mindful against finding "only what we are looking for or willing to see," which, as Wynter suggests, leaves black women off-stage.

NOTES

1. George Lamming, *The Pleasures of Exile* (London: Allison & Busby, 1971), 116.

2. For arguments in support of the liberative capacities of the Calibanesque tradition, see Kamau Brathwaite, "Caliban," in *Islands* (London: Oxford University Press, 1969), 34–38; Roberto Fernández Retamar, "Caliban: Notes Toward a Discussion of Culture in Our America," trans. Lynn Garafola et al., *Massachusetts Review* 15, nos. 1–2 (Winter/Spring 1974): 7–72; and Margaret Joseph Paul, *Caliban in Exile: The Outsider in Caribbean Fiction* (New York: Greenwood Press, 1992). Sylvia Wynter argues against this reading in "Afterword: Beyond Miranda's Meanings: Un/silencing the 'Demonic Ground' of Caliban's 'Woman,'" in *Out of the Kumbla: Caribbean Women and Literature*, eds. Carole Boyce Davies and Elaine Savory Fido (Trenton, NJ: Africa World Press, 1990), 355–72.

3. In his essay "Discovering Literature in Trinidad: The Nineteen Thirties," C. L. R. James reflects on what he considered to be the inevitable decision to leave, a decision many writers were forced to make for the sake of their own self-preservation.

Discussing these circumstances with Albert Gomes, James poignantly sums up the dilemma facing black West Indian intellectuals seeking to advance themselves in the Caribbean. He states that "We *had* to go, whereas Mendes could go to the United States and learn to practice his writing, because he (Mendes) was white and had money. We had to make our money"; C. L. R. James, "Discovering Literature in Trinidad: The Nineteen Thirties," *Savacou*, no. 2 (September 1970): 54–60. James's reflections on the social circumstances that necessitated the departure of so many West Indian writers paralleled the situation Lamming describes in *The Pleasures of Exile*. A generation of young, middle-class West Indian men left their respective islands in an effort to test their vision and their ability to *see* themselves from the other side of the colonial lenses they were so used to.

4. See Kenneth Ramchand, *The West Indian Novel and Its Background* (London: Heinemann, 1983), for a detailed discussion of the rise of West Indian literature outside of the Caribbean region. Ramchand offers an insightful account of programs such as the BBC's *Caribbean Voices* and other British literary institutions and their roles in the emergence of Caribbean literature in the metropoles.

5. For a more detailed discussion of the significance of the wave of migration on West Indian literature and more specifically on writers, see George Lamming, "The Occasion for Speaking," in *The Pleasures of Exile*, 23–34.

6. George Lamming, *Conversations: George Lamming; Essays, Addresses, and Interviews 1953–1990*, eds. Richard Drayton and Andaiye (London: Karia Press, 1992), 27.

7. Lamming, *Pleasures of Exile*, 107.

8. Aimé Césaire is one of many writers whose re-visions of *The Tempest* address the centrality of race, class, and gender in contemporary Caribbean literature. Césaire casts Ariel as a mulatto figure and Caliban as a black revolutionary. Césaire's revisions highlight issues of race (or caste) and class in the Caribbean. The relationship between Ariel and Caliban, though not fully realized, foreshadows the revolutionary possibilities in other Caribbean countries. See Aimé Césaire, *A Tempest*, trans. Richard Miller (New York: Ubu Repertory Theatre, 1992). A number of postcolonial critics have addressed this substantial tradition: see Rob Nixon, "Caribbean and African Appropriations of *The Tempest*," *Critical Inquiry* 13, no. 3 (1987): 557–78; Lemuel Johnson, "Shoeing the Mule: 'Caliban' as Genderized Response," in *Latin America and the Caribbean Geo-politics, Development, and Culture*, ed. Arch R. M. Ritter (Ottawa: CALACS Carleton University, 1984); O. Mannoni, *Prospero and Caliban: The Psychology of Colonization*, trans. Pamela Powesland (Ann Arbor: University of Michigan Press, 1990); Roberto Fernández Retamar, *Caliban and Other Essays*, trans. Edward Baker (Minneapolis, MN: University of Minnesota Press, 1989); and Houston Baker, "Caliban's Triple Play," *Critical Inquiry* 13, no.1 (1986): 182–96.

9. Anne McClintock, "'No Longer in a Future Heaven': Gender, Race, and Nationalism," in *Dangerous Liaisons: Gender, Nation, and Postcolonial Perspectives*, eds. Anne McClintock, Aamir Mufti, and Ella Shohat (Minneapolis: University of Minnesota Press, 1997), 89.

10. This statement is offered to Miranda in response to her question, "Sir, are you not my father?" Prospero's response here is peculiar because it proposes his paternity in relation to what Miranda's mother tells him about her daughter, suggesting that there may well have been some doubt about her words and therefore his paternity. Shakespeare's account leaves much to the imagination of the reader when he writes,

> Thy mother was a piece of virtue, and
>   She said thou wast my daughter; and thy father
> Was the Duke of Milan; and his only heir
> And princess—no worse issued.
> My brother and thy uncle, called Antonio—
> I pray thee mark me—that a brother should
> Be so perfidious!—he whom next thyself
> Of all the world I loved, and to him put
> The manage of my state, as at that time
> Through all the signories it was the first
> And Prospero the prime duke, being so reputed
> In dignity; for the liberal arts
> Without a parallel; those being all my study,
> The government I cast upon my brother
> And to my state grew stranger, being transported
> And rapt in secret studies. Thy false uncle—
> Dost thou attend me?

William Shakespeare, *The Tempest*, ed. P. Holland (New York: Penguin Books, 1999), 1.2.56–78. If we understand the "state" and government to include all aspects of his throne, the leap from throne to queen is not too far. In other words, if Prospero's neglect of "state" includes his wife, and if, indeed, he entrusted all matters of the state to Antonio, then readers should certainly consider his wife as part and parcel of his fiefdom.

11. George Lamming, *Water with Berries* (Port of Spain, Trinidad: Longman Caribbean, 1971), 38.

12. My reference here is connected both to Caliban's assertion in *The Tempest* that "this island's mine by Sycorax my mother" (1.2.331) and to the popular idea of the "motherland" as the source of inspiration and contestation in many nationalist movements. This constructed space is not uniform in its conceptualizations but is nonetheless a common point of reference as many of the cultural histories of Shakespeare's Caliban suggest. For two exhaustive historiographies of Shakespeare's Caliban and its various appropriations, see Alden T. and Virginia Mason Vaughan, *Shakespeare's Caliban: A Cultural History* (London: Cambridge University Press, 1991) and Roberto Fernández Retamar, *Caliban and Other Essays* (Minneapolis: University of Minnesota Press, 1989).

13. Shakespeare, *The Tempest*, 1.2.332–40..

14. Sandra Pouchet Paquet, "*Water with Berries*: Caliban in Albion," in *The Novels of George Lamming* (London: Heinemann, 1982), 34.

15. Lamming, *Water with Berries*, 38.

16. Abena Busia, "Silencing Sycorax: On Colonial Discourse and the Unvoiced Female," *Cultural Critique*, no. 14 (Winter 1989–1990): 86.

17. Shakespeare, *The Tempest*, 1.2.266.

18. Busia, "Silencing Sycorax," 87.

19. Busia, "Silencing Sycorax," 94.

20. Busia, "Silencing Sycorax," 94.

21. Gayatri Spivak, "Can the Subaltern Speak? Speculations on Widow Sacrifice," in *Marxism and the Interpretation of Culture*, eds. Cary Nelson and Lawrence Grossberg (London: Macmillan, 1988), 287.

22. Spivak, "Can the Subaltern Speak?" 308.

23. Lamming, *Water with Berries*, 148.

24. Stephen Orgel, "Prospero's Wife," *Representations*, no. 8 (Autumn 1984): 4. Orgel is citing the Arden edition of the play, edited by Frank Kermode.

25. Orgel, "Prospero's Wife," 7.

26. Emphasis mine. Lamming, *Water with Berries*, 226.

27. McClintock, "'No Longer in a Future Heaven,'" 89–90. McClintock is citing Frantz Fanon, *The Wretched of the Earth*, trans. Constance Farrington (London: Penguin, 1963), 30.

28. Lamming, *Water with Berries*, 228.

29. Lamming, *Water with Berries*, 229.

30. At this point in Lamming's narrative, Roger, another Calibanesque figure in the novel, begins to burn down various establishments around the city. All of the places he sets fire to seem to be significant gathering places for West Indian immigrants in Britain, including the Mona Pub and finally the Old Dowager's house.

31. Wynter, "Afterword," 360.

32. Teeton's attachment to an old dead tree trunk in Lamming's novel is a symbolic reference to Shakespeare's play and Sycorax's punishment. One is left to wonder whether his attachment to the trunk is also symbolic of his own internal struggle with Randa's imprisonment and death in San Cristobal.

33. In Lamming's introduction to *The Pleasures of Exile*, he describes the significance of the Haitian Ceremony of Souls for his reimaging of this historical narrative. According to Lamming, the celebrants are "mainly relatives of the deceased who, ever since their death have been locked in water. It is the duty of the Dead to return and offer, on this momentous night, a full and honest account on their relations with the living"; Lamming, *Pleasures of Exile*, 9.

34. Lamming, *Water with Berries*, 102.

35. Busia, "Silencing Sycorax," 95.

36. Lamming, *Water with Berries*, 110.

37. Lamming, *Water with Berries*, 117–18.

38. Busia, "Silencing Sycorax," 86.

39. Belinda Edmondson, *Making Men: Gender, Literary Authority, and Women's Writing in Caribbean Narrative* (Durham and London: Duke University Press), 145. Edmondson is citing Shari Benstock, "Expatriate Modernism," in *Women's Writing and Exile*, eds. Mary Lynn Broe and Angela Ingram (Chapel Hill: University of North

Carolina Press, 1989): 25; and she refers the reader to Samantha Heigh's reading of Freud's *Uncanny in Heigh*, "The Return of Africa's Daughters: Negritude and the Gendering of Exile" (paper presented at the African Literature Association Conference, Guadeloupe, 1993): 13.

40. Wynter, "Afterword," 365.

41. Wynter, "Afterword," 363–64. Wynter is engaging Foucault's *The Order of Things*, where he argues that "because 'Man' is an object of 'positive knowledge' in Western culture, he cannot be an object of science" (Wynter, "Afterword," 369 n40). Sylvia Wynter cites Foucault's use of this term in his discussion of the discursive limitations in various disciplines. In a lecture, delivered in December 1970 and published as Appendix to *Archeology of Knowledge*, Foucault notes that Mendel's findings about genetic heredity were not "hearable at first because they were not within the "'vrai'" of the discipline at the time" (Wynter, "Afterword," 369).

Chapter Three

Gender and Genre: The Logic of Language and the Logistics of Identity

> Speech, voice, language, and word—all are ways of being in the world, and the artist working with the I-mage and giving voice to it is being in the world. The only way the African artist could be in this world, that is the New World, was to give voice to this split I-mage of voiced silence. Ways to transcend that contradiction had to and still have to be developed, for that silence continues to shroud the experience, the I-mage and so the word.
>
> M. NourbeSe Philip,
> "The Absence of Writing or How I Almost Became a Spy," 16

> Does the inner space exist whole in any language? Other than "threat" and "fear?" What is the language of the inner space? To read the text that lies "missing" in the silence of the inner space, we needing new language—the language of jamettes, possessing their inner and outer space. The be-coming and coming-to-be of a jamette poet.
>
> M. NourbeSe Philip, "Dis Place—The Space Between," 100

FINDING A LANGUAGE FOR THE EXPERIENCE OF SPACE/PLACE

The phenomena described by M. NourbeSe Philip sit at the crux of contemporary debates about Caribbean literature and identity. Trapped in a discourse that simultaneously denied their humanity and emphasized their presence as a form of alterity, colonial subjects could only imagine and represent their Selves in a language of contradiction that made them what they were, in fact, not. In an effort to transcend these contradictions, Caribbean writers revised the categories/institutions of history and identity to create a space that could accommodate their lived experiences and their expressions of those experiences. These spaces, though reconstructed, still depend on the authority afforded by imperialist discourses and hierarchies. Appropriations of various traditions and tropes have been deployed effectively in a number of ways, one of which is to recenter black female subjectivity as a normative part of colonial and postcolonial Caribbean literature. Narrative representations of the nation as overtly gendered (female) and sexualized through the mapping of nationalist agendas onto women's bodies raise immediate questions about the possibility of transcending these contradictions without engaging the constructed silence of black women's histories, genealogies, and experiences in colonial and postcolonial Caribbean literature. Contemporary texts by critics and writers alike have argued that the logic of language and the logistics of identity have developed along an axis of masculinist discourses that police and appropriate black female sexualities in the service of black nationalist movements.

Literary representations of the lived realities of women remain locked within traditional notions of genre, identity, language, and gender, despite the ironic shift that saw women become a prominent part of the social landscape of Caribbean literature during the Trinidad Renaissance of the 1930s. The "discursive unities" between colonialist and post-independence nationalist narratives presented reading audiences with a discursive terrain endowed with canonical authority and political force, a discourse that constructed women as present yet silent historical subjects. This tradition was reproduced and disseminated in the new political and cultural landscape of the modern Caribbean nation-state. Writing a generation later, Caribbean women experiencing the pains (not pleasures) of exile needed to craft a political and cultural landscape that fit their own sense of logic, language, history, and identity. Despite the similarities in the geographic trajectories between contemporary Caribbean women writers and their male counterparts of the 1950s and 1960s, the cultural and political circumstances are worlds apart. Migrating for women writers at the end of the century was not heralded with the same sense of national pride as the previous exodus of the "sons of the nation." Moreover, the institutional assurances (island scholarships, jobs with the BBC, teaching posts, freelance reporting, etc.) available to young colonials like C. L. R. James, Eric Williams, and others were not as widely available for women migrating a generation later. The absence of these benefits, as well as the changing relationship between the metropoles and "foreigners," indicated the shift in racial politics in United States, Britain, and Canada.

No longer the benevolent provider, Britain took care of its own as cultural perspectives shifted, and part of this new responsibility involved preserving its sense of Britishness.¹ My interest in second-wave migration for women writers and discourses of identity is twofold. Firstly, I want to suggest that, for contemporary Caribbean women writers, migration meant coming to terms with their own experiences of alienation, oppression, and dispossession, first in their Caribbean homelands, and then in their new home lands—the places that were now home—in the African Diaspora. Secondly, I want to examine the extent to which women writers employ a gendered critique of genre by implicating form as well as the discourses of identity in the shaping of women's physical, linguistic, geographic, and existential spaces and places. The deconstruction of narrative form that, I argue, is becoming a characteristic of contemporary Caribbean women's literature (particularly in the case of Erna Brodber, M. NourbeSe Philip, Maryse Condé, and Merle Collins) complicates traditional relationships between language and identity. My engagement with M. NourbeSe Philip's writing examines her exploration of the inextricable links between traditional constructions of gender, sexuality, and identity. Philip's explicit linking of language, sexuality, and history in her poetry highlights the hegemony exercised and experienced through colonialist discourses. Her prose and poetry emphasize the psychological damage of language and History on black slaves; more specifically, she stresses the use of language as a tool of violence that represses the imagination while oppressing the physical body. The questions posed by Philip threaten the boundaries of our understanding of language and representation. She asks, "Does the inner space exist whole in any language? Other than 'threat' and 'fear?'"² To begin to formulate a response to this question, we need to reconceptualize the relationship between language and the environments language inhabits. Implicit in this question is a critique both of the means by which space is defined and controlled, and of the centrality of power in its representation and experience.

In her prose/diary/play/poem/letter, "Dis Place—The Space Between," Philip recenters a critique of power through her engagement with historical constructions of women, their lives, and their bodies within discursive "fields of play." These fields of play and production include colonial legal documents, historical records, scientific studies, personal letters, and colonial traditions. Philip's disregard for uniformity of genre reflects her desire to highlight the discursive and political dispersion of language that has disciplined women's bodies while also distancing them from language. This "voiced silence" is produced among discourses that operate in the "spaces between" disciplines, genres, histories, identities, and personal accounts. An awareness of these spaces, according to Philip, creates an environment where the "polyvocular text"³ can be engaged as an articulation of alter/native models for representing aspects of Caribbean history and identity.

This critical approach is as much a writing strategy for Philip as it is a mode of existence for feminist critic Teresa de Lauretis, who argues that female identity is "not unified or simply divided between positions of masculinity and femininity, but multiply organized across positionalities along several axes and across mutually contradictory discourses and practices."[4] Imagining identities within discourses of colonialism demands a critical approach that borrows from contradictory spaces, regardless of their relational proximity to the subject in process. This approach can best be described as a form of bricolage that brings together disciplines, histories, languages, and identities with the aim of exposing the intricate connectedness of each to the other.

"Dis Place—The Space Between" represents the "polyvocularity" of Caribbean discourses on identity, discourses that extend beyond traditional boundaries that separate disciplines, genres, lingustic and national communities, and historical periods. This community of voices includes personal letters from the author and Ferdinand, the sixteenth-century king of Spain; court records (presented as a play) from the trial of notorious "jamettes"[5] in Port-of-Spain, Trinidad; calypso songs and quotations from dancers and musicians such as Rex Nettleford and Miles Davis; critiques by intellectuals such as Michel Foucault, Gayatri Spivak, C. L. R. James, and Lucille Mathurin Mair; and commentary on cricket and carnival. Philip coins the term "s/place" to represent the interconnected nature of space and place throughout her work, bringing physical, sexual, and geographical domains into dialogue with one another. How does this s/place function, and how does it affect the ways black subjects, particularly female subjects, experience their Selves? Can this s/place provide what Belinda Edmonson succinctly describes as a "theory of Caribbean female writing that identifies an 'essential' Caribbean female subject?"[6] According to Philip, this s/place represents the postmodern realities of black women across the world:

> S/Place. Where the inner space is defined into passivity by, and harnessed to, the needs and functions of the outer space—the place of oppression. Run it down[7] even further into Caribbean English: s/place mutates into "dis place." "Dis place": the outer space—the plantation, the New World. "Dis Place": the result of linking of the inner space between the legs with the outer place leading to "dis placement." "Dis place"—the space between. The legs. For the Black woman "dis placed" to and in the New World, the inner space between the legs would also mutate to "dis place"—fulcrum of the New World plantation.[8]

This space, in between, is the physical experience of external space and how it is configured internally, through the mind and body. From Columbus's early exploits through the Trinidad Renaissance to the "brain drain" migrations of the sixties and seventies, the terrain of Caribbean literature has been defined through these spaces "in between." This space represents the sexualized landscape of national identity and the gendered discourses that instituted Caribbean literary traditions. Traversing geographies to gain the advantage of critical distance is one of the privileges of Caribbean male intellectuals, one that has borne itself out in the language used to describe Caribbean historical and cultural landscapes.

There can be no separation of gender and national identity because female sexuality has long been the context out of which the nation emerges in all its contradictions. Women's relationships to the physical landscape of their own bodies are mediated (to put it mildly) by the threat and fear of sexual violation, which has long been a staple in nationalist narratives of resistance and rebellion. In a subsection of "Dis Place—The Space Between" entitled "The Body," Philips describes the processes involved in displacing women from their physical, sexual, and political spaces through the threat of rape:

> In patriarchal societies (the only societies we have known), the female body always presents a subversive threat. By far *the* most efficient management tool of women is the possibility of the uninvited and forceful invasion of the space between the legs—rape. Which is a constant. A threat to *the* space—the inner space between the legs. Even if never carried out, this threat continually and persistently inflects how the female reads the external language of place, or public space—the outer space. One woman raped is sufficient to vocalize and reify the threat of outer space, and the need to protect this inner space means that the female always reads the outer space from a dichotomous position—safe/unsafe, prohibited/unprohibited. How the female poet interacts with the land, the countryside, or the urbanscape—with the outer space in all its variety, or place in its most physical sense is, therefore, entirely affected by gender. She must read place—the outer space—in a gendered language. Is the choice, therefore, either to accept the restriction in physical behavior and available space that the threat of rape brings—limit one's activities to the daytime, and to specific places? Or what? The female poet's understanding of place in its most physical sense will be different from and necessarily more restricted, than that of her male counterparts.[9]

The language of colonialism, in its earliest literary representations, was a language of oppression and violation, particularly sexual violation. The journals of great "explorers" make (in)famous the illusions of conquering "virgin territories" and "penetrating" deep into the "heart of darkness." The discourse and practice of rape as a "tool of efficient management of women" are fictionalized as a trope in colonialist narratives of discovery and in the lived reality of black women in the New World. The accounts of rape chronicled in the journals and diaries of travelers to the New World, as well as in the colonial legislation that granted slave owners power over black women's bodies, testify to the historical connections between women's bodies and the landscape under siege. Resolutions from the Council of War of 1665 express the historical power of the letter of the Law to govern black women's bodies.[10] In *A Genealogy of Resistance*, this legal doctrine forms a significant part of the body of the section entitled, "THE BODY FEMALE and black":

> *It Is Our Royal Will and Pleasure*
> If any number of persons shall find out the Pallenque of the said
> Negroes, they shall have and enjoy to their uses all the Women and
> Children and all the plunder they can find there for their reward.[11]

This legislation enacts the "efficient management" of rebellious blacks through the forceful invasion of women and children who are singled out as the recipients of any treatment that is the "pleasure and will" of those exercising the law. The invasion of the "inner spaces" of the New World enabled and empowered disciplinary discourses grounded in the language of conquest, penetration, and pillage in the name of "taming" the landscape, the savage, and the darkness "in between."[12] In so doing, it also produced the framework for nineteenth-century Victorian ideals of sexuality and womanhood that would be used to exclude and distance black female subjects from their identities as women.

Black women writing slave narratives in North America, such as Harriet Jacobs, had to revise their modes of expression in order to write out of the double bind of their race and gender.[13] In twentieth-century writing from the Caribbean, we see a similar formulation of this bind, articulated through Caribbean nationalism and nationalist politics. The integral connectedness of race and gender in early constructions of West Indianness is brilliantly expressed through the barrack-yard fiction of the 1930s. The allegorical nature of the barrack-yard and storefront narratives gives a face and a voice to the exploitation of the working poor. The nationalist landscapes mapped out above in chapters 1 and 2 represent women's bodies as tropes for embattled conceptualizations of Caribbean national identity.

It is not simply the appropriation of women's bodies that is significant here, however. These appropriations became a means of disciplining black female identity in other Caribbean nationalist narratives. The "inner space" of the barrack-yard and the women who reside there were defined in and through the "outer spaces" of colonial patriarchal society in Trinidad.[14] The financial dependence on keepers highlights the extent to which "outer spaces" determine the shape of power systems in the yard, if not its values. However, the power struggles in early barrack-yard narratives also provide the first glimpses of the discursive disciplining that emerges in the second wave of Caribbean literature written in exile. The women who inhabit the stories of the *Beacon* represent a wayward willfulness that tramples every social institution of Victorian colonial society in the interest of women's self-preservation. This radical positioning of women in relation to the nation-state is swiftly revised in order to make way for a more socially responsible and politically astute nation on the march toward independence.

The practice of embracing women's bodies as a trope for representing West Indian realities by writers of the Trinidad Renaissance was replaced by the backlash of nationalist politics that required that men have access to mobility and control over their social surroundings. While this mobility offered, on the surface, an equal opportunity for men and women, the dis/placement of women during this mid-century period of Caribbean writing would have a lasting effect on how women would occupy nationalist landscapes. The experience of displacement meant something significantly different for men than it did for women. For women, it amounted to their absent presence in the literature and landscape of the period. For men, however, this displacement was an opportunity to sharpen their insights. Lamming's *The Pleasures of Exile* and *Water with Berries* both characterize this displacement as a necessary stage of development for Caribbean artists. As exile emerged as a mode of representation in the second wave of Caribbean writing, there was a corresponding systematic marginalization and/or erasure of black women. Edmondson offers a convincing argument for reading the critical vantage point of "outer spaces" as a hegemonic category that can only be accessed through masculinist discourses of sexuality and national identity.

The power of "Elsewhere" historically endowed Caribbean male writers with (canonical, political, and cultural) authority to speak on behalf of the nation and its citizens, despite their distance from both. If ex/patri/ation is a necessity for Caribbean men to insure their presence as subjects on the national stage of history, what does this mean for Caribbean women writers attempting to formulate a black female subjectivity not predicated on this formulation? How do women writers represent the female body, which has been distanced from its Self through its use and misuse as a nationalist trope for colonial "virgin territory"? How do they begin to formulate a discourse to express their experiences of s/place? Can this language provide a means for revising the traditions that have disciplined their bodies and their language into silence?

Philip advances a complex critical response to these questions through her engagement with the "logic of language" in postcolonial discourses. Her collection *She Tries Her Tongue, Her Silence Softly Breaks* yokes discourses of sexuality, language, and oppression into immediate visual, spatial, and historical proximity on the page. In so doing, she translates narrative "form" into a vehicle for (dis)forming or exposing the cracks in and complicity across discursive communities and traditions. This approach pays particular attention to the configuration of human science and its construction of the female body through image and language.

IMAG(IN)ING THE WORD/WORLD THROUGH "VOICED SILENCE"

The intimate connections between sexual and physical spaces (or what Philip refers to as "scapes") informs the processes through which bodies of language and, indeed, physical bodies are disciplined into discourses that reflect the restrictions, genealogies, and conventions of the s/places from which they emerge. This metathetic representation of displacement, one that changes spaces to scapes, shows the extent to which language and meaning are linked visually. Moreover, the psychological, physical, and emotional distances between subject and place, space, and (land)scapes in Caribbean literature has traditionally been mediated by the "privilege" of exile. Philip's *She Tries Her Tongue, Her Silence Softly Breaks* challenges the structure and dispersion of discourses, as well as the traditional boundaries erected between poetry, prose, personal narrative, the humanities, and the social sciences. In her opening essay, "The Absence of Writing or How I Almost Became a Spy," Philip challenges her reading audience to confront the historical and cultural interconnectedness between the body and the word—more specifically, between the female subject's body and the Word (or the Law of the Father). Traditions of policing women's bodies through legislative, social, or religious institutions have been the discursive domain of men. The interconnectedness of gender, language, and power, therefore, is of singular importance throughout Philip's writing as it represents an effort to rehistoricize and delegitimate discourses that have subsumed and disrupted the processes of Be(come)ing for Africans in the New World. If, as Philip's asserts, "Speech, voice, language and word—all are ways of being in the world,"[15] then, to represent the experiences of Africans in the New World, the writer would have to forge a relationship to language different from that which has historically constructed black subjectivity and identity.

The image of "voiced silence" that Philip evokes captures the nature of the contradiction at work within discourses of identity that lock black subjects out of the processes of making meaning of their Selves in their own language. By highlighting the simultaneous expression and suppression of black subjects through erasure (silencing), Philip's deployment of the notion of "voiced silence" suggests that the black subject's utterances (or mother tongues) are transformed by the whips of slaveholders into unintelligible sounds. The intimate connection between language and labor in the New World ensured that the primary function of language was not to express, but to oppress and repress the experiences of Africans. The possibility of a language capable of "giving voice" to what enslaved people experienced, therefore, was never available to Africans in the New World:

> The African in the Caribbean could move away from the experience of slavery in time; she could even acquire some perspective on it, but the experience, having never been reclaimed and integrated metaphorically through language and so within the psyche, could never be transcended. To reclaim and integrate the experience required autonomous I-mage makers and therefore a language with the emotional, linguistic, and historical resources capable of giving voice to the particular I-mages arising out of the experience. . . . I would argue further that it is impossible for any language, which denies the humanity of any group or people to be truly capable of giving voice to the I-mages of experiences of that group without tremendous fundamental changes within the language itself.[16]

In such a situation, enslaved people learned a language (English) that kept them silenced and reduced (both language and) their bodies to units of production. The "voice" created out of this relationship, therefore, spoke nothing of (or to) the lived experiences of Africans in the New World, creating the "voiced silence" to which Philip refers.

How, then, would the writer, particularly the woman writer, begin to construct for herself an I-mage out of these layered contradictions? If Africans in the New World had (and still have) only English (or French, Spanish, or Dutch, depending on the colonizer's tongue) to express themselves, were they, as many Caribbean writers have suggested, doomed to Prospero's prisonhouse of language? Or was there another alternative, one that could bend the medium to meet the needs of Africans in the New World? Far from asserting the creation of a new language or resorting to a romanticized notion that African languages could be made to serve the needs of generations of African Caribbean peoples for whom Africa was only a distant memory, Philip asserts that "English, in its broadest spectrum must be made to do the job." In other words, somewhere between what we refer to as "standard" English and/or other colonial tongues would emerge a "demotic variant of English" representative both of the "havoc that Africans wreaked on the English language" and of the "metaphorical equivalent of the havoc that coming to the New World represented for the African."[17] The slippage and playfulness of Caribbean demotics, the "I" of Rastafarian language, the turns of phrases, and other representations of the "overstanding" are all examples of the how enslaved people "took night and made day," with language, making it work overtime for them.

The questions raised by Philip and many contemporary women writers are by no means new, nor do they represent a renewed interest in the age-old struggle for possession of Prospero's gifts or curses. The problematic of language for Caribbean writers is continuously documented, and the debates show no signs of abating, particularly as the long-term implications of colonialism and its new manifestation, globalization, continue to unfold.[18] As the capacity to express experiences and feelings in myriad languages goes, so too does the power to name and know the Self. The challenge for Caribbean writers is to exploit aspects of language and further subvert them to make the language truly belong to Caribbean subjects. In this last respect, Philip pursues forms of *métissage* in order to interrogate and resist conventions and institutions inherited from colonialist oppression, while simultaneously laying bare the integral workings of these conventions in order to better understand the relationship of the parts to the whole. These processes of subversion are instrumental if Caribbean subjects are to begin to endow their language with meanings of their own, to create their own I-mages. Exploring the structure of literary conventions within the Western canonical tradition, African mythology, and the Caribbean demotic provides Caribbean writers with an opportunity to formulate new patterns, systems, and modalities to represent African Caribbean realities. Highlighting the important uses of non-conventional literary forms, Philip asserts that

> The continuing challenge for me as a writer/poet is to find some deeper patterning—a deep structure, as Chomsky puts it—of my language, the Caribbean demotic. As James Baldwin has written, "Negro speech is not a question of dropping s's or n's or g's but a question of the beat." At present the greatest strength of the Caribbean demotic lies in its oratorical energies, which do not necessarily translate to the page easily.... To keep the deep structure, the movement, the kinetic energy, the tone and pitch, the slides and glissandos of the demotic within a tradition that is primarily page bound—that is the challenge.[19]

As Philip suggests, the contradictory forces so characteristic of Caribbean culture also trouble any attempt to find a "neat" conclusion. In this case, the greatest tool available for the Caribbean writer is also the difficulty facing any attempt at finding a solution. The response, however, has not been one of utter distress. Quite the contrary, Philip herself comments that the problematics and issues discussed in the opening essay of *She Tries Her Tongue* serve as "something of a blueprint" for her poetic engagement with the Caribbean demotic.[20] She successfully situates her critique of language, power, and identity within these contradictions, drawing on her colonial heritage, her mother and father tongues, and the other wisdoms from African cultures that have so infiltrated New World, Caribbean traditions.

The "deep structure" to which Philip refers, when read in all its complexities, includes both the "form" of language and the modalities through which language and meaning are constructed, disseminated, and interpreted. She also reminds us of the questions raised earlier about the black female body's relationship to language by explicitly linking the loss of control over language to black women's loss of control over their physical spaces and places. Disruptions of language inevitably affect the ability of the black female subject to express her experiences and thus her relationship to her histories, myths, I-mages, and identities. In the opening poem, Philip evokes an embodied language by reconfiguring the economies at work in myths such as Ovid's *Metamorphoses* and the tale of Proserpine and Ceres. The section "And over Every Land and Sea" includes a series of poems that repossess the language of mother/daughter relationships to consider the separation of black mothers from their children, first during slavery and then through the large-scale dispersion of immigrants in search of work. Above each poem in this section, Philip includes lines from Ovid's text:

> *Meanwhile, Proserpine's mother Ceres, with panic in her heart vainly sought her daughter over all lands and over all the sea.*
> . . . .
> *As for Cyane, she lamented the rape of the goddess...nursing silently in her heart a wound that none could heal...*
> . . . .
> *It would take a long time to name the lands and seas over which the goddess wandered. She searched the whole world—in vain . . .*[21]

These lines frame the subsequent poems and connect them across historical periods and discursive terrains. The narrative of Ceres, who is searching frantically for her abducted daughter, is rewritten. The landscape of the narrative is reclaimed to reflect the embodied realities of black mothers seeing their children bought and sold on the slave market. The mythic search in Ovid's tale becomes all the more impossible if we read it through the experience and ruptures that occur in Middle Passage and other forced migrations.

The poem, "Questions! Questions!" opens with the lines "Where she, where she, where she/be, where she gone?"[22] and recounts a mother searching madly for her daughter. Similarly, "Clues" implies a historical connection to the earlier poem by offering suggestions as to the location of the missing young woman:

> She gone—gone to where I don't know
>   Looking for me looking for she;
>   is pinch somebody pinch and tell me,
>   up where the north marry cold I could find she—
>   Stateside, England, Canada—somewhere about . . .[23]

Philip's appropriation of this mythic quest highlights the historical thread that connects traditions in Greek mythology to other power structures in which men, who exercise their will as though they were gods, transformed the landscapes of women's bodies and imaginations. By repossessing the historical landscape, the text embodies black women's experiences, forcing the same language of the mythological quest to take on a very different meaning in a racialized context. When mothers cannot find their children and do not have the right (of freedom) or the resources to search for them, who will search, inquire about their disappearance, and find them?

When Ceres discovers Proserpine's girdle, her worst fears are confirmed, and she laments the loss and rape of her daughter. Read in relationship to the sexual economy of colonial slave plantations, the romanticism of the mother/daughter relationship is starkly contrasted against the violation and exploitation of black women's bodies for profit and the "will and pleasure" of slave masters.[24] This contrast highlights the assumptions of Western feminism and its efforts to reclaim the female body without dealing with the specificities of black women's histories. In her rereading and rewriting of this myth, Philip undoes the uniformity of the sign of "woman" by articulating the experiences of black women, experiences that have been subsumed under the broad category of History or within women's history. Ceres's search, in this instance, is juxtaposed against the experience of a black woman whose child is sold away, generations dispersed, the lineage disrupted, scattered in space and time, irrecoverable.

Philip engages this same "deep structure" in her textual representations of the ruptures in English language(s) and its limitations as a mode of expression for black subjects. These limitations, however, leave room for creative reimaginings of language, I-maginings that provide for the possibility of speaking in tongues, "mother tongues" and "father tongues." Once more, the problem is precisely the key to the solution as the "trying" (or difficult) tongue of English also opens room for "trying" (experimenting) to decenter English as we know it. Philip's "Discourse on the Logic of Language" is a performative representation of the processes involved in the act of decentering or deconstructing language. Despite what Philip describes as "the anguish of English," her poetry explores the possibility for black subjects in the New World to speak, as it were, in tongues.

"Father tongues" have historically served as a means of alienating black subjects from their Selves and, more particularly, have been part of a history of violence and oppression. Therefore, language, sexuality, and identity are intimately connected through a rather intricate cartography of language acquisition, dissemination, and interpretation in "Discourse on the Logic of Language." The first page of the poem poses an interesting dilemma for its readers because of the unusual layout:

Discourse on the Logic of Language[25]

English
is my mother tongue.
A mother tongue is not
not a foreign lan lan lang
language
l/anguish
  anguish
—a foreign anguish.

English is
my father tongue.
A father tongue is
a foreign language,
therefore English is
a foreign language
not a mother tongue.

What is my mother
tongue
my mammy tongue
my mummy tongue
my momsy tongue
my modder tongue
my ma tongue?

I have no mother
tongue
no mother to tongue
no tongue to mother
to mother
tongue
me

I must therefore be tongue
dumb
dumb-tongued
dub-tongued
damn dumb
tongue

EDICT I

Every owner of slaves shall, wherever possible, ensure that his slaves belong to as many ethnolinguistic groups as possible. If they cannot speak to each other, they cannot then foment rebellion and revolution.

WHEN IT WAS BORN, THE MOTHER HELD HER NEWBORN CHILD CLOSE: SHE BEGAN THEN TO LICK IT ALL OVER. THE CHILD WHIMPERED A LITTLE, BUT AS THE MOTHER'S TONGUE MOVED FASTER AND STRONGER OVER ITS BODY, IT GREW SILENT — THE MOTHER TURNING IT THIS WAY AND THAT UNDER HER TONGUE, UNTIL SHE HAD TONGUED IT CLEAN OF THE CREAMY WHITE SUBSTANCE COVERING ITS BODY.

> THE MOTHER THEN PUT HER FINGERS INTO HER CHILD'S MOUTH—GENTLY FORCING IT OPEN; SHE TOUCHES HER TONGUE TO THE CHILD'S TONGUE, AND HOLDING THE TINY MOUTH OPEN, SHE BLOWS INTO IT—HARD. SHE WAS BLOWING WORDS—HER WORDS, HER MOTHER'S WORDS, THOSE OF HER MOTHER'S MOTHER, AND ALL THEIR MOTHERS BEFORE—INTO HER DAUGHTER'S MOUTH.

but I have
a dumb tongue
tongue dumb
father tongue
and english is
my mother tongue
is
my father tongue
is a foreign lan lan lang
language
l/anguish
  anguish
a foreign anguish
is english—
another tongue
my mother
    mammy
    mummy
    moder
    mater
    macer
    moder
tongue
mothertongue

tongue mother
tongue me
mothertongue me
mother me
touch me
with the tongue of your
lan lan lang
language
l/anguish
  anguish
english
is a foreign anguish

EDICT II

Every slave caught speaking his native language shall be severely punished. Where necessary, removal of the tongue is recommended. The offending organ, when removed, should be hung on high in a central place, so that all may see and tremble.

The polyvocularity of the text is created through both sight and sound, producing an effect of fragmented images that are constantly disrupted by the narratives that share the page as well as the same historical s/place. Philip's miscegenation of form disrupts the seemingly natural "order of things" that the reader and listener try to absorb. The difficulty of engaging the content as well as the multiple forms of representation forces audiences to question the relationship between the form and the discursive terrain that informs how we produce meaning and, therefore, knowledge. Philip's engagement with form, then, asks us to consider the ways each of these narratives always already contain traces of the other, whether verbally articulated or not.

The visual layout of the text in this poem reflects an ongoing engagement with the connections between form and function in Philip's writing. By positioning an array of textual representations on the same page, Philip forces the reader to make certain decisions about which he or she will read first, and that decision will ultimately shape the way the narrative is experienced and interpreted. Brenda Carr asserts that "In *She Tries Her Tongue*, miscegenation of form runs a kind of textual interference, incites a collision of discourses, that reveals language to be anything but indeterminate in its material effects. This text activates engagement with the mutual implication of discourses and bodies."[26] The bodies that inform "Discourse on the Logic of Language" assert historical and cultural links between language, sexuality, and oppression; these links manifest in a variety of physical and disciplinary discourses.

Philip's engagement with form deconstructs the "sensible" terms of sociohistorical institutions by closely examining processes involved in producing and disseminating this "sense" through coercion, terror, and legal and cultural practices and discourses. The capitalized text that that flows vertically, down the left-hand margin of the page where the poem and "EDICT 1" appear, reconstructs the locale of power and language in shaping identity through its physical proximity to the other narratives on the page. This prose constructs an-Other narrative that expresses the care administered by a mother to her child and the importance of the tongue as an object used to remove the afterbirth from the mother's newborn daughter. It is a text that leans on the other discourses for its authority, depending on the reader's ability and willingness to connect it to the other representations on the page. The mother (tongue) is the progenitor of language and a source of protection:

WHEN IT WAS BORN, THE MOTHER HELD HER NEWBORN CHILD CLOSE: SHE BEGAN THEN TO LICK IT ALL OVER. THE CHILD WHIMPERED A LITTLE, BUT AS THE MOTHER'S TONGUE MOVED FASTER AND STRONGER OVER ITS BODY, IT GREW SILENT—THE MOTHER

TURNING IT THIS WAY AND THAT UNDER HER TONGUE, UNTIL SHE HAD TONGUED IT CLEAN OF THE CREAMY WHITE SUBSTANCE COVERING ITS BODY.[27]

Although this quotation is presented here in the reading format common to English and most romance languages (from left to right), in Philip's book the text is positioned perpendicular to the rest of the page, written down the side, in what is traditionally considered the margin. The visual layout of this piece of writing requires readers to read from top to bottom, not left to right, because of its appearance on the page. The difficulty of reading the text might also require the reader to turn the book counterclockwise (east to west) in order to read the passages that flow from north the south. By replacing the traditional layout of the words on the page with this unorthodox style, Philip challenges her audience to critically consider literary conventions, the processes involved in printing texts, and the implicit assumptions of authors and readers alike.

The multiplicity of meaning in this narrative contributes to the dialectic created among the other texts on the page. As such, the different genres and discursive representations of the edict and the poem make two primary readings possible. One reading suggests that Philip's spatial arrangement provides a visual and discursive juxtaposition of possible meanings between the texts, forcing us to imagine the relationship of each text to the other. Tonguing, in this instance, becomes a verb in the sense of "giving words." However, as we will see later, this same act of tonguing takes on a different meaning if we consider the imposition of a "father tongue" as the edicts alert us to the violence, where the act of licking now has to be read in relation to acts of violence that discipline the subject into silence. The second edict prescribes "removal of the tongue" for slaves caught speaking in their native languages.[28] The tongue, therefore, is seen as a weapon, a tool of resistance, and certainly a means of oppression as is suggested in later in the poem.

The visual proximity of the different narratives transforms nurturing acts into acts of aggression against the physical and discursive body of the subject. In her essay "En/Gendering Spaces: The Poetry of Marlene Nourbese-Philip and Pamela Mordecai," Elaine Savory asserts that

> The text which runs along the page vertically is entirely in capital letters and describes a mother's tongue licking a newborn child clean of the white substance which covers its body. As she does this, the child falls quiet. Within these two different scripts and meanings, lies the poem, which takes the idea of the mother tongue and father tongue and plays them against each other. . . .[29]

The implicit critique of the "father tongue" or nation(al) language, which is said to be the voice of the larger community, is not only challenged, but (dis)formed through Philip's engagement with the multiplicity of meaning and language in this poem. Although the mother's agency gives words to her daughter, it does not guarantee the context or conditions through which the daughter's utterances will be received, or the field of play onto which they will enter. This s/place is a point where negotiations of power can, and have, dis/placed the female subject from her modes of expression.

Philip's engagement with the discursive terrain of colonialist discourses considers another aspect of the "trying" nature of language and the politics of "trying tongues" that resist oppression at every turn. Her critical examination of the phrase "mother tongue" pushes the construction of the "mother" as the progenitor of language. The question Philip raises (of what we call a language that is a foreign language, or foreign tongue) recognizes the implications of a power that can circumvent the intimate act of "tonguing" and giving language, to impose a foreign language. Moreover, her engagement with scientific discourse brings our attention to the complicity between science, sexism, and racism. The poem's opening statement is meant to highlight the "authority" of science and scientific discourse, and influence how we think about language and identity:

> Those parts of the brain chiefly responsible for speech are named after two learned nineteenth century doctors, the eponymous Doctors Wernicke and Broca respectively. Understanding and recognition of the spoken word takes place [*sic*] in Wernicke's area—the left temporal lobe, situated next to the auditory cortex; from there relevant information passes to Broca's area—situated in the left frontal cortex—which then forms the response and passes it on to the motor cortex. The motor cortex controls the muscles of speech.[30]

The scientific discourse, which appears on a page by itself, offers another complication in how we are to interpret this act of "giving words." Distinguishing between the functions of Wernicke's and Broca's areas of the brain, Philip highlights the separation between the spoken word and the act of actually speaking the word, while the "motor cortex," she tells us, "controls the muscles of speech."[31] The positioning of this passage in the center of the page is significant for a number of reasons. First, it disrupts the tri-genre poetic on the preceding page without introduction, heading, or any indication that it is related to the edict, prose, or poetry of the first page of the poem. Secondly, Philip's appropriation of this piece of scientific prose is an implicit commentary on language and its origins in the human brain.

The Broca and Wernicke areas of the brain are responsible for different aspects of language and speech. The Broca area of the brain is named after Pierre-Paul Broca, a French surgeon and anthropologist, while the Wernicke area of the brain is named after the German neurologist Carl Wernicke. For the purposes of my essay, the significance of these parts of the brain is not so much how they function as what happens when they do not function (dysfunction). When a patient suffers a trauma to the brain, either in the form of a blow or from a stroke, these particular parts of the brain are extremely susceptible to what, in neurological parlance, is called "aphasia." Aphasia refers to a group of language disorders that can occur when the language-dominant hemisphere of the brain is damaged.[32] There are two kinds of aphasia: Broca's aphasia, in which a patient omits small words such as "is," "and," and "the," and Wernicke's aphasia, where patients tend to speak in long meaningless sentences and create new "words." The first page of "Discourse on the Logic of Language" shows us an example of this kind of language pattern:

> English
>   is my mother tongue.
>   A mother tongue is not
>   not a foreign lan lan lang
>   language
>   l/anguish
>   anguish—a foreign anguish.[33]

This pattern *sounds* similar to those of a patient with symptoms of aphasia. The repetition, in particular, duplicates the series of words that, though seemingly related to one another, are not sequenced in a sensible order. Neurologists describe these words "meaningless neologisms," which are more often than not associated with psychological illnesses, most notably schizophrenia.

In light of Philip's earlier claims about the challenge she faces as a writer, Wernicke's and Broca's characterization of aphasia as a form of illness complicates the relationship of the black subject to science, language, and expression. The black subject's relationship to language is defined through medical and social discourses. Paul Broca's research in physical anthropology during the late 1800s and his development of craniometers were significant in developing the pseudoscience of phrenology that emerged as the basis for racist scientific claims about the cranial size differentials between blacks and whites.[34]

As a text engaged in mapping the terrain of language production and representation, "Discourse on the Logic of Language" is an exercise in discursive and epistemological *métissage*. The visual and discursive layout of the array of texts produces a field of power relations that include a variety of hierarchies, contradictions, symmetries, and disconnects across cultures, disciplines, and histories.[35] The scientific research of Broca and Wernicke, the legal discourses of the edicts, the myths, and the educational lessons are all related and yet dispersed across a number of "spaces" and "scapes."

The power they exercise, from their respective (and sometimes fluctuating) positions, when brought together in this context, provides a useful index of logistical relationships.

If we consider the trauma and terror expressed through the edicts and enacted on the bodies of enslaved people what are we to make of the Caribbean demotic in the face of several hundred years of scientific inquiry that has disciplined certain voices and expression into the realm of psychosis? The trauma that produces aphasia, for example, could well result from sexual, linguistic, and physical violence. We are asked, then, to consider the impact of being separated (whether through physical violence or psychological terror) from your linguistic community and the impact it has on the "muscles of speech," or the tongue. Certainly, there must be extensive damage to the language dominant hemisphere of the brain. As Philip argues, "our revelation to ourselves in the New World was simultaneous with a negative re-presentation of ourselves to ourselves, by a hostile imperialistic power, and articulated in a language endemically and etymologically hostile to our very existence."[36] The Caribbean writer, therefore, rather than writing about kinky hair and flat noses, "should be writing about the language that kinked the hair and flattened the noses."[37]

By placing the scientific definitions in the same context as historical and social discourses, Philip closes the constructed gaps between the language of science, as "fact" or "truth," and the language of sociocultural discourses, thereby creating a space for conceptualizing science as both informed and produced by social and cultural agendas. In so doing, she bridges the disciplines of history, sociology, anthropology, and medicine. Her appropriation of Broca's and Wernicke's findings on the difference in brain size (in a short scientific treatise on the left and right brain) as "proof" of the superiority of white males in comparison to "women, Blacks, and other peoples of colour" opens the sacred space of science, exposing it as a discourse overtly shaped by the racist ideologies of the nineteenth century.[38]

By providing her reading audience with visual representations of the connections between the physical/neurological traumas imposed on enslaved people, science and scientific discourses, and legal discourse, Philip implicates these epistemologies in the functional damage inflicted on the psyche because of the inaccessibility of the "mother tongue." "EDICT I" argues that *"if they cannot speak to each other, they cannot then foment rebellion and revolution."*[39] However, assuming the natural desire to speak in the mother tongue, "EDICT II" suggests a "cure" for any breach in the earlier proclamation:

EDICT II
*Every slave caught speaking his native
tongue shall be severely punished. Where*

*necessary, removal of the tongue is
recommended. The offending organ,
when removed, should be hung on high in
a central place, so that all passing may
see and tremble.*⁴⁰

The discursive terror represented across these genres is pushed further when we consider the history of colonialism that constructed communities in order to prevent any means of communicating while, at the same time, imposing a language used to define labor and oppression.

Philip's poem effectively visualizes the impact of what, in neurological parlance, is called a "conversion disorder." Conversions are bridges between the physical/neurological (aphasia) and the functional (where there is an illness with no neurological injury).⁴¹ The psychoanalytical roots of conversion provide another productive lens through which to consider the discursive connections mapped in Philip's poem: "According to psychoanalytical theory, conversion disorder is caused by the repression of unconscious intrapsychic conflict and the conversion of anxiety into a physical symptom. The conflict is between an instinctual impulse [like speaking in your native tongue] and the prohibitions against this expression [removal of the tongue]. The symptoms allow partial expression of the forbidden wish or urge but disguise it...."⁴² This passage helps us to consider how the Edict functions as a disciplining form of repression, despite its positioning in the margin on the page. It functions as an authoritative voice that reaches into the internal body of the text and the subject. Philip's representation of "EDICT II," its visual appearance in font and heading, is meant to signify specific power of the "patria" or "Law of the Father" to dis/place the subject from expression. Although the use of italics may seem to be a non-authoritative visual representation, the content of the Edict succeeds in making the point clear and forceful. It is not the presentation of the law itself, but the practice of upholding its recommendation that leaves the lasting impression. The visual and physical "space in between" the poem and the Edict becomes a space of dismemberment, disempowerment, and disembodiment.

In the same manner, Philip invites her audience to consider the distance and difference between the definitions of the tongue, the whip, and the penis, and how they function discursively in systems of power and signification:

A tapering, blunt tipped, muscular, soft, and fleshy organ describes
(a) the penis.
(b) the tongue.
(c) neither of the above.
(d) both of the above.

In man the tongue is
(a) the principal organ of taste.
(b) the principal organ of articulate speech.
(c) the principal organ of oppression and exploitation.

The tongue
(a) is an interwoven bundle of striated muscle running in three planes.
(b) is fixed to the jawbones.
(c) has an outer covering of a mucous membrane covered with papillae.
(d) contains ten thousand taste buds, none of which is sensitive to the taste of foreign words.[43]

The examination format is particularly effective in the context of her critique of language, science, and oppression as it suggests that the practice of exercising choice presumes a certain relationship, power, and authority in the knowledge of the subject matter. Each of the questions highlights the similarities in the answers, depending on the perspective and vantage point of the reader. The inherent contradictions represented in choices that bridge the social and the scientific draw attention to analytical "blind spots" in our interpretations of power relations and the interconnected nature of these discourses.

Because the questions are each followed by a selection of correct answers, the "freedom" of choice in the poem becomes a precarious one; readers, like the colonized speakers of English, can only work out of their knowledge of this language that is at once their inheritance and their anguish. Freedom, in this context, can only be read through the implicit privileges on which these discourses depend, in much the same manner that the "freedom" to search for a lost child presupposes a mother's "right" of possession of her body and her children. All choices are filtered through the authority of discursive communities, laws, and landscapes that impose limits upon "freedom" for black female subjects. The tongue, as an organ of taste, speech, and expression, is simultaneously a part of the anatomy of oppression and exploitation. In the plantation economy, linguistic oppression and sexual exploitation both (en)act the language of violence and Law (black mothers equal black children, and black children are property) on the body of enslaved black women. The tongue and the penis are the same in this act of rape since both violate the spaces "in between" the legs, the imagination, and experience/expression.

Philip's writing focuses on decentering the language and authority of the Law of the land/nation/patri/Father. While previous debates about language and identity assumed a telos of Being constructed through imperialist discourses, Philip's poem subverts the logic of language to allow multiply voiced expressions of identity, authority, and power; her poem speaks in tongues, as it were. The multivocal, multigenre style exposes how the discursive deployment and dispersions of language work to construct the "knowledge" of certain objects and subjects of History. In so doing, she exposes language and the knowledge produced from these vantage points as constructed and implicated in the hegemonic practices of linguistic and cultural oppression. The emphasis on language and knowledge in contemporary Caribbean women's writing reflects the significance of addressing the Law of the land and language, which Philip describes as "nine-tenths possession, and one-tenth the legitimization process."[44] Her engagement with "hard" science ensures a firm footing in one of the most authoritative discourses in the history of Man. The links between "hard" science, anthropology, and sociology become clearer, less attributable to occurrences based on a predetermined system of signs.

Philip identifies the task of the writer in relation to the processes at work in various communities and contexts; this is a notable shift from the notion of consolidated identities that reside and emerge within a particular set of historical or social circumstances (slavery, emancipation, postcolonialism). These processes, she argues, range across diverse landscapes of experiences and:

> refines the entire experiential life and world view of the tribe, the race, and consequently of society at large; and if we accept that the poet, the story-teller, the singer or balladeer (through their words), express this process in their work then we must accept that this process becomes one way in which the society continually accepts, integrates and transcends its experiences positive or negative.[45]

This genealogy of "living language" and the creative process of self-expression links the subject to her or his surroundings and to processes that make translating experience through language possible. The emphasis for Philip, however, is on the continuity of movement, negotiations, and articulations between the subject and her or his surroundings, not simply a process progressing toward an end. Her emphasis, therefore, is on the movement between the discursive spaces and the possibilities that emerge as a result of the engagement of the productive capacities of the imagination.

Rather than conceptualizing the discourses of identity through what words "mean," Philip's texts argue for a relationship to language that permits subjects to "speak in tongues" that have emerged as a result of generations of "trying tongues," tongues that are now key to breaking silences. This process of speaking in tongues, however, cannot occur without the re-membering of stories, myths, and figures, and the continual reintegration of experiences that have been disciplined out of our histories and landscapes. These myths, stories, songs, and poems, according to Philip, are part of the "grammar of dissent" for unvoiced generations of blacks in the New World. These utterances, though unvoiced for generations, are part of the performative aspects of language that emerge in the "kinopoesis" of the written word on the page.[46] Capturing this movement in written language can be achieved only by pressing back the boundaries that restrain genre, structure, form, and voice in literature.

Discussing the processes and objectives involved in the production of *She Tries Her Tongue, Her Silence Softly Breaks*, Philip asserts that her aim is to subvert the lyrical voice in order to make the text more "polyvocular." By subverting the lyrical voice in a textual context, Philip develops a model that disrupts what Edouard Glissant refers to as a "forced poetics" that is obsessed with silencing the "din" of discourse.[47] As a noun, "din" is a loud annoying noise; as a verb, the word "din" is the act of forcing information into a person by continually repeating it.[48] Philip preserves this "din" in all its meanings by manipulating the visual layout of her text so that it reproduces the multiplicity of voices being heard at once. Her emphasis on the rhythm and movement of these sounds reflects the systematic production of meaning in the Caribbean demotic. Each reading, hearing, voicing of her text therefore represents a new experience between speakers and audiences.

For Caribbean women writers, this mode creates another continuum of expression. However, in the face of History, one is left with a similar problematic in the region's literature. If representing the I-mages and experiences of blacks in the New World requires a demotic, can Caribbean histories be written through such a model? If language is a reflection of the environments that subjects inhabit, is there a model for writing a history that can accommodate the rapid movements that have shaped Caribbean reality? If, as Philip argues, the voice that speaks the subject and its experiences is best expressed through this polyvocular narrative form, what are the implications of this assertion for how we write the histories of black subjects in the Diaspora? Can history be written with a similar subversive, creative voice and still maintain its disciplinary, social, and cultural authority? Or do such narrative leave the realm of "history" and migrate toward fiction because it is not rooted in "facts" that can be substantiated by others in the same voice? If this polyvocular voice is the modality for expressing the realities of black subjects, how does this performativity manifest itself in the processes of Be(come)ing in the world? The answers to these questions, as we will see in the next chapter, have their roots in historical and cultural pathways that define "home" in the African Diaspora.

NOTES

1. For example, Merle Collins writes a poem entitled "No Dialects Please" in response to a call for submissions to a poetry contest. The advertisement, according

to Collins, ends by stating that submissions in "dialects" would not be considered because, "after all we are British"; Merle Collins, "No Dialects Please," in *Watchers and Seekers: Creative Writing by Black Women*, eds. Rhonda Cobham and Merle Collins (New York: Peter Bedrick Books, 1988): 118–19. The implicit assertion, that those who might speak or write in dialects—English dialects—were, first and foremost, not British and not a part of the British landscape, would become a major obstacle facing Caribbean writers (particularly women) in the 1990s.

2. M. NourbeSe Philip, "Dis Place—The Space Between," *A Genealogy of Resistance and Other Essays* (Toronto: Mercury Press, 1997), 100.

3. M. NourbeSe Philip, "Notes on the Completion of Potentiality," *A Genealogy of Resistance and Other Essays* (Toronto: Mercury Press, 1997), 126.

4. Teresa de Lauretis, "Displacing Hegemonic Discourses: Reflections on Feminist Theory in the 1980s," *Inscriptions* 4, no. 3 (1988): 136.

5. The term "jamette" refers to a woman from a low and disreputable class, belonging to the slums. The members of this group rejected the norms of society in their way of life. They were the reverse of the upper-class elite, and the ethos of this jamette subculture reflected the conditions under which they lived. Richard Allsopp, *Dictionary of Caribbean English Usage* (London: Oxford University Press, 1996), 195.

6. Belinda Edmonson, *Making Men: Gender, Literary Authority, and Women's Writing in Caribbean Narrative* (Durham: Duke University Press, 1999), 83.

7. "Run down," "come down," or "oil down" all refer to Caribbean dishes that include a variety of meats, yams, coconut milk, and other spices boiled down into a stew. Once boiled down, the coconut milk changes and the individual tastes become indistinguishable and mutate into one creamy flavor.

8. Philip, "Dis Place," 77.

9. Philip, "Dis Place," 75–76. Anthony Giddens, in *The Transformation of Intimacy*, writes that in "pre-modern development of Europe rape flourished mainly on the margins, at the margins, at the frontiers, in colonies, in states of nature amongst marauding invading armies." Allegations of mass rape of Bosnian Muslim by Serbian forces in 1992, as a way of spreading terror and asserting control, suggests that these practices defy a simple linkage to "pre-modern" times. In a March/April 1993 *Ms.* editorial on the rape of Bosnian women, Robin Morgan asks, "If rape in war is a weapon, what is it in peace time?" (quoted in Philip, "Dis Place," 110).

10. Resolutions from the Council of War, Article of War by Governor Sir Thomas Modyford and Council, August 15, 1665, occasioned by "the Rebellion of the Carmahaly Negroes and Other Outlying Negroes"; quoted by Philip, "Dis Place," 98.

11. Resolutions from the Council of War, 1665, quoted by Philip, "Dis Place," 98.

12. The phrase "inner space" is used throughout Philips's "Dis Place—The Space Between" to indicate the continuous relationship between sexual spaces and physical geography. Traditional representations of physical landscapes and colonial excursions into these spaces in sexual terms have long since shaped discourses of imperial conquests. The connections between land as geography and sexual space continued into nationalist struggles, sectarian warfare, tribal wars, world wars and, most recently, wars against terrorism.

13. Harriet Jacobs, *Incidents in the Life of a Slave Girl* (New York: Dover, 2001). Jacobs's narrative includes numerous references to her sexual abuse and exploitation at the hands of her master. Writing to an audience of white women, has to maintain the ideals of the "cult of true womanhood," which denied the sexuality of all women, and held black slave women to an impossible standard of respectability given their conditions as slaves, Jacobs is forced to finesse the explicit details of her abuse to gain the trust and empathy of her reading audiences.

14. "Outer spaces" is used here to represent the power of external forces that are, more often than not, controlled by patriarchal institutions such as newspapers, unions, armies, legal systems, governments, medical establishments, etc.

15. M. NourbeSe Philip, "The Absence of Writing, or How I Almost Became a Spy," in *She Tries Her Tongue, Her Silence Softly Breaks* (Charlottetown, PE: Ragweed Press, 1993), 16.

16. The term "I-mage" versus "image" is used by Philip to represent the deconstructive elements of her engagement with language and the Rastafarian practice of privileging the "I" in many words. This unconventional use of orthography enables her to represent the processes of giving meaning through the experience of the "I" who possess the language and, therefore, the ability to engage I-magining or I-magination; Philip, "The Absence of Writing," 15–16.

17. Philip, "The Absence of Writing," 18.

18. See, for example, Sandra Pouchet Paquet, *The Novels of George Lamming* (Kingston: Heinemann, 1982); Ngugi wa Thiong'o, *Decolonizing the Mind: The Politics of Language in African Literature* (London: Heinemann, 1986); Patrick Taylor, *The Narrative of Liberation: Perspectives on Afro-Caribbean Literature, Popular Culture, and Politics* (Ithaca: Cornell University Press, 1989); and Margaret Paul Joseph, *Caliban in Exile: The Outsider in Caribbean Fiction* (New York: Greenwood Press, 1992).

19. Philip, "The Absence of Writing," 23; Philip is citing James Baldwin from *Conversations with James Baldwin*, eds. Fred L. Stanley and Louis Pratt (Jackson, University Press of Mississippi, 1989).

20. Philip, "The Absence of Writing," 22.

21. M. NourbeSe Philip, "Questions! Questions!" in *She Tries Her Tongue, Her Silence Softly Breaks* (Charlottetown, PE: Ragweed Press, 1993), 28; "Adoption Bureau," 29; "Clues," 30.

22. Philip, "Questions! Questions!" 28.

23. Philip, "Clues," 30.

24. Resolutions from the Council of War, 1665, quoted by Philip, "Dis Place," 98.

25. Philip, "Discourse on the Logic of Language" (Original page numbers from the poem are undeleted on both pages 99–100).

26. Brenda Carr, "To 'Heal the Word Wounded': Agency and the Materiality of Language and Form in M. Nourbese Philip's *She Tries Her Tongue, Her Silence Softly Breaks*," *Studies in Canadian Literature* 19, no. 1 (1994), http://www.lib.unb.ca/Texts/SCL/bin/get.cgi?directory=vol19_1/&filename=Carr.htm (accessed October 15, 2006).

27. Philip, "Discourse on the Logic of Language," 56.

28. Philip, "Discourse on the Logic of Language," 58.

29. Elaine Savory, "En/Gendering Spaces: The Poetry of Marlene Nourbese-Philip and Pamela Mordecai," in *Framing the Word: Gender and Genre in Caribbean Women's Writing*, ed. Joan Anim-Addo (London: Whiting & Birch, 1996), 18.

30. Philip, "Discourse on the Logic of Language," 57.

31. Philip, "Discourse on the Logic of Language," 57.

32. D. Joanne Lynn, Herbert B. Newton, and Alexander D. Rae-Grant, *The 5-Minute Neurology Consult* (Philadelphia: Lippincott, Williams, & Wilkins, 2003), 2.

33. Philip, "Discourse on the Logic of Language," 56.

34. Stephen Jay Gould, *The Mismeasure of Man* (New York: W. W. Norton, 1996), 124–39.

35. Françoise Lionnet, "*Logiques métisses*: Cultural Appropriation and Postcolonial Representations," in *Postcolonial Representations: Women, Literature, Identity* (Ithaca: Cornell University Press, 1995), 6.

36. Philip, "Absence of Writing," 20.

37. Philip, "Absence of Writing," 20. Philip is quoting from her own journal entry of December 11, 1986, entitled "Testimony Stoops to Mother Tongue."

38. Philip, "Discourse on the Logic of Language," 57.

39. Philip, "Discourse on the Logic of Language," 56.

40. Philip, "Discourse on the Logic of Language," 58.

41. Benjamin J. Sadock and Virginia A. Sadock, *Kaplan and Sadock's Concise Textbook of Clinical Psychiatry*, 9th ed. (Philadelphia: Lippincott, Williams, & Wilkins, 2002), 250.

42. Saddock and Saddock, *Kaplan and Sadock's Concise Textbook*, 250.

43. Philip, "Discourse on the Logic of Language," 59.

44. Philip, "Absence of Writing," 21.

45. Philip, "Absence of Writing," 14.

46. M. NourbeSe Philip, "African Roots and Continuities: Race, Space, and the Poetics of Moving," in *A Genealogy of Resistance and Other Essays* (Toronto: Mercury Press, 1997), 231. Philip coins this term in relation to Ezra Pound's systematization of languages according to their varying qualities. She notes that Pound, in his work *The ABCs of Writing*, defined languages in this manner: "phanopoesis: beautiful to look at (Chinese); melopoesis: beautiful sounding (Greek); and logopoeisis: logical (English)." To this system of classification, Philip adds her term "kinopoesis": dynamic and quick moving (African languages and their demotics).

47. Edouard Glissant, *Caribbean Discourse: Selected Essays*, trans. J. Michael Dash (Charlottesville: University Press of Virginia, 1989), 123. Glissant uses this term in his discussion of the manner in which syntax, as well as language, was imposed during communication between master and slave. He argues that, for Caribbean people, the word takes on its meaning from sound or the pitch of a word as well as a continuous stream of language, which to white slave masters resonated as "unstructured" use of language. Philip has commented about this quality in Trinidadian English, describing it as a "language that moves, like the Carnival band, through space rhythmed by time" (Philip, "African Roots and Continuities," 203).

48. *Oxford American Dictionary*, 1980 ed.

Chapter 4

Routes and Roots: Re(in)scribing the Meaning of Home

> If the project of Imperialism is violently to put together the episteme that will "mean" (for others) and "know" (for the self) the colonial subject as history's nearly selved other, the example of these deletions indicate explicitly what is always implicit: that meaning/knowledge intersects power.
>
> Gayatri Spivak, *A Critique of Postcolonial Reason*, 215

The most persistent and yet most under-theorized element in Caribbean nationalist literature is the "anxiety" produced by black female subjectivity. Hence, thinking through the epistemic and ontological implications of reading black female subjectivity as the abject Other in Caribbean literature poses very specific challenges to foundational debates such as the Quarrel with History, Prospero, Caliban and language, concepts of creolization, and certainly the problem/pleasure of exile. I want to begin by re(in)scribing Spivak's assertions in the epigraph, in order to focus on the specific ways black female subjects function as nationalism's "nearly selved" other, particularly through the practice of alienating black women from the processes of their subject formation. This alienation makes their bodies *mean* (or signify) differently as Others in ways that are counterproductive to their processes of Be(come)ing. While I am not asserting that imperialism and nationalism are equivalent, I want to suggest that black female subjectivity is appropriated in a similar fashion in both contexts, but for very different ends. The question of how meaning is produced is of crucial importance, as Spivak suggests, because it lies at the root of both imperialist and nationalist projects. Postcolonial subjects know their Selves based on their relationship to their surroundings; from these spaces they mimic, revise, challenge, and perform different ways of being in the world. However, as Spivak observes, there is a consistent struggle for access to the system of signs that make the Self, the nation, and the world, mean.

This chapter engages Erna Brodber's *Louisiana* (1994) to consider the precarious nature of those "unhoused" (nearly selved) subjects of the Caribbean literary landscapes imagined by women writers. Caribbean women writers tell very different stories about the conditions and possibilities of existence for black female subjects whose "unhomeliness," or alienation from "home," is the condition of a new generation for whom the experience of exile is lived in demonstrably different ways than their male counterparts. Narratives that focus on migration to the "seat of the Empire" have historically situated women in margins or in positions antithetical to Caribbean nationalist agendas at home and abroad.[1] Far from seeing themselves as "unhoused" or, to borrow Homi Bhabha's term, "unhomely," women writers engage the meaning of "home" in their writing with a broader understanding of the relationship between the intersection of these two spaces/places (home and diaspora).[2] Marginalization does not necessarily mean exclusion or erasure, as I assert in chapter 1. It also manifests itself through a "smallness" of space that is reflected both in narrative positioning and in the nation-state. Therefore, as Bhabha asserts, critical interpretations of these hidden, secluded spaces require a more inquisitive analysis than previously considered, an inquisitiveness that has less regard for traditional lines of demarcation between public and private, masculine and feminine, home and abroad. The idea of being outside of these discursive structures has to include an understanding that

> To be unhomed is not to be homeless, nor can the "unhomely" be easily accommodated in that familiar division of social life into private and public spheres. The recesses of the domestic space become sites for history's most intricate invasions. In that displacement, the borders between home and world become confused; and uncannily, the private and the public become a part of each other, forcing upon us a vision that is as divided as it is disorienting.[3]

The "unhomely" subject of fiction describes the state of (non)existence for female subjects in most nationalist narratives. Thus, women writers have redrawn the boundaries for discussions about cultural identity in order to recognize elements of home while also translating these moments of recognition beyond the limited scopes of defining "Self" in relation to the State. This process of recognition and movement, *beyond*, necessarily takes place in the spaces "in between" home and diaspora, spaces that resist totalizing political and cultural experience in favor of new performances of black, female subjectivity that transgress the boundaries of the nation-state.[4]

In many narratives by women writers, black female subjects are represented as exiles within the nation-space they call "home"; and they then experience this exile again during their immigration as they are alienated from their Selves as women. Within the context of Caribbean nationalism and the racial and cultural landscapes of the "host" countries to which they immigrated, women writers of the seventies and eighties emerged with critical perspectives informed by the "double vision" that their new identities demanded. This capacity to see themselves as both homeless at home and "unhomely" in the world beyond the borders of their homelands has become an integral part of Caribbean women's contemporary literature. The deeper historical displacement experienced by women is the focus writers engaged in writing home (from abroad). Acts of the imagination serve as the proving ground for different visions and critical paradigms that interpret the currency and valuation of "home," discourses of belonging and identity, and the circulation and exchange of those discourses in the Caribbean subject's route to Be(come)ing. The project of building a nation, like that of building a Self (discussed in chapter 1), involves imaginary narratives that do not reflect the lived reality of citizens. However, the (literary and cultural) imagination is the primary site where the popular image of selfhood is performed, revised, and perfected, only to be revealed as a myth that is constantly under the threat of erasure.

Where writers of the Trinidad Renaissance sought to constitute their identities by engaging the elements of their lived experiences or "realities," George Lamming's narratives of the 1940s sought to revise the nature and impact of the subject's lived experiences by insisting on the ontological possibility of a reality beyond Empire. However, Erna Brodber's novel, *Louisiana*, proposes that we reconstruct how we exist and understand existence, the "real" and history. Both the narrative and its structure disrupt what we have come to think of as the "normative" or "objective" conventions and discourses of history that have endowed History with the authority to institute and legitimate identity. Brodber's narrative is concerned with how the "real" is constructed and experienced ontologically.

In *Louisiana*, the metaphysical impact of memory manifests itself through realities that occur within the mindscape of the protagonists, suggesting that the power of thought and imagination determine the possibility for Be(come)ing. However, like other women writers, Brodber places a tremendous emphasis on language as a cross-cultural and cross-historical signifier. The import of language, for Brodber, lies not in its articulation (as words) but in its various forms and capacities in systems of knowledge production. Her emphasis, therefore, is on making explicit the processes and significations through which the subject participates in its Be(come)ing. By taking up the issue of metaphysics, Brodber implicates the disciplines of sociology and anthropology for their efforts to construct the histories of black subjects without much attention to the nature of Being for black subjects.

Brodber's protagonist is forced to mobilize her "faculties" and embark on a journey into "knowing" that challenges her to consider an alter/native epistemological model for her ontological existence. Ella Townsend, a graduate student in anthropology, is charged with the project of putting Selves back together through "interior" historical research. This political, metaphysical, and spiritual approach is part of an ongoing project begun in Brodber's earlier novels *Jane and Louisa Will Soon Come Home* and *Myal*. The main protagonist in *Louisiana*, who curiously shares the same first name as the protagonist in *Myal*, is sent to Louisiana to record the history of the "blacks of South West Louisiana" for the Works Project Administration (WPA) narratives of the Federal Writer's Project. The project was started by Franklin D. Roosevelt in the 1930s to employ artists during the Great Depression. The historical aim of the project was to institutionalize knowledge about the day-to-day lives and experiences of enslaved people as told by blacks themselves; this methodology was one of the more revolutionary aspects of this new field of social science. In the novel, Ella is offered a job at Columbia University to gather this "firsthand" information. Before taking this job, Ella's relationship to words and word crafting is already well established from her published writing, much to the dismay of her Jamaican parents, who are concerned because she has decided not to attend medical school and is now "mixed up" in American race politics:

> I, their offspring, had fallen in love with words and chose to be a word smith. Can a poem take the place of a stethoscope cum office with a brass name plate? That my works and my name—their name—got into *Crisis* and *Opportunity* meant nothing. "'Crisis?' What crisis? These American Negroes expect goodies to be put in their laps." "'Opportunity'? One of them burial schemes nuh. How you get mixed up in that?"[5]

If the circumstances and historical trajectory of Brodber's novel seem similar to those of Zora Neale Hurston, another notable scholar and researcher coming of age during the 1930s, it is no coincidence. As we piece together the geographic, political, and literary landscape of Louisiana, the narrative "doubling" of cultural and epistemological signposts is slowly revealed to Ella and the reading audience, as Brodber parallels Ella and Hurston, who was also a graduate student in anthropology, at Barnard College (the sister campus to Columbia University), and a student of famed anthropologist Franz Boaz. Hurston received a six-month grant to collect black folklore in the South. Like Brodber's protagonist, Hurston published in *Opportunity*, a magazine edited by Charles Johnson, dedicated to giving voice to black culture in America. Hurston's short story, "Spunk," appeared in *Opportunity* in 1925, and that same year several pieces were published in another monthly magazine focusing on Black culture, *Crisis*, which was founded and edited until 1935 by W. E. B. DuBois. In fact, it was at an awards dinner sponsored by *Opportunity* that Hurston met Fannie Hurst, who hired her as a secretary and later assisted her in attaining a scholarship to attend Barnard College.[6]

The most significant connection between Brodber's protagonist and Zora Neale Hurston is their connection to St. Mary, Jamaica, and St. Mary, Louisiana. Both places share a history of creolization in the African Diaspora that attests to the far-reaching implications of imperialism, which exceed all borders and boundaries (cultural, geographic, and metaphysical). After receiving a Guggenheim Fellowship in 1935 to collect folklore from the West Indies, Hurston traveled to Haiti and then to Jamaica where she observed the practices and traditions from the Balm Yards to Pocomania. Her experiences while in the Caribbean were published in a collection of travelogues entitled *Tell My Horse: Voodoo and Life in Haiti and Jamaica*. Hurston's descriptions of St. Mary, Jamaica, reappear in a cross-cultural transformation in Brodber's novel as she recounts Ella's trip to Louisiana to conduct field research and interviews about blacks in the South.

These doublings, beyond functioning as a narrative strategy, raise the question of scientific methodology that plagues both scholars. Hurston, like Ella Townsend, comes of age as an anthropologist at a period when the social sciences (specifically sociology and anthropology) in American institutions of higher learning were under a great deal of scrutiny. Ideological battles about the scientific credibility of the methodology deployed in the social sciences emerge in all their contradictions in Brodber's novel when Ella is faced with the prospect of associating herself as a participant observer as she records the lives of blacks in the South. The authority of "science," along with its uses, aims, and methodology, are all called into question when they collide with the "higher science" of New Orleans and Jamaica. When Ella's object of study (Mammy King) dies suddenly, Ella begins to hear her voice. Ella is faced with the problem of developing a new scientific methodology capable of representing, or rather translating, her experience of Mammy's voice as something other than a sickness of the mind. The struggle takes the form of a constant effort to try to arrive at a "scientific" explanation and to accept the events as part of an-Other epistemological order.

The WPA narratives involved the most authentic sources for empirical research: scientific methodology, recording equipment, and firsthand accounts. Ella is one of the first researchers to be given a tape recorder, the primary tool for ensuring the "authenticity" of the Other. Brodber's novel suggests that, in spite of these scientific processes, the task of recording history depends on an imposed uniformity and on translations of events that rarely take into consideration the cultural contexts within which these events unfold. Ella's initial efforts to "observe" Mammy King (a.k.a. Louise) serve as a prime example of this approach to writing history. As we read *Louisiana*, it becomes clear that, structurally, the text is a map of the improbability (if not the impossibility) of "capturing" subjects through the "anthropological eye/I."[7]

Mammy King's account of her life includes the first-person accounts of several dead friends who insist on having their say in this project. One of the narrators/intruders is Mammy's longtime friend Lowly, who arrives in Louisiana at the same time as Ella, albeit on different existential plane. Their simultaneous arrivals prove to be as confusing for the reader as they are for Mammy King, who seems to be delusional in her old age. However, by the time we leave the first chapter, entitled, "I Heard a Voice From Heaven Say," and move on to the second chapter, "First the Goat Must Be Killed" (which precedes the first chapter temporally), the narrative becomes more clear. The "voice" from heaven is Lowly describing to her friend what her "translation" (or death) is like, with the hope that Mammy will give up her fight to remain among the living. There are, therefore, two translations under way at the beginning of the novel, although they are notably different in their aims and intentions. Lowly, who misses her friend deeply, shares her experience with Mammy:

> Anna I was seeing every corner of the scene. Being translated is like that. You can see from every angle.
>
> ....
>
> Then only the voice, Suzie Anna, carrying you now in the chute, keeping you company through the waters, over the rainbow's mist, into seventh heaven and back to fete through the days of dinkie minie, to see this thanksgiving and the nine-night to come and without a tired muscle. Back with every faculty—all hands, feet, eyes, ears a body could need for higher service.[8]

Rather than naming the faculties themselves, Lowly names the physical parts of the body through which these faculties are made possible. Moreover, the all-seeing eye/I in this passage suggests an over-endowed critical position. As the novel progresses, Ella's perspective is slowly being retrained to exercise a more "concerned" critical vision, but not in the manner we expect. The "nine-night" ritual Lowly refers to, as Ella learns later, is a significant part of her shifting epistemic location. This shift in Ella's being is visually represented in the shifting line of a song that haunts her. The line "***Ah who sey Sammy dead***,"[9] is set off from the rest of the narrative in the first chapter and begins shifting into the "body" of the text (and the subject) as the narrative of self-discovery progresses.

In "Night Song after Death," an account of her travels to St. Mary Parish, Jamaica, Hurston describes the nine-night ceremony as one of the cross-cultural links between blacks in the Diaspora:

> In reality it is old African ancestor worship in fragmentary form. The West African tradition of appeasing the spirit of the dead lest they do the living a mischief. I made bold to ask the reason for the nine night. With everybody helping out with details they told me. It all stems from the firm belief in survival after death. Or rather, that there *is no death*. Activities are merely changed from one condition to the other. "Why is it that he [the dead] cannot do what the living do? It is because the thing that gave power to these parts is no longer there. That is the duppy, and that is the most powerful part of any man. Everybody has evil in him, and when he is alive, the heart and the brain controls him and he will not abandon himself to many evil things. But when the duppy leaves the body, it no longer has anything to restrain it and it will do more terrible things than any man ever dreamed of. It is not good for a duppy to stay among living folk. So, we make nine night to force the duppy to stay in his grave."[10]

The explanation, given to Hurston by an older Jamaican, makes the trajectory of Ella's new critical perspective clearer. Ella acquires the ability to hear and talk with the dead through Mammy King's lifeline. Seemingly in spite of her "nine night," Lowly's duppy has arisen from the grave to bring her closest friend across to the other side. Mammy, however, has a project to complete before she leaves—a project she will continue from the other side if Ella is willing to do the work of translating her experiences out of her current mode of being into an-Other transmigratory state of being.

Once Ella and her husband, Reuben Kohl, begin to decipher the events following Mammy's death and Ella's fitful possession by Mammy King's spirit during her funeral, they discover that the tape Ella thought was empty is, in fact, filled with stories. The tapes contain conversations about Mammy King's life that have, apparently, been recorded in Ella's absence. While listening to the recordings, Ella recognizes that

> Some words control large spaces. They sit over large holes.
> . . . .
> After we had learnt that the reel was full, not of silences but of words, not of someone like Jack Johnson meddling or playing tricks or of Mammy reeling out her life story as a parting gift to a well-favoured me, but of conversations between two women, one of them Mammy, with interjections from me in words I didn't know, we immediately forwarded the spool to Lowly's song right through the end. We fell off the end of the reel right through those word holes.[11]

Ella's task as scientist, subject, and ultimately "translator" is to make this project significant at an experiential level. She begins to piece together the information on the reel based on the relationship between her life as a subject/object of study and the voices and experiences from the other side (of history, her Self, and the Other world). When Ella begins her research, her understanding is limited by her perception of former slaves as a group of people to whom history happens, not people who participate in the forming and (dis)forming of historical discourses on black identity. Boundaries that are supposedly fixed, and thus preserved for study, turn out to be more permeable than anticipated. The world of the dead suddenly intervenes in that of the living; "science" and technology (represented by the tape recorder) encounter "higher science" (as represented by the voices from the other side). The "fact" of death as an immutable end is turned into a fiction, one that Ella has to accept if she is to make sense of what she is experiencing. She has to accept the limitations of her knowledge and surrender her faculties to "higher science" to fill in the epistemological gaps.

It becomes clearer that the transcript of the novel is an account of Ella "feeling her way to" her Self. With each new development, Ella, like the reading audience, begins to piece together and fill in the gaps in the narrative that is her life. Another piece of the puzzle is solved when Ella discovers a picture from Mammy's funeral that triggers a re-membering in her unconscious. That is, it triggers a recollection as well as the bringing together of two strands of history and experience; this manifests in a change in the form of the novel:

> "*Ah who sey Sammy dead*," I heard myself say just about the same time as my very weak voice on reel whispered it. So this was somehow about the dead. Two different women. Two different places. Two different times. Buried in similar rites. Was that it? So why was I there? Why was I in their conversation and how and why was I moved in this my other self—I obviously had two—to say this, "*Ah who sey Sammy dead*?" No answer came. Only another seepage from an experience I hadn't realized had had such an impact on me. . . .[12]

Ella's own remembering begins when her subconscious triggers a figurative (textual) and literal (psychological) recollection of her grandmother's death as a child in Jamaica. This event occurred when Ella was four years old, an age that allows her faculties to be more open to the "higher science" that surrounds her in Jamaica. She recalls hearing the song "Sammy dead, Sammy dead, Sammy dead oh" during her grandmother's burial, the same song she hears at Mammy King's burial. Her subconscious response, as a child who is unable to articulate what she is experiencing, is to think to herself, "*Ah who sey Sammy dead*? Sammy no dead yah.*"[13] This response, then and now, frees Ella's repressed memory of the trauma, loss, and grief over her grandmother's death. The shift from the bold font, which stands outside of the rest of the text in the first chapter, to an italicized font within the body of the text here, suggests a transitional moment in Ella's development. The transition is not complete, however. The line from the song, though incorporated in the text, is still not part of Ella's ontological landscape. It remains buried as an epistemic experience that cannot be realized until she comes to terms with its relationship to her ontological existence. This repressed memory, or as Ella terms it, a "hegemony of the spirit," has blocked Ella's path as she attempts to "feel her way" to translating the information on the tape, dreams and other signs left her by Mammy King.[14] This remembering and remaking of the "truth" she remembers is a significant turning point in Ella's emergence as a subject in the process of Be(come)ing.

The "truth" of national space, once preserved by discourses of citizenry that excluded blacks, is also exposed as a fiction when migratory links between Africa, the Caribbean, Europe, and North America are revealed. The "contamination" of Ella's basis for "reality," knowledge, methodology, and historical scope opens a space for considering the transmigratory nature of black identity in the Americas. Throughout the novel, songs, folktales, and dances appear as cultural markers that confirm the historical and political links between blacks in the Diaspora:

> There were times when there was a great dispute. "But Madam that's our song" or "Fellows where'd you hear that. That's ours" and the battle royal went back and forth with madam telling how far in her distant pass she had heard it and it couldn't possibly be West Indian, "Who carried it to you?"
>
> . . . .
>
> Madam said that her folks told her that the civil war soldiers passing by could be heard singing that song like they knew they were marching to their death. The crew didn't argue: they apparently had no past for that song as publicly sad and therefore as large as hers. I couldn't get the shared experience of those two sets of negroes from two different parts of the world out of my head. I couldn't get it out of my head how Lowly and Mammy had been buried to the strains of the same song.
>
> . . . .
>
> Upon the hill, the rising sun.
>
> . . . .
>
> It is the voice that calls me home.[15]

Although Ella's project doesn't appear immediately connected to blacks in the Civil War, the focus of this historical event as a North American phenomenon is disrupted by competing accounts that suggest that this song crossed the sea and reappeared in similar sociopolitical contexts a generation later, in World War I. Songs like "Just Before the Battle Mother" speak here to a shared historical and political past for African people in the Diaspora. Mammy's death and subsequent passing to the other side, the songs sung by the soldiers in the Civil War, and Ella's own arrival in Louisiana all represent a return, not to a history based on origins, but to a history of disparate memories, journeys, worlds, and discourses.

Even though, in Ella's mind, these people may have "had no past for that song," the lyrics represent a historical and geographical continuum that encompasses the struggles between blacks in the United States and black (West Indian) soldiers fighting for the Union Jack of Great Britain. Their struggle for freedom, while occurring in different parts of the world, emerging from different political ideologies, and deploying different strategies and narratives of independence, yoked Africans in the Diaspora to this "past." This brand of anthropology sought to re-member disparate cultural traditions, signs, and experiences that were fragmented by the trauma of slavery and then reinvented, anew, in the Americas and the New World. As Mammy King's translation progresses, so too does Ella's journey toward recuperating the soul of her dearly departed Jamaican Self and, ultimately, her Being as such. In the process of translating her past Selves, Ella begins to re-member or piece together the life of Mammy King (a.k.a. Miss Grant King) in the novel. Inquiring about the circuitous route to the identity she has been trying to translate, Ella is forced to acknowledge the relationship between memory, repression, and trauma, which work to provide a protective shroud around the subconscious.

The doubling, backtracking, repetition, and disruption of temporal and spatial boundaries leads us to an elaborately constructed psychoanalytical mapping of Ella's unconscious, such that the "gaps" and impediments begin to show themselves in a strange temporality. From her unconscious emerges a re-memory of her Self and her relationship to the scientific study in which she is engaged. This "discovery," since this is what we have to call it in spite of its presence in her past, affords Ella a glimpse of an area of her experience that has been beyond her reach. This new insight into herself manifests itself in her construction of a methodology for re-membering the life of Sue Ann Grant King:

> Week 6. I felt I had all the words down. Analysis, I had got no further with Mammy's history. Let me scour the reel again for any escaped gem. On separate pieces of paper list names of people mentioned, list names of places mentioned, list cultural items, then add data as found. This was my analytical frame, so I had sheets of paper headed Lowly, Ezekiel, Silas, Donna Claire, the mistress, Ramrod Grant and of course Sue Ann Grant King. This was file 1. File 2 had of course Louisiana, St Mary (Jamaica), St. Mary, Louisiana (USA), Chicago. Chicago Southside. In file 3 were sheets headed Dinkie mini, john-crow-blow-nose, the bannered groups by name, shepherd, rag-songs, victrola, units—"units set up", she had said—Arkansas devilment, coon can, longshoreman's strike. The only date given me was the earthquake (Jamaica) 1907. I would rinse and rinse

until everything was down, then with my one little date I would try the historical reconstruction of the life of Mrs. Sue Ann Grant-King.[16]

Ella's research methodology expresses the contradictory discourses at work in her efforts to construct this history. First, she makes a "list . . . of places mentioned, list [of] cultural items, then add[s] data as found." Far from sounding like a description of analytical methodology, Ella's approach is extremely eclectic with respect to her cultural and scientific interests. Her methodology, therefore, contains those things that appear in the "gaps" of her memory and in the disjointed conversations with the "venerable sisters." Hers is not a science of certainty, nor is it one of doubt, as she is determined to put down the "facts" though she "can't prove them to be so."[17]

Brodber brings competing scientific and historical discourses into contact with one another in a field of "free-play" (the unconscious), allowing the productive capacities of the imagination to realize their potential. Her use of fiction (both as a genre and in Kant's definition of the term) constructs a theory of history that is at once "free" and "lawful" to the Self being constructed in *Louisiana*.[18] She subverts the rigidity of narrative form and epistemological and ontological boundaries through discussions between characters who appear in quotation marks without any reference to who is speaking, thus suggesting a collective articulation: dialogues are not introduced; first-person narratives lack any identification of the speaker. The rules that govern narrative and performance shift, depending on the sociohistorical agendas at work in the construction of narratives of identity. The figurative and literal consumption of Ella's mind and body by the "venerable sisters"[19] (and the historical project) is a necessary step, an epistemological shift that opens a space for Ella to conceive (or engage her faculties with) an-Other Self, one that is not confined to the laws of association outlined by her methodological training as a scientist.

Brodber's representation of history and imagination is, therefore, productive rather than reproductive, because it assumes that the possibility for Be(come)ing depends on the limits of the imagination, not of history, science, or other institutional modes of knowing. The unquestioned continuities produced in the WPA narratives emerge as symptoms of un-represented historicities that are repressed or forced into inaudible registers within the "field of study," or, in this case, black subjectivity. Brodber's narrative exposes the extent to which discourses of cultural identity and political action are "covered over," constructed as silent, insignificant utterances within larger historical and national projects that attempt to construct identities that "fit" into the overarching inclusivity of nationalist projects.

Despite their long-standing exclusion from institutional discourses of difference and identity, Caribbean women writers have long been concerned with the problematic of existing (in the existentialist sense) in the tight spaces of these projects. In this regard, Brodber's revision of the narrative form in *Louisiana* shares some of the same unconventional properties discussed previously in the works of M. NourbeSe Philip. Like Philip, Brodber uses visual layout to disrupt the reader's expectations of the text, and both deploy constantly shifting locations of time, geography, and space. This representation has the same displacing effect discussed earlier in relation to Philip's use of metathesis, where spaces becomes scapes. In Philip's "Dis Place—The Space Between," this dislocation alienates the reader from the practice of reading, forcing the reader to reconsider her or his positions of power in relation to the text. What is most interesting about Brodber's text, however, is the degree to which both the reader and the novel's protagonist are being simultaneously transformed through their reading practices. The narrative itself is invested in modeling a new mode of interpretative strategies for readers engaged in making meaning of the African Diaspora.

Brodber's examination of the anthropological eye/I highlights the shift in the positioning of blacks as objects of scientific knowledge to be measured and categorized first as scientific objects and then as anthropological subjects whose experiences could be captured through empirical methodology. The problematic of anthropology as a science of immutable "truths" emerges more clearly when we consider the relationship between Ella and the empirical evidence she gathers about Mammy King, the subject under construction. Arguably, subject formation is not "technically" part of her research; it is not what she is sent to gather data about. The problem of how to translate this information into a meaningful narrative of experience proves to be far more complex than initially anticipated. Brodber's narrative creates a space for her readers to consider the question of transcendence as part of the scientific inquiry taking place between Ella and her "subject" matter. Ella's efforts to "know" herself in relation to her "field of study" are not directed at a particular ending, but at the possibility of a change in her current mode of being. This distinction is significant for the connections between thinking and being in Brodber's narrative. Her book suggests that the possibility of coming into being lies in the subject's understanding of what thought makes possible in metaphysical and political contexts.

The "translators" here are Ella and the reader, as both are (de/re)constructing meaning through their engagement with a set of textual representations. The task of the translator is to negotiate the authoritative discourses of anthropology, sociology, theology, and the "higher sciences." Brodber's narrative demystifies the processes of creation (or re/production) through which subjects institute their existence. In so doing, the sphere of "reality" is exposed as a field of play constructed through sociohistorical institutions in much the same manner that scientific and social discourses generate knowledges about objects of study. Brodber's emphasis on the interconnectedness between science and subject formation provides a fruitful occasion for considering her project as a strategic response to the kind of alienation and displacement under investigation in Philip's "Discourse on the Logic of Language." If we consider the social and scientific project under way in *Louisiana*, we are encouraged to ponder its value as a textual enactment of the reconstruction of the Selves displaced through years of discursive, historical, and existential oppression.

Louisiana posits cultural cross-fertilization among immigrants throughout the Black Atlantic as an example of the historical and cultural performativity of African Diaspora. Brodber contextualizes the practice of Diaspora politics and the centrality of migration and mobility in all facets of black politics in America. However, the status of immigrants and the conditions that prompt mass migration of West Indians are not as easily translatable in the American racial and political landscape. Kezia Page raises this issue when she argues that several crucial boundaries are overlooked in these cross-cultural celebrations. Page's point here is that the historical aims of the WPA narratives depended on the immobility of a generation of poor blacks in the southern United States:

> Brodber's Louisiana . . . explores trans-cultural alliances as important psychic and cultural progress for black people, but even more so, because Louisiana is set in the 1930's, in the USA, in the South. While diaspora affords these cultural spaces, such spaces do not exist outside of place and nation. That is, in the same way difference is celebrated as part of the cultural mecca that is diaspora, this difference can exist in the form of national and political borders (immigration law) and can affect the extent of cultural mergings in diaspora.[20]

De-emphasizing the vehicles of the nation-state does not inhibit movement or cross-cultural dialogue among blacks in the Americas. Brodber seems to be aware of this tension, but reroutes this potential conflict through a cultural displacement rather than through gender, sexuality, and class, all of which play a significant role in bringing Ella's parents to the United States in the first place. When Ella finds her parents' marriage certificate and "his address was given as Colon and hers, Windsor Castle, St. Mary, Jamaica," a crucial aspect of Caribbean/American diaspora politics is introduced but it is left to the reader to postulate about its relevance.[21] This Caribbean/American endeavor and all the inequities of power implicit in the building of the Panamá Canal represented the new emergence of American imperialism in the Caribbean region. Ultimately, these tensions highlight the degree to which cultural cross-fertilization depends on unequal distribution of resources and power.

Ella, a first-generation Caribbean American, middle-class woman, does not yet comprehend the meaning of her own social mobility in the United States.

Her father's address on a marriage certificate signifies his class mobility, connecting his work as a Panamá Canal worker in the early 1900s and her mother's mid-1940s "nurse's uniform—white dress, white shoes, white cap, stalking through the know, sleet and the heart of the summer street" to a growing market demand for labor.[22] Laborers in the Panamá Canal Zone, domestic workers, health care workers, and machinists of various sorts swelled the ranks of black immigrants who came to America in search of a better future; they sought ways to improve their conditions through economic and social mobility. However, countless undocumented workers were being exploited in order to complete a project that would redefine commerce and trade in the United States.[23]

Brodber acknowledges the limitations faced by "immigrants" not exiled of their own choosing. The intersecting histories of colonialism and the various technologies of the state, designed to manage and control movement, are arguably the source of Ella's epistemological block when she arrives in Louisiana. She is unable to imagine herself or her past in relation to the poor black people she encounters. When her husband, Reuben, who was taken from the Congo and raised in Europe by a priest, decides to leave Columbia University to join her and begin research in the South, she reminds him, "you know the kind of visa you have; you can only work with Columbia."[24] The tenuous conditions of mobility, which Page calls "material restrictions," are always already present in the margins of this narrative, but are sublimated in service of the loftier cultural and national project that privileges the cross-cultural links among blacks in the Diaspora.

While Brodber's novel actively constructs a tradition of border crossing in the African Diaspora, gender identity and national identity seem determined by prescribed notions of the family or its surrogate, the (black) nation; but what is the nature of this family, and how will its branches be replenished in the absence of children? This is indeed the problem at the center of nationalist projects that depend on women's wombs as the battleground upon which the nation's future depends. Brodber's project offers us an intriguing reformulation and interpretation of reproduction and black nationalism through a radically transformed genealogy of black female subjectivity. From the "silenced spaces" in the histories of blacks in the Diaspora emerges a narrative that has been covered over by the privilege of masculinity: the fragmented recollection of Lilieth, a young woman who is pregnant for her teacher, Benjamin Johnson. When she informs him of her condition, his lack of response and unwillingness to take responsibility for his actions seals her fate:

—Lilieth I don't know what to say. What is to be done? How far are you on? It doesn't matter. It doesn't matter. What shall I do?—rhetorical questions under the sound of the organ. Then the sobbing under the notes of the organ for a life that had spelt foreign travel, further study and maybe somewhere down the line a settled family with this said Lilieth or someone like Lilieth, for you liked her, really did, sobbing over the notes of the organ.[25]

Lilieth dies as a result of a forced botched abortion, and there seems to be little or no recourse for her family and their loss. This historical fragment speaks volumes about the masculine privilege that emerges as another "material restriction" limiting the future of black female subjects; but there is an equally disturbing silence about this particular shard of history. Reaching into the past to bring forward the full breadth of this memory when Ben comes to tell her his story, Ella re-enacts Lilieth's abortion when she "[gets] up... on the nearby couch with [her] legs apart. There is so much pain. I scream." Once this painful past is brought forward, Ella leaves Ben to do the work, saying, "my job was to help him re-live his painful past. He had to take it from there."[26] One is left to wonder if this re-enactment is not also relevant for Ella's own understanding of her own sexual consciousness as a woman who hopes for children, but resigns herself to a higher purpose. The question emerges later when she wonders whether "female prophets are allowed to have children?"[27]

We might pose the question differently, and ask whether female sexuality and reproduction can transcend the biological limitations of childbirth to engage in an-Other interpretation of Being-in the-world based on giving birth to subjectivity. The peculiar muting of female sexuality and reproduction in Brodber's narrative proves to be one of the more complex problematics that also emerge in novels like *Crown Jewel*, written during the Trinidad Renaissance. Though distinctly different from the earlier barrack-yard stories, which overtly positioned black women's sexual bodies in direct correlation to the development and prosperity of West Indian nation-states, Brodber's fiction shares a similar vision of black women whose political aspirations seem at odds with their sexual identity as women and with their desire to be mothers. The interesting difference, however, is that Ella's physical and psychic body becomes the domain of the "venerable sisters" first, and is nearly wholly consumed by the project in which she is engaged.

Ella Townsend marries to become Ella Kohl, and is later "reborn" as Louisiana when "two women [Louise and Sue Ann] sire another."[28] There is no doubt that the gender politics of the novel center on women's political participation in black nationalist politics. When, at the end of the novel, we learn that Mammy King is a Garveyite, organizing on behalf of the movement while she is in Chicago, we know Ella will join this long tradition of psychic, cultural workers. We are left with the notion that "two places can make children! Two women sire another?"[29] The spiritual underpinning of Brodber's novel proves to be a particularly vexing problematic for women who give themselves over, mind, body, and soul, to this cultural and political project. The holy trinity can indeed be reproduced as two women sire another on a metaphysical level, suggesting that the generations of women displaced and alienated from their spiritual selves can indeed be rerouted (and indeed rerooted) through collective relationships to the Divine. However, questions posed by feminist critics like Jacqui Alexander ask readers to reconsider the relationship between political consciousness and spiritual consciousness, not as separate modalities of existence, but as parts of an integrally linked praxis of the Sacred.[30] Ella and Reuben do not have any children after ten years of marriage, but Ella's work as a psychic enacts the birth and rebirth of black female subjectivity in the African Diaspora.[31] She is the diasporic subject of the Americas, one represented in the Spanish word "ella" (which translates in English as she or it), a subject that gives birth to its Self, her Self (Ella). The subject birthed by the end of Brodber's novel is a Self once diverted and "unhoused" through the processes of exile, immigration, and cultural and spiritual dislocation. She is a subject that has returned home from her alien/nation.

NOTES

1. The phrase "seat of the Empire" is a translation of a line from Louise Bennett's famous poem "Colonisation in Reverse" from her collection *Jamaica Labrish* (Kingston, Jamaica: Sangster Book Stores, 1995), 179–80. In the poem, Bennett describes the growing patterns of migration between Jamaica and England:

An week by week dem shippin off
  Dem countryman like fire,
  Fe immigrate and populate
  De seat o' de Empire
  What a devilment a Englan!
  Dem face war and brave de worse,
  But I'm wondering how dem gwine stan'
  Colonizin' in reverse.

2. Homi Bhabha, *The Location of Culture* (London: Routledge, 1994), 9–18.
3. Bhabha, *Location of Culture*, 9.
4. In thinking about imagining identity beyond boundaries, one cannot escape the appropriation or even the recognition of C. L. R. James's *Beyond a Boundary* as a major literary and cultural contributor to all discussions of performance, identity, and national identity. While his contributions to these discussions are unmistakable, I bring James into the discussion at this point in order to make a point about the crucial elements involved in engaging identity (national, political, gendered) as always in process. In an interview with David Scott, George Lamming makes a rather interesting claim about the title of James's book, *Beyond a Boundary*: "Now there is something I can't get explained, I don't know if we can find the original, but *Beyond*

a Boundary was not the title. The title was *Beyond the Boundary* not *Beyond a Boundary*. The original title had *the* Boundary. And that was my choice. But it was with a *definite* article not the indefinite. . . . But it was incorrect because it should have been 'the.' Because if you said 'a,' you'd deconcretize what we're talking about. But if you say 'the' and 'boundary,' you have both the concrete and the movement beyond the concrete"; George Lamming, "The Sovereignty of the Imagination: An Interview with George Lamming," by David Scott, *Small Axe: A Caribbean Journal of Criticism* 12 (September 2002): 110 (emphasis mine). Far from being a simple splitting of grammatical hairs, this distinction (between "the" and "a") is central to any formulation of Caribbean cultural identity, particularly because the past of the region is always already bound up with colonial pasts and postcolonial futures. The future, in this instance, is always in progress toward the next boundaries of the horizon.

5. Erna Brodber, *Louisiana* (London: New Beacon Books, 1995), 40.

6. Lillie P. Howard, "Zora Neale Hurston," *Afro-American Writers from the Harlem Renaissance to 1940*, eds. T. Harris and T. M. Davis, vol. 51 of *Dictionary of Literary Biography* (Detroit: Gale, 1987), 135.

7. For a more detailed discussion of this phrase, see Uzo Esonwanne, "The Madness of Africa(ns): Or, Anthropology's Reason," *Cultural Critique*, no. 17 (Winter 1990–1991): 107–26; Mary Louise Pratt, "Scratches on the Face of the Country; Or, What Mr. Barrow Saw in the Land of the Bushmen," in "'Race,' Writing, and Difference," ed. Henry Louis Gates, Jr., special issue, *Critical Inquiry* 12, no. 1 (Autumn 1985): 119–43; and Michelle V. Rowley, "Crafting Maternal Citizens? Public Discourse of the Maternal Scourge in Social Welfare Policies and the Services in Trinidad," *Social and Economic Studies* 52, no. 3 (September 2003): 31–58.

8. Brodber, *Louisiana*, 10–11.

9. Brodber, *Louisiana*, 16, 28.

10. Zora Neale Hurston, *Tell My Horse: Voodoo and Life in Haiti and Jamaica* (New York: Harper & Row, 1990), 43–44.

11. Brodber, *Louisiana*, 43–44.

12. Brodber, *Louisiana*, 51.

13. Brodber, *Louisiana*, 92.

14. Brodber, *Louisiana*, 98.

15. Brodber, *Louisiana*, 85, 86–87.

16. Brodber, *Louisiana*, 64.

17. Brodber, *Louisiana*, 102.

18. Kant, in *The Critique of Judgment*, defines fiction as the "actual fantasies with which the mind entertains itself as it is continually being aroused by the diversity that strikes the eye." Immanuel Kant, *The Critique of Judgment*, trans. Werner S. Pluhar (Indianapolis: Hackett Publishing, 1987), 94.

19. Brodber, *Louisiana*, 32.

20. Kezia Page, "'Two Places Can Make Children': Erna Brodber's *Louisiana*," *Journal of West Indian Literature* 13, nos. 1–2 (April 2005): 57.

21. Brodber, *Louisiana*, 69.

22. Brodber, *Louisiana*, 70.

23. Rhonda Frederick, *"Colón Man a Come": Mythographies of Panamá Canal Migration* (Lanham, MD: Lexington Books, 2005), 35–36. Frederick discusses the extent to which Canal Zone workers were the most "ubiquitous and invisible people" in the U.S.-controlled work zone. She points out that, "because of the number of undocumented workers secured by the [Isthmian Canal Commission], the 'circular migrants' who frequently traveled between the isthmus and their home countries when their Panamá Money ran low, and the inordinate numbers of undocumented deaths, it is impossible to determine the actual number of Colón Men who worked in Panamá"; Frederick, *"Colón Man a Come,"* 36.

24. Brodber, *Louisiana*, 68.
25. Brodber, *Louisiana*, 104.
26. Brodber, *Louisiana*, 105.
27. Brodber, *Louisiana*, 106.
28. Brodber, *Louisiana*, 17.
29. Brodber, *Louisiana*, 17.

30. For a more extensive discussion on the relationship between political consciousness and spiritual consciousness, see Jacqui Alexander, "Pedagogies of the Sacred: Making the Invisible Tangible," in *Pedagogies of Crossing: Meditations on Feminism, Sexual Politics, Memory, and the Sacred* (Durham: Duke University Press), 287–332.

31. I am deeply indebted to Michelle Rowley for her insight and direction that challenged me to think more broadly about how reproduction functions, not just in Brobder's narrative, but in larger debates about black female subjectivity. My reading of reproduction in this chapter comes directly out of conversations about reproduction as an ontological and epistemological undertaking, not simply a biological one.

Chapter 5

Boundaries, Borders, and the Unhoused: Re-Routing Black Identity in North America

> Unlike exile and nationalism, *immigration* and nationalism are not perceived to have any relationship to each other. The immigrant's motives are to make money (often, in the case of West Indian women—who constitute the largest portion of West Indian immigrants to the United States—to support families "back home"); her focus is on "making it" in the metropole, as opposed to the apparently loftier aims of the exile, who remains preoccupied with the *meaning* of the native land in one way (Naipaul) or another (Lamming).
>
> Belinda Edmondson, Making Men, 141

The title of this book, *Alien-Nation and Repatriation*, suggests that there are several integral components to any discussion of Caribbean identity: alienation, repatriation, and the patriarchal privilege implicit in most forms of nationalism (the *patri* of repatriation). Each aspect of this project, therefore, is intimately concerned with the s/places where these experiences and expressions of nationalism intersect, but more specifically, with the locations where they rupture, diverge, contradict, and threaten the discursive performances upon which the idea of the nation depends. The epigraph from Belinda Edmondson's *Making Men* highlights a critical difference between exiles and immigrants while offering a lens through which to read Caribbean women's writing in a (new) nationalist context. Women writers have examined more closely the intersections between race, class, and gender in the intimate spaces "in between" home and abroad where they fought for education and opportunities they did not have access to in the Caribbean region. In many instances their novels stand in stark contrast to those of Lamming, Naipaul, and James.

Edmondson's observation about the relationship between immigration and nationalism provides an occasion to consider what "making it" meant (economically and socially) for women castigated at home, what their "unhomeliness" meant at home, and how these meanings would translate in the landscapes they encountered abroad. Building on Spivak's earlier assertions "that meaning/knowledge intersects power" and that black female subjects function as nationalism's "nearly selved other,"[1] I engage Edmondson's observations in order to consider how her interpretations of gender and power might signify differently when read through one another, particularly insofar as they are concerned with theorizing about power negotiations and positionalities of black female postcolonial subjects.

The implicit possibilities of migrating are among the "acts of imagination" required to begin the journey into an-Other mode of being for Caribbean women. Migration allowed them an opportunity to explore the terrains of "pleasure/privilege" that were part of Empire. Efforts to "make it" for women living in the metropoles involved a tremendous effort to make themselves, both out of what they left behind (possibly to return to later), and in the new landscapes they encountered as immigrants. While giving expression to the various complexities of what "making it" in America meant, women also had to make meaning of their identities in an effort to reconstruct and represent them in relation to new cultural, political, and historical terrains. Without the institutional authority of canonical representation (Caliban, Sycroax, Miranda, or Ariel), no matter how problematic, finding even a trace of their Selves (epistemologically and ontologically) meant interpreting their experiences of "home" differently, in their own language and from their own political vantage points. In other words, they needed to make meaning (race, nation, sexuality, and class) *mean* differently without reinscribing themselves within the "absent presences" of the Caribbean canon they were resisting and revising. My reading of Edmondson emphasizes the fact the black women's bodies are always already the central object/subject of concern in Caribbean nationalist literatures; yet their absent presence is essential for the black, male subject of history. As a result, women emerge as wholly outside of and yet integral to nationalist literature: they are the subjects of nation-states, but can never quite fully become citizens. However, lest we believe that it is only the black female subject whose precarious positioning of subject and citizen leaves her "homeless," I want to return, momentarily, to the geographical setting of Erna Brodber's novel as an opportunity to consider how the race and class nexus shapes the experiences of immigration, migration, citizenship, and national belonging.

In the aftermath of Hurricane Katrina in 2005, the world witnessed the singular extent to which material restrictions limit mobility and the right to protection under the law. The cultural and geographical landscape of Louisiana now serves as a monumental reminder of the tenuous nature of home and belonging for black Americans who became refugees within their own nation and state precisely because they did not have access to mobility in all its complex forms (i.e., transportation, jobs, insurance, and education). The sudden (and seemingly permanent) mass migration of poor New Orleanians shed a blinding light on the meaning of race and class in American discourses of identity. The media spectacle exposed inequities and fissures in the idea of one indivisible nation (as the American pledge of allegiance suggests) and forced many to re-examine the underlying assumptions informing narratives of looting and chaos that unfolded on national television. There was the assumption that the poor of New Orleans did not have the right to expect assistance from the federal government. Somehow, the fact that they were poor and predominantly black took precedence over the fact that they were American citizens and, therefore, entitled to protection under the law from natural and national disasters.

Some of the earliest reports of the national disaster resorted to the kinds of narratives usually reserved for immigrants and refugees from "underdeveloped" countries. Images of looting in the streets and dark hands outstretched begging for help appeared on the television; and, as Wolf Blitzer's CNN telecast of *The Situation Room* noted, "tragically, so many of these people, almost all of them that we see, are so poor and they are so black."[2] When the living conditions that turned a natural disaster into a national disaster floated to the surface (along with the dead bodies of those left behind), many in the United States stood aghast, while others questioned the "right" of these Americans to demand assistance from the federal government. There are countless interpretations of what Hurricane Katrina revealed about the American racial and political landscape; but in the end, as the migration of Katrina survivors/refugees continued, reports flooded television stations about the possible "threats" that the communities hosting the victims would face.[3] There is no doubt that the images of New Orleanians arriving in remote parts of the United States and the constant evocation of the phrase "Third World" by media reporters evoked memories of images of black refugees from other countries (Haiti, Rwanda, Somalia). Put in the plainest terms, the designation "refugee," once reserved for those fleeing persecution because of their race, religion, or political affiliation, was readily mobilized and mapped onto the people pleading for help on television daily. The irony, of course, is not that the term was used at all, but that it was used because the victims were poor and black, and not because the media saw them as persecuted people whose government refused them protection and assistance. The United Nations definition of a refugee suggests that an essential part of this designation is that the parties fleeing their "country" are doing so because they are unwilling or unable to avail themselves of the protection of the country of their citizenship.[4] The media missed the irony of this semantic slippage, focusing instead on the "unhoused" subjects who had fallen victim first to the hurricane and then to the U.S. government. There is much to be learned from considering the ways in which the semantics of identity worked to translate poor and black bodies into alien, nationless, expatriated people within their homelands.

When mass migration from Caribbean countries to the United States took place in the 1930s, there was a similar sense of drastic and immediate change in the demographics and cultural climate of major American cities. Winston James chronicles the dramatic shift: "from a population of twenty thousand in 1900, the foreign-born black population in the United States had grown to almost a hundred thousand by 1930. The overwhelming majority of these migrants came from the Caribbean islands, over 80 percent of them...between 1899 and 1932."[5] Paule Marshall's *Brown Girl, Brownstones* describes the same migration trend in a language that, almost fifty years later, yokes the lives and experiences of West Indian immigrants of the 1930s and poor blacks in Louisiana early in the twenty-first century:

> Like a dark sea nudging its way onto a white beach and staining the sand, they came. The West Indians, especially the Barbadians who had never owned anything perhaps but a few poor acres in a poor land, loved the houses with the same fierce idolatry as they had the land in their obscure islands. But, with their coming, there was no longer tea in the afternoon, and their odd speech clashed in the hushed rooms, while underneath the ivy the old houses remained as indifferent to them as to the whites, as aloof. . . .[6]

Marshall situates her narrative during the 1930s in New York, one of the primary sites of migration for West Indians and a city where Bajans, seeking access to land, property, and opportunities, cast their lot in the hope, not so much of becoming American, but of becoming successful. Winston James's observations about the sudden increase in migrants from the Caribbean region are reflected in Marshall's description of the slow but certain "threat" of West Indians (and other immigrants) "darkening" the landscape of the United States. Like these West Indians who immigrated to the United States well over seventy years ago, the victims of Hurricane Katrina were quickly, but hesitatingly, translated into a discursive system that characterized them as "refugees" rather than "migrants" because of their race and class. Semantics are of crucial importance here: the word "migrant" implies a person who is moving *willingly* from one place toward something in another. The implicit assumption of resources at the heart of this definition is one of the things that fueled the disaster of Katrina. The centrality of class must remain always at the center of all debates about Katrina and its aftermath. The "threat" posed by these "unhoused" subjects is clearly framed by a similar set of colonial/state policies that reflect white political power and privilege, then and now.

When we are introduced to Silla Boyce in *Brown Girl, Brownstones*, her desire to "buy house" seems irrational, motivated primarily by a desire to obtain her "piece" of the American dream at any cost. However, a closer examination of migration patterns and histories reveals the conditions and policies from which Caribbean people (but more specifically Barbadians) were fleeing in the Caribbean region. The acquisition of homes, far from simply representing efforts to establish themselves as "American," speaks more directly to their desire to escape their "unhomeliness" and the racist policies that ultimately led to increasingly impossible living situations in West Indies. The combination of a declining sugar economy, a series of natural disasters, increasingly racist land ownership policies, and a growing population all pointed to an increasing need for land reform throughout the region, but more specifically in Barbados. As Winston James suggests, Barbadian immigration to the United States needs to be considered through "the balance of forces on the land, not through counting black heads on the island, but by recognizing white power and black oppression."[7]

This last point should have been the first frontier of engagement and discussion about Katrina and the subsequent national disaster. However, in the face of strained national resources, donor fatigue, and finger-pointing across the spectrum of government agencies, the numbers of black people disbursed across America soon gave way to the amount of "green backs" and "brown bodies" it will take to rebuild New Orleans for wealthy patrons and residents.[8] The invisibility of immigrants (legal and illegal), particularly in times of national crisis, is not a twenty-first-century phenomenon. In the 1940s setting of *Brown Girl, Brownstones*, Deighton Boyce reminds us that "if they don have some kind of record or something so on you, you don exist. You can be walking 'bout like other men, breathing like everybody else, but not existing fuh true."[9] Then as now, the key to survival for all of these undocumented workers and other "aliens" lies in remaining within the confines of their individual communities, regardless of the similarities in the states (and nations) of (non)existence between themselves and black Americans. As non-citizens, they belong primarily to themselves and to their communities.

In her afterword to Marshall's novel, Mary Helen Washington argues that these communities of fiercely competitive Barbadians saw insularity as the key to their survival.[10] Silla is, unequivocally, a picture of the hardness of life, a woman turned "man" by life's unbearable weight; she is the antithesis of her effeminate and promiscuous husband, Deighton, who spends his money on sweets and ice cream for his children, fine silk shirts for his evening strolls along Lenox Avenue, and long naps in the family's sunroom. Silla's selectivity and single-mindedness become the source of her family's downfall, but her objectives remain firmly rooted in her plan "to buy house." Her mobility depends largely on exercising power over those she sees as lacking in ambition, education, and cultural grounding:

> "Lord, lemme do better than this, Lemme rise!" Silla cries when she is down on her knees scrubbing "the Jew floor" and she feels it is the inevitable nature of power to give way to the next group forceful enough to seize it. Like the other Barbadians in her community she has staked out a claim to power with this carefully conceived plan: work night and day to buy house; rent out every room, overcharge if necessary; sacrifice every penny to maintain property; keep strict vigilance on the children so they will enter high-paying professions; stick close to other Bajans, and exclude African American blacks who are only a "keep-back"; as soon as one house is paid for, move to another desirable location—preferably Crown Heights; imitate the Jew.[11]

West Indian immigrants like Silla Boyce believed that working like a dog would, at the very least, open windows of opportunity for their children. The desire to "imitate the Jew" is repeated throughout the novel as West Indians see financial security and owning property as the keys to belonging in America. The vision of home ownership reflects Silla's every motion in the novel; not a single movement is wasted on what she sees as the frivolities of life: nice clothes, walks in the park, making love. However, many of these West Indian immigrants underestimated the far-reaching implications of the color line in America.

In Marshall's novel, there is an unmistakable separation of black Americans and Black West Indians, but this separation "yields the peculiar themes and images of this novel."[12] As Mary Helen Washington notes,

> These people came to "this man country," as they call it, on purpose, as willfully as many white immigrants; and they exercised their collective force to get what they need and want. Their power and literacy and community strength are essential to the tragic vision of *Brown Girl, Brownstones*; for like the brownstones they inhabit, the are a formidable army—huge, somber, watchful, ancient and beautiful—but "doomed by the confusion of their design."[13]

If we consider the brownstones to be architectural symbols of a newly emerging American identity, then the confusion in the design is something that continues to threaten the foundation of the entire structure of national identity. The reality of subjects who exist in the "spaces in between" the rooms in these brownstones requires—almost demands—a large-scale renovation of the entire structure, from the foundation up.

The brownstone houses are the physical structures built on the foundations of a complex nexus of race, gender, and class that spans Barbados, England, and the United States. Silla's desire to "buy house" is more aptly a desire to impose her own meaning on the landscape of America and, in so doing, redefine her Self in relation to Barbados. Silla's struggle to acquire property is aimed at proving the limitations of "home" prevented her from "making it" in Barbados. If property is the means of translating identity for West Indian immigrants in Marshall's novel, what are the markers of belonging for the first generation of Afro-Caribbean Americans? Early in the novel there is already the suggestion that the brownstones are insufficient to contain their experiences. Selina is constantly migrating between the rooms of the house, lurking in the stairwells. Her mother, in contrast, seems anchored in the engine room, the space that produces energy to keep the machine moving; her spaces are the kitchen and the factory where she bends words and machines to her will.

Like her literary predecessors who people the barrack-yards of the stories of C. L. R. James, Alfred Mendes, and others, Silla's body signifies on the entire Bajan community. In the barrack-yard narratives, women's physical and sexual bodies represented a parallel silencing in the larger political landscape; in contrast, Silla's sexuality is erased, leaving only a mild trace of desire that eventually emerges as one of her tragic flaws. The one instance in which she succumbs to her sexual desire and makes love to Deighton, she bears the cost for this weakness in her otherwise impenetrable armor: Deighton spends all of the money from the sale of his land on frivolous gifts for their children. Though she is represented as "the mother" in *Brown Girl, Brownstones*, she is the antithesis of traditional definitions of motherhood and femininity.

The sign of the "mother" functions similar to the way the Law of the Father does in psychoanalysis, but with a particularly telling subversion. Silla (the mother) separates her children from the body of their "beautiful-ugly" father because of his refusal to accept the social structures he is born into as a black Barbadian. In psychoanalysis, the appearance of the Father separates the child from the body of the mother. However, Marshall subverts the psychoanalytical model as Selina is separated from her father (symbolically) when his dream of returning home is dashed by Silla when she sells his land. Later, Selina is further separated (literally) from Deighton as Silla exacts her revenge by having him deported to Barbados because he joins a religious cult and refuses to acknowledge and participate in his own community. Before Deighton reaches Barbados to face what is for most West Indians an unforgivable crime—returning from abroad with nothing to show for your time there—he drowns after falling (though it is strongly suggested that he jumps) overboard. His symbolic death occurs long before he jumps (or falls) overboard because he is, in effect, unrecognizable within the Barbadian community and also within the African American community. Arguably, his death is performed each time he attempts to gain entry into the system of signification where he is unrecognizable to whites in Barbados and whites in America because of both his class and race.

Silla and the other members of the Barbadian community continuously reprimand Deighton for "putting himself up in these white people face asking for some big job and yuh's not even a citizen."[14] Marshall's cartography connects the faces of white Americans with those of white Barbadians who refuse to recognize anything besides Deighton's black skin.[15] In contrast, Silla assumes that her blackness means she will always have to work harder than most, and it is this recognition that marks the class differences between blacks in Barbados. While Silla was in the "Third Class" picking grass in the cane fields, "working harder than a man at the age of ten," Deighton's mother dressed him in white shirts and shoes and sent him to Harrison College.[16] This difference explains why Deighton recalls Barbados with nostalgic memories while Silla's recollections are primarily of brutal oppression and exploitation. Her desire and disdain for her husband (the "beautiful ugly father") are fueled by her recognition that, as the only son in his family, Deighton has more opportunities that she could ever imagine, far less realize.[17] This same gender structure also makes it possible for him to inherit land while she works "like a dog" to secure property in the United States.

When she is finally confronted with the "meaning" of her black skin, their daughter Selina, proves to be ill prepared for the harshness of the reality of the color line in America, a line that had remained sketchy within the confines of the Barbadian Association. One of the Association's members announces during a meeting, "You need to strike out that word *Barbadian* and put *Negro*. We got to stop thinking about just Bajan. We ain't home no more. Our doors got to be open to every colored person that qualify"; however, the resistance and indignation at such a request can only be measured in relation to the ferocity of rains in the West Indies, without warning and full of fury.[18] Unable to lay claim to the voices of the women gathered around her mother's kitchen table, Selina is voiceless (silenced) when she comes face to face with the cold reality of what her black skin signifies to whites in America:

> "Oh, it's not their fault, of course, poor things! You can't help your color. It's just a lack of the proper training and education. I have to keep telling some of my friends that. Oh, I'm a real fighter when I get started! I wish they were here tonight to meet you. You . . . well, dear . . . you don't even act colored. I mean, you speak so well and have such poise. And its wonderful how you've taken your race's natural talent for dancing and music and developed it. Ettie used to

say the same thing. We used to have these long discussions on the race problem and she always agreed with me. It was so amusing to hear her say things in that delightful West Indian accent . . ."[19]

Faced with these words, the individuality Selina has fought for so viciously against her mother, sister, and the Bajan community is shattered. She realizes that, in the eyes of white people like Margaret's mother, her "blackness" always makes her one with all of "them," the people this woman fears and is fascinated by. Despite her constant association with the transitional places (the staircase and the doorways) in the brownstone in which she lives, and regardless of her struggle to define herself against both the Bajan community and the African American communities on Fulton Street, Selena realizes that she is always already a permanent part of both of these communities in the eyes of white America. She recognizes that "like all her kinsmen, she must now prevent it from destroying her inside and find a way for her real face to emerge."[20] If the brownstones symbolize the complex negotiations for space and belonging, then Selina's struggles may well be contained in "the castle of her skin as Lamming's novel, *In the castle of My Skin* implies."

By situating this moment of recognitions in the context of the "double consciousness" DuBois identified as the inheritance of black Americans, Marshall extends the critical lens of interpretation by bridging Selina's father's experiences in Barbados and the social and political structures at work in pre-Civil Rights America. What does double consciousness mean for the first generation of Caribbean Americans? How will Selina begin to bridge the multiple positionalities of black America and the Barbadian community to which she still belongs, even if only marginally? Does her encounter with racism effectively interpolate her into the same racial landscape of black Americans who are refused access to the economic, social, and cultural opportunities and institutions available to Caribbean immigrants? How are we to read this encounter in light of the consistent refusal to include black Americans in the Association, or even to engage the institutional oppression that denies them access to their rights as "citizens" of the United States? The conclusion of the novel suggests that Selina's recognition and interpellation into the American racial landscape is only partially complete because her lesson must also be contextualized in relation to an "unhomely" space (Barbados) left empty by her father's death.

At the end of the novel, Selina poses a question to her self as she walks the streets of the dilapidated projects: "What was at the center?"[21] Was there something that could sustain her as she sought to mold a space for herself in this s/place she was born into? She decides to begin her search for an answer to this question in two places, with two visions of her Self. First, she will travel to Barbados, possibly to recuperate the memory of the place that died with her father and was already dead to her mother. However, her final act of tossing one of her silver bangles from "home" (which every Bajan girl wore from birth), is one of connection and departure, a double visioning of her future and past.[22] Marshall does not provide the closure we might expect now that Selina Boyce has come into her own Selves (as Bajan, African American, woman, daughter of Deighton and Silla Boyce). The sound of the bangle hitting the stone is "a frail sound in that utter silence" of the projects.[23] Thus, Selina's struggle for her own voice and presence in the Barbadian community and in the United States, though emerging, does not and arguably cannot have the same strength she admires and despises in her mother and women of their generation. They have become like her father and the brownstones, beautiful and ugly simultaneously. Thus she plans to remove herself from this setting to seek out an-Other space to imagine and perform her self-identity.

BETWEEN BLACKNESS AND BEING: UPROOTING HOME AND NATION

The marked tension between gender, class, race, and belonging continues to dominate the works of Caribbean women writers, particularly those writing from abroad. Erna Brodber's *Louisiana* manages to maneuver the complexities of this nexus by focusing on cartographies of black nationalist politics. Her project of writing the historical landscape of the United States through a South-South dialogue between cultures in the Caribbean and in the southern states allows a more seamless narrative of cultural belonging, regardless of time and dis/placement. Marshall does not assume the "loftier aims of the exile"[24] (black nationalism) as her point of origin and therefore has to reckon with other immigrant communities and American-born blacks, with whom West Indians share a historical past, and yet from whom they strive to be different. Like Marshall's *Brown Girl, Brownstones*, Elizabeth Nunez's novel *Beyond the Limbo Silence* suggests that this tradition is rooted in a colonial past that insists upon recognition, if only as part of a colonial inheritance bequeathed to "the sons of the nation." Written almost fifty years after *Brown Girl, Brownstones*, *Beyond the Limbo Silence* traces a similar historical and political trajectory to arrive at distinctly different, though equally open-ended, conclusions about the experiences of black West Indians in the United States. Where Marshall evokes Barbados as an unrealized, even unrecognizable signification of home, Nunez roots her protagonist in Trinidad and the United States, replete with multiple histories (writ small) within the larger historical narratives of these nation-states.

The novel opens with a clear sense of England's waning authority in the colony, but the impending construction of an American military base in Trinidad marks the emergence of the United States as the neocolonial presence in the region. By situating the historical and cultural backdrop for the novel in pre-independence Trinidad, Nunez explicitly connects the geopolitical territories and social struggles of black Americans with Indo-Caribbean and Afro-Caribbean people in the region. Nunez's other two female protagonists, Angela Baboolalsingh, an Indo-Caribbean student from British Guiana, and Courtney Adams, a working-class Afro-Caribbean from St. Lucia, represent the broader cultural, class, and regional geographies of the Caribbean region. Angela brings to the novel the complexities of East Indian ethnic identity in a nationalist context, particularly when read through the American political lens of "racial unity," a concept that *means* something very different in the ethnically diverse Caribbean region. Courtney, in contrast, is situated as a kind of foil to Angela in terms of their different approaches to surviving the experience of migrating to the United States. Much is made of the fact that Courtney has to work in order to send money back to her mother in St. Lucia. Unlike Angela, who makes time to sit around and talk to her classmates, Courtney's routine is described as "work, study, work, study. That's all [she] ever does."[25] Courtney is, as Edmondson suggests, one of those women who are focused on "making it," but with the different motivation that higher education opens other avenues for her to support her family back home. Thus, although Courtney is an Afro-Caribbean woman at the College of the Sacred Heart, her class status marks her as different from Angela and Sara, and this, as Sara knows, is important in the class-stratified colonial societies of Caribbean. The nuances of racial, ethnic, and class identity should, however, not be new to Sara because her grandmother's experiences in Trinidad are framed by some of the same complex issues of difference; but in her grandmother's case, gender difference adds another level of complexity to the race/class/ethnicity nexus.

Sara Edgehill's nameless grandmother, like Marshall's Silla, bears the "mark" of difference as woman because her body is a constant reminder of the cartography of neocolonialism; hers is a body too significant for the other women in the community to bear:

> The women said she was mannish. At least my mother and my mother's sisters did. It was not a compliment. When I was a child I thought this characterization of my father's mother had to do with her size and color and the fact that with six sons she was surrounded by men. She dwarfed my grandfather by what seemed to me to be at least two feet, but what I knew later, with the eyes of an adult, to be merely inches. Then, too, she had a body unlike that of any other woman I knew in Trinidad. My grandmother's body was unyielding. The parts of her legs that I saw beneath her knee length skirts were sinewy, too, and the short boots she wore rainy season or dry gave the impression that she had just finished, or was about to do, man's work.[26]

This physical description of Sara's grandmother resembles the cartography of racial politics in Trinidad and in the United States between 1950 and 1970. This "mannishness" that Sara first measures in size and stature is slowly revealed to be more than a physical difference; the label is earned by Sara's grandmother's position in the family as a woman who made men (gave birth only to boys), by her light skin color (which gives her more power in Trinidad), and by her insistence on making meaning out of her surroundings in a way that is antithetical and culturally opposed (in its African and indigenous groundings) to her family's beliefs. Sara's grandmother's difference stands in opposition to systems of knowledge and the production of nation in Trinidad. The project of nation building was the domain of men who had just returned from studying abroad, men who had the advantage of the critical distance that travel brings and who had indeed pondered the meaning of home under colonial rule and returned to assume their roles in the struggle for independence. Sara's grandmother challenges the knowledges that their supposed expertise constructs.

The grandmother's "unyielding" body of Sara's childhood also symbolizes an unyielding body of knowledge that she refuses to relinquish. The similarities between the way in which her physical body signifies through "the parts of her legs . . . beneath her knee-length skirts . . . and the short boots she wore rainy season or dry" suggest that her physical presence and appearance remind her family of that which they would most like to forget: that she is a woman who has the power to make men, and to make their lives and deaths mean differently in the memories of family members. When her grandson Alan departs for England, she is the only one in the family who knows that his departure is a symbolic death because, while his parents say he is off studying in England, "everyone knew he had no scholarship and his family had no money."[27] Without the mark of class privilege, black men like Alan can only climb so far before they are forced either to embrace their non-existence in the "unhomeliness" of countries abroad or to return to their mother/lands to face another form of social death.

Long before her grandson dies after a mysterious diving accident, Sara's grandmother understands that he is already dead, his Self is beaten into submission during his years of suffering in England:

> Finally my youngest uncle, Melvyn, gathered up the courage to explain. He was with my cousin when he died. "We had a warning," he began cautiously. "I told him so I told him—"
>
> . . . .
>
> "What warning?" My grandmother's voice, soft but firm, stopped Mervyn midsentence. "Go on tell me. Talk."
>
> . . . .

"A big black fish like a giant dolphin. I saw it in the distance when out boat was out at sea. I saw it break through the water. It looked...[like] a woman."

. . . .

"With arms like a woman?" she asked. "Short? Stunted? But like a woman?"

My dead cousin's father stared at my grandmother in disbelief, his lower lip shaking, but he did not dare cross her. He unleashed his fury on Melvyn instead.

"Like a woman! You goddamn liar! You stupid fool! This is what you have to say when my son is dead."[28]

Sara's grandmother insists on telling everyone that the Orehu called her grandson to his physical death since he had already been killed spiritually in England.[29] The men in the family are furious at her unwillingness to accept his death as a tragic accident, and that night Sara recalls the men bellowing "loudly in impotent rage."[30] In both Marshall's and Nunez's novels, the reality of this "death" is manifested through reclamation by the same routes/passage ways that brought their ancestors to the New World hundreds of years ago. For the less-traveled generation of women in Nunez's novel, the absence of institutionalized knowledge of the world does not represent a "lack" or void in their perceptions of the world—quite the contrary. For Sara's grandmother, her granddaughter's imminent departure for the United States is part of a continuous historical cycle win which she loses loved ones "to those big countries."[31]

In light of this sense of loss, Sara's news of winning a scholarship is met with a reaction that she is wholly unprepared for as her grandmother bursts into tears; but her grandmother is not so undone by grief that she cannot pass on some words of wisdom and learned experience. Although she has never visited America, Sara's grandmother has an acute understanding of the perils of the American racial landscape and insists that Sara will not leave until she has been warned about what she faces. Standing in the kitchen, with a towel in hand, Sara's grandmother tells and then shows her what happened to her great-uncle, Thomas, who had gone to live in America:

> She stopped waving the towel, pulled it taut and wrapped one end around her neck. The other, longer end, she stretched above her head. She stood there like an animal about to be slaughtered. Her head dropped on her shoulder.
>
> "Do you understand now child?" she asked. Her voice seemed to carry the mysteries of the past... "Do you understand me big child?"
>
> I said what I did not believe. "He was hanged?"
>
> She laughed and brushed the towel back and forth across her shoulders. "And you want to go to America?"
>
> "The word is lynched," she said. "Lynched. Your great-uncle Thomas was lynched. Strung up on a tree American style."[32]

Sara's education begins when she realizes that her family's definition of her grandmother as "mannish" is not a compliment. Her education continues when she witnesses her family's response to her grandmother's interpretation of Alan's death, but particularly the response of the men in the family. However, her grandmother's choice of words, first "child," and then later "big child;" and then later, "lynched" instead of Sara's term "hung," suggest a completion of a lesson for which her journey to America will be the test of her full comprehension.

When Sara raises her great-uncle's death with her grandfather, he dismisses her grandmother's re-enactment, and tells her that her great-uncle was accidentally shot in Georgia because he "resembled a colored man who had raped and strangled five white girls."[33] However, the distinctive mark of difference in these two (political and epistemological) bodies of knowledge is her grandfather's insistence that what happened to his brother in the South in 1950 would have nothing at all to do with her going to Wisconsin in 1963. In other words, her grandmother's difference is marked by her epistemological reordering of the bodies of knowledge she encounters; she pays the price for this reordering by being marked as "mannish" and is, in turn, made "unhomely" in the eyes of her family through the physical sign of her "lack" of femininity. Sara's mother, in contrast, has arrived at her own way of making her surroundings mean what she needs them to, in order to achieve her own goals, regardless of any obvious incongruity between her text and reality. She bases her interpretative strategies in her firm belief in the church and its representatives, among whom priests and the American soldiers in Trinidad are numbered.

The arrival of a "blue eyed black priest from Mississippi" in Trinidad during the 1950s, like the American military base, represents a shift in the imperial history of the Americas. The emerging strength of the American dollar in the Caribbean region marked a changing relationship between former British subjects of the crown and "Yankees" who felt their money could buy them anything, especially the deference of West Indians. This sense of benevolence extends to their missionary projects to "discover raw talent in the primitive world."[34] Despite the fact that Sara's mother does not see herself or her daughter as "primitive," she does not challenge this representation. Instead she forgives the priest and rewrites his narrative to fit her own desire by deciding that Sara is selected for the scholarship because she is bright and studious. Despite her appreciation for what the Americans have done for her family, particularly providing them with the vaccine to stem the polio epidemic ravishing the youth in their community, Sara's mother realizes in her own quiet way that West Indians are considered inferior, even by black Americans. She reminds her daughter that "Father Jones was like us and not like us" and "colored or white, all Americans were the same. When push came to shove, they would band together."[35]

It is clear, however, that for Nunez, this warning is not potent enough to take hold in Sara's imagination when she arrives in the United States because, after all, her mother had never traveled to America. For this reason, when Sara encounters Mrs. Clancy, who migrated to the United States thirty years earlier, she expects a certain degree of sympathy because Mrs. Clancy is West Indian. When Sara tells Mrs. Clancy that her grandmother did not want her to come to America because "America killed my great-uncle," Mrs. Clancy's responds, "You monkey chasers from the banana bush. Yes you monkey chasers from the banana bush think you know everything. Well you don't know anything."[36] This encounter draws the first clearly articulated boundary between Sara and other blacks in the United States. Mrs. Clancy's outburst serves as a warning of that which Sara's mother is unwilling and arguably unable to teach her daughter: Americans (both black and white) see West Indians as "primitive." While dominant discourses of race in America attempt to consolidate black unhomeliness in order to protect the possessions (votes, education, property, white women, jobs, power) of white men, the mass movement of legal and illegal immigrants makes the fissures of this national myth more immediately visible. Sara's experience with Americans in Trinidad encourages her to believe the myth of America as one nation and one people. Her mother warns her, however, that regardless of the similarities between the black priest and black middle class West Indians, when push comes to shove, Americans would band together. Read within the discourses of "First and Third Worldism" that are an intrinsic part of nation building in the West, Mrs. Clancy's comment highlights the extent to which class privilege shapes how black immigrants are coded within American racial discourses.

Racial codification is translated (by West Indian immigrants) into class and cultural signs of difference that disrupt the fluidity of boundaries and force Sara, Angela, and Courtney to make their marks on the American landscape in pencil, rather than permanent markers. Where Angela decides to emphasize her ethnic difference by wearing saris and singing calypsos to entertain her classmates, Courtney repeatedly calls herself a "voudoun priestess" and is known to keep "little black dolls in the bottom of her drawer."[37] Courtney's insistence on practicing obeah marks her as Other and African, which is what Angela seeks to distinguish her Self from and what Sara knows she is bound to by blood, but seeks to transcend through class. The binaries of blackness/whiteness, Caribbean/United States, Alabama/Wisconsin are exploded by histories that share similar elements of power and privilege. As a foreign student in the United States, Sara reads her arrival through a double lens of difference and alien/nation. Her cultural and political distance from policies that bar African Americans from the same educational institutions she, as a black West Indian, is permitted to attend marks her difference from "Other" blacks. The "civilizing mission" of the benevolent philanthropists of the College of the Sacred Heart effectively balances their hatred of American blacks with their support of more deserving, less threatening West Indians. The irony of a black (blue-eyed) priest from Mississippi acting as a foot soldier for the same racist ideologies that produce black Americans as Other than white, and therefore Other than human, is one of the lessons that Sara's mother rewrites in order for her dream of her daughter's education to be realized. Whether through the myth of "independence without bloodshed" that allows her white benefactors in Wisconsin to feel safer around blacks from the Caribbean, or the equally problematic fiction of happy-go-lucky "natives" of the West Indies espoused by Sam (her African American boyfriend), Sara experiences the United States in a liminal space quite similar to that of her grandmother, whose mixed blood condemns her to an existence of alienation and unhomeliness at home in Trinidad.[38]

The shared historical and political elements of American racism and colonial imperialism produce a variety of mistranslations of West Indian identity by *both* white and black Americans; but through these mistranslations we can begin to see intersecting interests in white America's revisionist narratives of "bloodless" independence and the efforts of middle-class West Indians (both black and white) who felt that the labor union struggle posed a threat to their inheritance, or what "belonged" to them by right. When Sara encounters the distancing produced by her cultural identity, she recognizes it immediately as part of the middle-class value system in Trinidad, which she was raised to appreciate and respect:

> Then, during my last year in school, just a few months before our bloodless independence, my history teacher, a French Creole, infected me with her nightmares, and that crowd in Woodford Square mushroomed into the unruly rabble my mother had claimed it was. "They are organizing to take what we have worked for," the teacher told my class. "Let them find jobs. They won't have the time to be loitering at Woodford Square in the middle of the day. The next thing you know they'll be in our schools sitting next to you. How'd you like to have the daughter of your mother's maid sitting next to you in class?"[39]

The recollection of the labor movement in Trinidad emerges in Sara's unconscious in response to Sam's accounts of the brutal efforts of George Wallace and his police force to "stop black children from going to the same schools that whites attend."[40] While Sara certainly feels Sam's pain and suffering, she still refuses to accept the implications of what this means for her, a woman who is black like those same children, to be attending a white college. Despite her recognition that there is a connection between what she learns in Trinidad about the differences between "them" and "her," "the brutality in

Alabama, the bloody beatings of children in Birmingham, had that cinematic quality of make-believe. Nothing in Oshkosh gave validity to the painful pictures he was painting or the feeling he was trying to convey."[41]

Sara's incapacity to reconcile her own race and class identity with the Civil Rights Movement in America produces ongoing crises between her and Sam. These crises come to a head when Sara discovers that she is pregnant, at the same time that three of Sam's friends and activists in the Civil Rights struggle; James Earl Chaney, Michael Schwerner, and Andrew Goodman, go missing in Meridian, Mississippi. These two developments in the novel coincide with the growing racial tension in the United States and suggest that both will determine the long-term relationship between the protagonists. Sara's personal agenda of romance and love simply cannot stand up to the brutality Sam has witnessed in the South. Her identity as female, woman, and mother is no match for all of the other identities she has to negotiate at this point in the narrative. In fact, her other identity, as a national (Trinidadian) subject has to be considered also: what would the nuns, her parents, and her grandmother think? The weight of all of these identities is so great that it pushes her into a silent space from which she is forced to react.

Sara decides to abort her pregnancy, but does not tell Sam until he returns from Mississippi after the bodies of the three men are found and buried. When Sara tells Sam about the pregnancy, she is completely undone by his response. In his estimation, given what has just transpired in Mississippi, "having a baby wasn't possible. Not at a time like this."[42] In what can only be described as a depressed state of existence, Sara becomes a witness/participant in a descent into a timeless past in which she, with the aid of Courtney and the bag of herbs her mother gives her before she departs for the United States, retraces the routes of her African, Caribbean, and British ancestors, from the experiences of the Middle Passage to *Jane Eyre's* Bertha and her madness, and back to the sound of calypso and resistance in the Caribbean where slave ships transported cargo to Virginia, Mississippi, and Louisiana. Her experience leaves us with a scattered subject caught in the liminality of homelessness, without a nation and without a Self. She comes to terms with the end of her relationship with Sam, acknowledging that her own suffering could not persuade him to return to her because "he had his work to do."[43] The reader is left to ponder what Sara understands as her own "work" in the context of the American landscape she must now negotiate without Courtney and without her grandmother.

If Marshall's *Brown Girl, Brownstones* ends optimistically, with the possibility of Selina crafting her Caribbean/African American identity from the multiple s/places to which she belongs, the conclusion of *Beyond the Limbo Silence* suggests that this possibility is not as readily or easily available to

Caribbean women immigrating just twenty years later in the 1960s. The young women in both novels occupy politically fraught spaces, couched between significant periods of historical and political change and turmoil: World War II, the push for independence in the Caribbean, and the Civil Rights Movement in the United States. The novels' conclusions are notably different, however. Marshall ends with the suggestion that Selina's journey to Barbados will open up more possibilities in her journey toward self-definition. Nunez's novel ends with Courtney being put out of school. Sam writes to Sara to tell her that his friend "Jesse Chrisman" was "lynched by a mob of white men"; this is the last letter she receives from him and she resigns herself to the end of their relationship.[44] Sara has been hospitalized for two weeks in a psychiatric ward, having, according to the nuns, suffered a nervous breakdown. She returns to school, but is now armed with a new source of knowledge and identity as Courtney gives her the dolls before leaving for St. Lucia.

How then are we to interpret the distinct differences between the conclusions of these two novels, which share the same political and social agendas? We might begin by looking closely at the fundamental differences between the two texts and their protagonists, differences that, as Edmondson argues, are linked to the relationship between immigration and nationalism. The timelessness of *Brown Girl, Brownstones* rests in Marshall's unapologetic critique of class and gender privilege within Caribbean culture. This critique is not spared when it comes to her American-born protagonists. Selina's decision to refuse the scholarship money from the Barbadian Association is crucial in moving her into another location, one in which she can assert her own power without being limited by the material comforts of home. This is the difference between the two novels. From the outset of *Beyond the Limbo Silence*, Sara's investment in her middle-class upbringing in Trinidad limits the possibilities of her experience in the United States. Despite the constant barrage of political and cultural signs that invade the sanctuary of the College of the Sacred Heart and her family's middle-class values, Sara refuses to read these signs as part of the same system of racial oppression in colonial Trinidad. Whenever there is an opportunity for her to break with the middle-class respectability that her mother has instilled in her as essential to any sense of being in the world, Sara chooses instead to focus on these values: the shame, the responsibility of being privileged, and most definitely, the love and attention of men to concretize a women's existence in the world.

Prior to refusing the Association's scholarship, Selina is also faced with a number of equally difficult decisions to make. She decides to leave her boyfriend and knows that she will leave her family in order to impose her own order and *meaning* on her landscape. In contrast, the fragmented conclusion of Nunez's novel represents the conflict between Self and s/place: Sara's ordered world as a black, middle-class, West Indian woman fragments when her presence in the American landscape is unrecognizable beyond the walls of the College of the Sacred Heart. There is a cautionary tale in my analysis of these two texts: Sara is reminded when she attempts to give up her scholarship that "no scholarship, no college. No college no student visa. You can't stay in America without a visa."[45] In contrast, Selina's belonging is guaranteed in the United States because, despite the racism that treats her as second class, she is nonetheless an American citizen. Selina can *willingly* leave the United States for the Caribbean; Sara is reminded of her status as a guest in "this man country" of America,[46] and therefore she must weigh heavily the cost should she decide not to return to school. Although it is not at all clear at novel's end how Selina will define home, it is clear that she belongs in America (in the sense of having lived there a long time and coming of age in the reality of her "double consciousness"). Sara, in contrast, is in a much more precarious position, one that will be buoyed by her middle-class respectability and the privilege that the College of the Sacred Heart will offer her, but one that is far less clear in terms of her cultural and political identity.

The crucial difference in the novels, however, is the writer's emphasis on how the experience of migration differs from exile and *means* something very different for these two women in the same systems of signification. Like Selina, whose father's dreamy stories keep Barbados alive in her imagination, Nunez's female protagonist is also caught between two worlds struggling to carve out spaces and relationships that are uniquely hers. These "in between" spaces are the battlegrounds where histories of oppression migrate through memory and performance no matter the translocations of colonial subjects. Arguably, Nunez's concluding epilogue can be read as a gesture to these s/places, nestled somewhere between the obeah man of San Souci, Mad Bertha's dark attic, and the soft red clay of Olen Burrage's farm, which held the secrets and the bodies of James Earl Chaney, Michael Schwerner, and Andrew Goodman. What lies buried within, beneath, and between these s/places is eventually unearthed and revealed as part of a shared historical experience that transcends geographical boundaries in the African Diaspora. The more difficult transmigrations, however, appear to rest in the class boundaries that seem a great deal less permeable and that inevitably shape the way in which gender and race are translated.

NOTES

1. Gayatri Spivak, *A Critique of Postcolonial Reason* (Cambridge, MA: Harvard University Press, 1999), 215.

2. Wolf Blitzer, Transcript of *The Situation Room*, aired on September 1, 2005. "Transcripts," *CNN.com* http://transcripts.cnn.com/TRANSCRIPTS/0509/01/sitroom.02.html (accessed on November 22, 2006).

3. For a more detailed discussion of the perceptions of the Katrina disaster in New Orleans, see Michael Dawson, Melissa Harris Lacewell, and Cathy Cohen, *2005 Racial Attitudes and the Katrina Disaster Study* (Chicago: University of Chicago Center for the Study of Race, Politics and Culture, 2006).

4. The 1951 United Nations *Convention Relating to the Status of Refugees* (the Refugee Convention) defines a refugee in the following manner:
Article 1. Definition of the term "refugee"
A. For the purposes of the present Convention, the term "refugee," shall apply to any person who:
(1) Has been considered a refugee under the Arrangements of 12 May 1926 and 30 June 1928 or under the Conventions of 28 October 1933 and 10 February 1938, the Protocol of 14 September 1939 or the Constitution of the International Refugee Organization;
Decisions of non-eligibility taken by the International Refugee Organization during the period of its activities shall not prevent the status of refugee being accorded to persons who fulfill the conditions of paragraph 2 of this section;
(2) As a result of events occurring before 1 January 1951 and owing to well-founded fear of being persecuted for reasons of race, religion, nationality, membership of a particular social group or political opinion, is outside the country of his nationality and is unable, or owing to such fear, is unwilling to avail himself of the protection of that country; or who, not having a nationality and being outside the country of his former habitual residence as a result of such events, is unable or, owing to such fear, is unwilling to return to it. United Nations Office of the High Commissioner for Human Rights, *Convention Relating to the Status of Refugees* (Geneva: UNOHCHR, 1951). http://web/amnesty.org/pages/refugees-background-eng#refugee (accessed on November 18, 2006).

For obvious reasons, the victims of Hurricane Katrina do not fit into the definitions of refugee stated in the letter of the convention. There are, however, several fundamental ways in which this definition of refugee is applicable, particularly the "well-founded fear of being persecuted for reasons of race, membership of a particular social group." The irony of the situation, however, is highlighted in the problematic reality that black and poor people in Louisiana lived in conditions that were not recognized—in practical terms—as a part of America. While we know that "technically" this is not accurate, the aftermath of Hurricane Katrina suggests that this was, in fact and outcome, the case, particularly because Homeland Security was unable (and, arguably, unwilling) to give aid to those stranded in dire situations.

5. Winston James, *Holding Aloft the Banner of Ethiopia: Caribbean Radicalism in the Early Twentieth Century* (London: Verso Books, 1998), 12.

6. Paule Marshall, *Brown Girl, Brownstones* (New York: Feminist Press, 1981), 4.

7. James, *Holding Aloft the Banner of Ethiopia*, 37.

8. While post-Katrina debates about race relations in America are still raging, very little has been said about the large populations of Hondurans, Mexicans, Salva-

dorians, and other Latinos who call Louisiana home. Displaced illegal immigrants, afraid to turn to FEMA or any other governmental agency for help in the aftermath of Katrina, are being doubly victimized: first by Katrina and then again by government agencies. As the cleanup begins, these same displaced workers are being further exploited as laborers working under dangerous conditions with little protection and even less compensation. For a more detailed discussion about the invisibility of Latinos and illegal immigrants in the post-Katrina race relations debate, see Marissa Kantor, "Viewpoint: Katrina's Invisible Victims," September 22, 2005, *BBC News* http://news.bbc.co.uk/2/hi/americas/4266892.stm (accessed 21 October 2006).

9. Marshall, *Brown Girl, Brownstones*, 66.

10. Mary Helen Washington, afterword to *Brown Girl, Brownstones*, by Paule Marshall (New York: Feminist Press, 1981), 312–13.

11. Washington, afterword, 312.

12. Washington, afterword, 312.

13. Washington, afterword, 312.

14. Marshall, *Brown Girl, Brownstones*, 82.

15. The first mention of this class difference is related in almost identical language earlier in the novel when Silla recounts how, in Barbados, Deighton was always "putting himself up in the face of the big white people in town asking for some big job— and they would chuck him out fast enough"; Marshall, *Brown Girl, Brownstones*, 33.

16. Marshall, *Brown Girl, Brownstones*, 45.

17. Marshall, *Brown Girl, Brownstones*, 44.

18. Marshall, *Brown Girl, Brownstones*, 222.

19. Marshall, *Brown Girl, Brownstones*, 288–89.

20. Marshall, *Brown Girl, Brownstones*, 291.

21. Marshall, *Brown Girl, Brownstones*, 308.

22. Marshall, *Brown Girl, Brownstones*, 5; Washington, afterword, 310.

23. Washington, afterword, 310.

24. Belinda Edmondson, *Making Men: Gender, Literary Authority, and Women's Writing in Caribbean Narrative* (Durham and London: Duke University Press, 1999), 141.

25. Elizabeth Nunez, *Beyond the Limbo Silence* (New York: One World/ Ballantine Books, 2003), 81.

26. Nunez, *Beyond the Limbo Silence*, 3–4.

27. Nunez, *Beyond the Limbo Silence*, 15.

28. Nunez, *Beyond the Limbo Silence*, 7.

29. "Orehu" is a word used by both the Arawak and the Warrau Indians to describe water spirits. Some tales describe the physical form of the Orehu as being similar to that of a water cow or manatee. Other accounts, particularly those from African-Creole folklore, refer to the Orehu as the "Water-Mama." In Nunez's account, the description of the Orehu is most similar to the descriptions found in the tales of the Warrau (or what Nunez calls the Waraos) Indians, who compare it to a manatee.

30. Nunez, *Beyond the Limbo Silence*, 7.

31. Nunez, *Beyond the Limbo Silence*, 15.

32. Nunez, *Beyond the Limbo Silence*, 17.
33. Nunez, *Beyond the Limbo Silence*, 18.
34. Nunez, *Beyond the Limbo Silence*, 28.
35. Nunez, *Beyond the Limbo Silence*, 41.
36. Nunez, *Beyond the Limbo Silence*, 41–42.
37. Nunez, *Beyond the Limbo Silence*, 81.
38. Nunez, *Beyond the Limbo Silence*, 172.
39. Nunez, *Beyond the Limbo Silence*, 172.
40. Nunez, *Beyond the Limbo Silence*, 155.
41. Nunez, *Beyond the Limbo Silence*, 156.
42. Nunez, *Beyond the Limbo Silence*, 271.
43. Nunez, *Beyond the Limbo Silence*, 316.
44. Nunez, *Beyond the Limbo Silence*, 316.
45. Nunez, *Beyond the Limbo Silence*, 213.
46. Marshall, *Brown Girl, Brownstones*, 23.

Conclusion:
Mapping Meaning and Identity

Literary representations of West Indian identity that appeared in magazines like *Trinidad* and the *Beacon* sought to distinguish an identity that had been obscured, devalued, and silenced by British colonialism. The cartography of this representation offered readers a space to imagine Self and native spaces within the lived realities of their cultural and political surroundings. The next generation of writers, many of whom came of age during the push for independence in the region, sought to reflect on the relationship between colonial subjects and the mother country (Britain) that had such a remarkable hold on how they imagined their Selves. For writers like C. L. R. James, George Lamming, and Ralph de Boissière, who migrated to Britain during this period, self-imposed "exile" from newly emerging Caribbean nation-states created the critical distance they felt was necessary to reflect on their conditions of existence as postcolonial subjects. Rereading these texts through the critical lens of black female subjectivity allows us to consider the extent to which gender and sexuality have shaped nationalist discourses in Caribbean literature. More importantly, a gendered analysis opens a space to consider the ways in which interpretative strategies depend largely on institutional discourses of identity that, more often than not, render black female subjects and citizens unrecognizable in postcolonial systems of signification.

This analysis engages traditions of representation in Caribbean literature that are wholly preoccupied with black women as political, sexual, and historical subjects, as producers and disseminators of knowledge and culture, and, last but not least, as citizens/subjects engaged in the processes of Be(come)ing in the world. M. NourbeSe Philip's writing contributes a new cartography of form and content through which to consider the political, scientific, creative, and cultural landscapes that women have had to traverse in order to exist as subject, citizen, and Self in the Caribbean and the ever-expanding African Diaspora. By revising the reader's spatial relationship to words on the page, Philip exposes the extent to which scientific, political, and cultural discourses have effectively disguised the interconnections of language, sexuality, and oppression. Like Erna Brodber, Paule Marshall, and Elizabeth Nunez, Philip is engaged in remapping literary and discursive landscapes by providing alter/native narratives about the exile and migration of female subjects who sought their fortunes abroad. In so doing, these writers are radically transforming the way we interpret how men are "made," to borrow Belinda Edmondson's formulation, and how masculinity functions as a stabilizing discourse in Caribbean literature.

Despite these writers' shared interests in reconstructing the discursive representations of migration, exile, and identity, their individual approaches vary significantly. The recurrence of male protagonists who meet their watery demise after being broken by "big countries" suggests that there are sea changes underway. The waves of migration have given way to a new generation of Caribbean "exiles" whose bodies are washed ashore, or as is more often the case, deported by plane to "homelands" that can scarcely recognize them, let alone accommodate them as guests and workers subjected to new forms of globalization. While there were those who certainly made their mark on the landscapes of America and England, for many migrants, ex/patriation meant disempowerment and alienation from the privileges they enjoyed while at home. The class structure in the British colonies, as Edmondson argues, afforded middle-class black West Indian writers entrance into British society by virtue of their education. The writers of the Trinidad Renaissance, by virtue of their colonial status as "gentlemen," could integrate more easily into British society, but not as easily into the United States:

> For [Albert] Gomes to write in America is for Gomes to continue to be white; that is, he joins white immigrants in the United States who effectively used whiteness as a class option by establishing their difference from American blacks, regardless of their socioeconomic background. For [C.L.R.] James to go to the United States would be for James to lose even the class privilege he possesses in the Caribbean by submergence into the underside of the monolithic American racial equation. By contrast, England contained a history whereby black middle-class men from the Caribbean and Africa could be granted privileged status there as gentlemen.[1]

The literary texts I have engaged here are concerned with addressing both sides of this equation through their attention to the way the race/class/gender nexus complicates translations of black Caribbean identity across different diasporic locations. What was once the "pleasure" of exile has been reborn as a stark reality in which men (emotionally, socially, and ontologically) broken by "big countries" are forced to repatriate to the nation they once called home. The contemporary reality of these forced repatriations is such that the place one calls home bears little or no resemblance to the state of existence encountered as a result of their alienation.

When prodigal sons return home, there is a space still open for them in the nation-state, but what of the woman whose alien/nation makes return an increasingly impossible existential condition? She is, more often than not, masculinized for her desire and efforts to make meaning while "making it" in the world around her, and is at the same time locked out of the power brokering afforded through masculinity. Her efforts to impose her Self and her meaning on the landscape, whether through travel or thought, are part of the new discursive landscapes under investigation here. While class does indeed offer some protection, it does not make "gentle(wo)men" of black female subjects—quite the contrary. Current trends, especially the growing backlash against "male marginalization," suggest that a retrenchment of colonial ideologies about black female subjectivity is poised to force itself into the literary and political landscapes of the Caribbean region. There is an impending "double jeopardy" on the horizon, one in which black women are increasingly visible workers whose products are consumed on the larger stage of global markets, while they are simultaneously "disappeared" and silenced, through physical and sexual violence, policy, and legislative decisions or culture. The irony, noted by all of the writers under consideration in this analysis, is that the need to "make men," even of women, is so pervasive that women writers also struggle mightily against this overdetermined location in their representations of West Indian identity at home and abroad.

The cartographies of these discursive representations by the women writers discussed in this book are as distinctly different as the social and political agendas that inform them. However, they share a particular attention to s/ places and processes characterized by "the spatial and temporal copresence of subjects previously separated by geographical and historical junctures, whose trajectories now intersect."[2] This space, which Mary Louise Pratt refers to as "the contact zone," functions in a notably different manner in the writing of Caribbean men. Where this zone has served historically as an occasion to reinscribe the privileges inherited as part of the colonial tradition, women writing in the twentieth century from their own alien and national locations are using these transitional zones in order to translate their trajectories into new textual and discursive modes of representation. In order for "the spatial and temporal copresence" of black female subjects to mean something other than what it has historically signified—the subject silenced and subsumed/consumed under the sign of the nation or black male subjectivity, or as surrogate mother to masculinity—women's subjectivity needs first to be translated out of dominant colonial and neocolonial discursive registers and traditions.

Considering what this transitional critical lens might entail, Curdella Forbes suggests the work might well begin with shifting ideologies of "belonging" from one generation to the next among Caribbean immigrants:

> Many have felt more entitled and more politically empowered to assert their sense of equal contribution and therefore of "belonging"—their equal right "to be there" as it were. Not infrequently, the feeling of right and "belonging" (right to place) is shared and, even more so, experienced by second-generation children of migrants, born or brought up in these metropoles; these in practice know no other place but the country of their birth to call home. The net effect is that not only nationalism, but also related issues of exile and geographic displacement, while not absent, are no longer the distinguishing marks of West Indian fictions of migration or the literary discourses of migrant West Indians.[3]

While the specter of nation may be subsumed under the more particular concerns of its citizens, the experience of displacement has taken on new forms that are more specific to the cultural and political terrains encountered by immigrants (both legal and illegal) who are never really at "home" within the nation-state. This is the most significant shift in discourses of identity in contemporary Caribbean literature. The growing anxieties about the relationship of Others (non-citizens) to metropolitan centers around the globe coincides with global trends that demand docile "working" bodies to strengthen and maintain the power of nation-states. However, as we well know, the mass movement of bodies, particularly black and brown bodies, cannot be contained by the technologies of globalization or by the boundaries of nation-states. If, as Forbes suggests, displacement, nationalism, and exile are no longer the prominent discursive markers of West Indian literature, the need for new interpretative models that will allow us to translate the lived experiences of subjects who are alienated at home, as well as (forcefully) repatriated nationalists and uninvited guests/workers like the historical C. L. R. James and the fictional Deighton Boyce is obvious. Within this literary landscape, however, we must also imagine critical spaces for those "nearly housed" women who reside in the short stories upon which Caribbean literary traditions rest so comfortably.

While displacement, nation, and exile might not represent the contemporary exigencies of West Indian literature and identity, we should pause reflectively over other ways we can engage what these terms have meant before we retire them as productive sites of engagement. We might find that these terms have been deployed too rigidly and, therefore, have too narrowly defined the borders of our imaginations. My brief engagement with the natural/national disaster Hurricane Katrina serves as an immediate reminder as to why we cannot be so easily distracted by historically fixed definitions of citizenship, alienation, displacement, and identity. As Jacqui Alexander argues,

> The neo-imperial state's cordoning off of the originary citizen from the immigrant in order to delineate the legal loyal heterosexual patriot has implications for radical political projects, including political organizing. If the very terms on which we organize are constituted through the ideology of the secure citizen—the very construct that the state deploys to position the loyal patriot—then we will continue to make invisible the widespread detention of immigrants and their criminalization, and we will mystify the ways in which these detention practices work to secure the secure citizen. As Carole Boyce Davies has argued, citizenship is far too fragile, indeed, it is far too fraught and far too subject to state manipulation and co-optation for it to become the primary basis on which radical political mobilization is carried on.[4]

My analysis of the production of racial minorities and poor people as "second-class subjects" and, therefore, second-class citizens draws heavily on Alexander's critique of the discursive production of sexual minorities within nationalist systems of signification. In the aftermath of Katrina, the status and security of the "originary" (American) citizen was circumvented by the state, and the privilege of belonging (by birth) to America was exposed as a myth. Just as sexual minorities and immigrants are produced as "unhoused" and "unhomely" subjects within nationalist discourses, so too were poor black Americans. What always existed, but had been made invisible within the American landscape, was figuratively and literally washed onto television screens across the globe. Shortly after the waves of water from Katrina hit the shores of Louisiana, the great race to distance black and poor citizens discursively from their homeland, by referring to them as refugees, was underway. The process of criminalization, which Alexander highlights, followed shortly thereafter as reports of looting and shooting began airing while thousands of people were left stranded or to die in what certainly proved to be spaces of detention: overpasses, stadiums, flooded hospitals, house roofs, and attics.

Despite our best efforts to reimagine national identity in the wake of September 11th, we have become complacent about state-sponsored separations designed to consolidate subjectivity and belonging. This critique combines an analysis of reading and writing strategies concerned with complicating how we interpret emerging global landscapes, and how we produce and disseminate knowledge and, through it, meaning. The impulses to secure "homelands" through state-sponsored policies of Othering are the same that govern the firewalls of the information highway: the desire to control the traffic, access, and transportation of those bodies of knowledge and working/laboring bodies who belong and those who do not. As a result of these efforts, meanings and new modes of engaging and performing Caribbean identity emerge and others are covered over, silenced, or disappeared under the debris of History and other fast-paced, unequal processes of identity de/construction in these contact/border zones. Some are indeed displaced, exiled to places they have never known or called "home," for various trangressions in places in which they are only considered guests who must always labor to belong.

Like the critical analyses of Forbes and Alexander, the body of reading and writing under consideration here asks readers to imagine the task that lies ahead in more thoroughly interdisciplinary approaches to interpreting literature. Such an approach, however, will have to "fashion simultaneous articulations with radical political movements in ways that bring the necessary complexity to the multiple narratives about how history [and subjectivity] are made."[5] The task of translating these textual locations of engagement has to include a mindful attention to the dis/placement of bodies who labor in the spaces "in between" public and private enterprises (i.e., seasonal workers, domestics, and sex workers who toil in the "all-inclusive" resorts, the New World plantations of free-trade zones) and those "cultural workers" (men and women) who, like a generation of intellectuals before them, read home closely, and make it mean differently from so very far away. In other words, it is not their physical proximity to home or to the nation that allows them to make meanings. Technology has made it possible to bridge the gap between space and time, home and abroad. However, the development of the information highway, the answer to all (social, cultural, historical, cultural, but doubtfully economic) divides, has also meant clearing spaces for these expanding notions of self, belonging, and identity. In these instances, the task of the translator, when reflecting on these seemingly settled discursive systems, is similar to that of the hacker: use creative and even unsanctioned disciplinary approaches and forms to challenge, revise, or exploit the integrity of these discursive systems to ensure the continuous traffic, trade, and dialogue among alien, nation, diaspora, and self, all of which are essential to the subjects Be(come)ing.

NOTES

1. Belinda Edmondson, *Making Men: Gender, Literary Authority, and Women's Writing in Caribbean Narrative* (Durham: Duke University Press, 1999), 152.

2. Mary Louise Pratt, *Imperial Eyes: Travel Writing and Transculturation* (New York: Routledge, 1991), 7.

3. Curdella Forbes, *From Nation to Diaspora: Samuel Selvon, George Lamming, and the Cultural Performance of Gender* (Kingston: University of the West Indies Press, 2005), 20.

4. M. Jacqui Alexander, *Pedagogies of Crossing: Meditations on Feminism, Sexual Politics, Memory, and the Sacred* (Durham: Duke University Press, 2005), 249. See also Carole Boyce Davies, "'Half the World': The Transnational Black Socialist Feminist Practice of Claudia Jones." Paper presented at the conference by African American Studies: Transnationalism, Gender, and the Changing Black World, Syracuse University, April 2002.

5. Alexander, *Pedagogies of Crossing*, 253.

Bibliography

Adorno, Theodor, Walter Benjamin, Ernst Bloch, Bertolt Brecht, and Georg Lukacs. *Aesthetics and Politics.* London: Verso, 1998.

Ahmad, Aijaz. *In Theory: Classes, Nations, Literatures.* London: Verso, 1992.

Alexander, M. Jacqui. *Pedagogies of Crossing: Meditations on Feminism, Sexual Politics, Memory, and the Sacred.* Durham: Duke University Press, 2005.

Allsopp, Richard. *Dictionary of Caribbean English Usage.* London: Oxford University Press, 1996.

Anderson, Benedict. *Imagined Communities: Reflections on the Origins and Spread of Nationalism.* London: Verso, 1983; rev. ed., 1992.

Anim-Addo, Joan, ed. *Framing the Word: Gender and Genre in Caribbean Women's Writing.* London: Whiting and Birch, 1996.

Archibald, Kathleen. "Clipped Wings." Pp. 79–86 in *From Trinidad: A Selection from Fiction and Verse of the Island of Trinidad, British West Indies,* edited by Albert Gomes. Port-of-Spain: Frasers Printerie, 1937.

Ashcroft, Bill, Gareth Griffith, and Helen Tiffin. *The Empire Writes Back: Theory and Practice in Post-Colonial Literatures.* London: Routledge Press, 1989.

Ashcroft, W. D. "Constitutive Graphonomy: A Post-Colonial Theory of Literary Writing." *Kunapipi* 11, no. 1 (1989): 58–73.

———. "Intersecting Marginalities: Post-Colonialism and Feminism." *Kunapipi* 11, no. 2 (1989): 23–35.

Azim, Firdous. *The Colonial Rise of the Novel.* London: Routledge Press, 1993.

Baker, Houston. "Caliban's Triple Play." *Critical Inquiry* 13, no. 1 (1986): 182–96.

Balibar, Etienne, and Immanuel Wallerstein. *Race, Nation, Class: Ambiguous Identities.* Translated by Chris Turner. London: Verso, 1991.

Baugh, Edward. *Critics on Caribbean Literature.* New York: St. Martin's Press, 1978.

———. "Towards a West Indian Criticism." *Caribbean Quarterly* 14, nos. 1–2 (1968): 140–44.

Behar, Ruth, and Deborah A.Gordon, eds. *Women Writing Culture*. Los Angeles: University of California Press, 1995.

Belmont, James, "James Belmont Condemns Local Magazine, Shocked Readers Write to the *Guardian*." *Trinidad Guardian*, December 22, 1929, 4, 10.

Benítez-Rojo, Antonio. *The Repeating Island: The Caribbean and the Postmodern Perspective*. Translated by James Maraniss. Durham: Duke University Press, 1992.

Beverley, John. *Against Literature*. Minneapolis: University of Minnesota Press, 1993.

Bhabha, Homi K. *The Location of Culture*. London: Routledge, 1994.

———. *Nation and Narration*. London: Routledge, 1990.

———. "Of Mimicry and Man: The Ambivalence of Colonial Discourse." *October*, no. 28 (Spring 1984): 125–33.

———. "Representation and the Colonial Text." Pp. 93–122 in *Theory of Reading*, edited by Frank Gloversmith. Brighton, Sussex: Harvester Press, 1984.

Blocton, Lula Mae. "Miscegenation as Metonymy: Sexuality and Power in the Colonial Novel." *Journal of Ethnic and Racial Studies* 9, no. 3 (July 1986): 360–72.

Blocton, Lula Mae, et al., eds. "Third World Women: The Politics of Being Other." Special Issue, *Heresies* 2, no. 4, issue 8 (1979).

Blundell, Margaret. "Caribbean Readers and Writers." *BIM*, no. 11 (July–December 1966): 163–67.

Bolles, A. Lynn. "'Goin' Abroad': Working Class Jamaican Women and Migration." Pp. 56–84 in *Female Immigrants to the United States*, edited by D. M. Mortimer and R. S. Bryce-Laporte. Washington, DC: Smithsonian Institute, 1981.

———. *We Paid Our Dues: Women Trade Union Leaders of the Caribbean*. Washington, DC: Howard University Press, 1996.

Boyce Davies, Carole. "'Half the World': The Transnational Black Socialist Feminist Practice of Claudia Jones." Paper presented at the conference by African American Studies: Transnationalism, Gender, and the Changing Black World, Syracuse University, April 2002.

Boyce Davies, Carole, and Elaine Savory Fido, eds. *Out of the Kumbla: Caribbean Women and Literature*. Trenton, NJ: Africa World Press, 1990.

Brantlinger, P. *Rule of Darkness: British Literature and Imperialism, 1830–1914*. Ithaca: Cornell University Press, 1988.

Brathwaite, Edward Kamau. "Caliban." Pp. 34–38 in *Islands*. London: Oxford University Press, 1969.

———. "Caliban's Garden." *Wasafari*, no. 16 (Autumn 1992): 2–6.

———. *History of the Voice: The Development of Nation Language in Anglophone Caribbean Poetry*. London: New Beacon, 1984.

Brathwaite, Edward L. "The Love Axe/L: (Developing a Caribbean Aesthetic, 1962–1974)." Pts. 1 and 2. *BIM*, no. 16 (June 1977): 53–65; no. 16 (December 1977): 100–106.

———. "The New West Indian Novelists: Part One." *BIM*, no. 8 (July–December, 1960): 199–210.

Breiner, Laurence A. "Is There Still a Caribbean Literature?" *World Literature Written in English* 26, no. 1 (Spring 1986): 140–50.
Brodber, Erna. *Abandonment of Children in Jamaica.* Kingston, Jamaica: Institute for Social and Economic Research, 1974.
———. "Fiction in the Scientific Procedure." Pp. 164–68 in *Caribbean Women Writers: Essays from the First International Conference*, edited by Selwyn Cudjoe. Wellesley: Calaloux, 1990.
———. *Jane and Louisa Will Soon Come Home.* London: New Beacon Books, 1980.
———. *Louisiana.* London: New Beacon Books, 1995.
———. *Myal.* London: New Beacon Press, 1988.
———. "Oral Sources and the Creation of a Social History of the Caribbean." *Jamaica Journal* 16, no. 4 (November 1983): 2–11.
———. *Perceptions of Caribbean Women.* Kingston, Jamaica: Institute for Social and Economic Research, 1984.
———. *A Study of the Yards in the City of Kingston.* Kingston, Jamaica: Institute for Social and Economic Research, 1974.
Brown, Paul. "'This thing of darkness I acknowledge mine': *The Tempest* and the Discourse of Colonialism." Pp. 48–71 in *Political Shakespeare*, edited by Jonathan Dollimore and Alan Sinefield. Ithaca: Cornell University Press, 1994.
Bruner, Charolette. "The Meaning of Caliban in Black Literature Today." *Comparative Literature Studies* 13 (September 1976): 240–53.
Buhle, Paul, and Paget Henry, eds. *C. L. R. James' Caribbean.* Durham: Duke University Press, 1992.
Busia, Abena. "Silencing Sycorax: On Colonial Discourse and the Unvoiced Female." *Cultural Critique*, no. 14 (Winter 1989–90): 81–104.
Campbell, Elaine. "The Dichotomized Heroine in West Indian Fiction." *Journal of Commonwealth Literature* 22, no. 1 (1987): 137–43.
Carby, Hazel. "Proletariat or Revolutionary Literature: C. L. R. James and the Politics of the Trinidadian Renaissance." *South Atlantic Quarterly* 87, no. 1 (Winter 1988): 39–52.
Carr, Brenda. "To 'Heal the Word Wounded': Agency and the Materiality of Language and Form in M. Nourbese Philip's *She Tries Her Tongue, Her Silence Softly Breaks.*" *Studies in Caribbean Literature* 19, no. 1 (1994): 72–94. http://www.lib.unb.ca/Texts/SCL/bin/get.cgi?directory=vol19_1/&filename=Carr.htm (accessed October 15, 2006).
Castoriadis, Cornelius. *The Imaginary Institution of Society.* Cambridge, MA: Massachusetts Institute of Technology, 1987.
Césaire, Aimé. *A Tempest.* Translated by Richard Miller. New York: Ubu Repertory Theatre, 1992.
Cliff, Michelle. *Claiming the Identity They Taught Me to Despise.* Watertown, MA: Persephone Press, 1980.
Cobham-Sander, Rhonda. *The Creative Writer and West Indian Society: Jamaica 1900–1950.* Ann Arbor: University Microfilms International, 1982.

———. "Dr. Freud for Visitor?" *Women's Review of Books* 8, no. 5 (February 1991): 17–18.

———. Introduction to *Black Fauns*, by Alfred Mendes. London: New Beacon Books, 1984.

———. "Revisioning Our Kumblas: Transforming Feminist and Nationalist Agendas in Three Caribbean Women's Texts." *Callaloo* 16, no. 1 (1993): 44–64.

Collins, Merle. *Angel*. London: Women's Press, 1987.

———. *The Colour of Forgetting*. London: Virago Press, 1995.

———. "No Dialects Please." Pp. 118–19 in *Watcher's Seeker: Creative Writing by Black Women*, edited by Rhonda Cobham and Merle Collins. New York: Peter Bedrick Books.

———. *Rain Darling*. London: Women's Press, 1990.

Columbus, Christopher. *The Four Voyages*. Translated by J. M. Cohen. London: Penguin Books, 1969.

Coombs, Orde. *Is Massa Day Dead? Black Moods in the Caribbean*. Garden City, NJ: Anchor Press, 1974.

Cooper, Carolyn. *Noises in the Blood: Orality and the "Vulgar" Body of Jamaican Popular Culture*. Warwick University Caribbean Series. London: Macmillan Caribbean, 1993.

———. "Science and Higher Science: Transmigration in Erna Brodber's *Louisiana*." Paper presented at the Caribbean Studies Association Meeting, 1996.

Cudjoe, Selwyn. *Caribbean Women Writers: Essays from the First International Conference*. Wellesley: Calaloux, 1990.

———. *Resistance and Caribbean Literature*. Athens: Ohio University Press, 1980.

Cummings, James. "What the Planter Plants." *Beacon* 1, no. 8 (November 1931): 22.

Dash, Jean Michael. "The World and the Word: French Caribbean Writing in the Twentieth Century." *Callaloo* 11, no. 1 (Winter 1988): 95–110.

———. "In Search of the Lost Body: Redefining the Subject in Caribbean Literature." *Kunapipi* 11, no. 1 (1989): 17–26.

de Boissière, Ralph. *Crown Jewel*. London: Allison & Busby, 1952, 1981.

———. *Rum and Coca-Cola*. London: Allison & Busby, 1984.

de Lauretis, Teresa. "Displacing Hegemonic Discourses: Reflections on Feminist Theory in the 1980s." *Inscriptions* 4, no. 3 (1988): 127–45.

Donnell, Alison. "Difficult Subjects: Women's Writing in the Caribbean pre-1970." Paper presented at the Sixth International Conference of Caribbean Women Writers and Scholars, Grenada, 1998.

———. "Dreaming of Daffodils: Cultural Resistance in the Narratives of Theory." *Kunapipi* 14, no. 2 (1992): 45–52.

Dreyfus, Hubert L. *Being-in-the-World: A Commentary on Heidegger's Being and Time, Division I*. Cambridge, MA: MIT Press, 1994.

Dubey, Madhu. *Black Women Novelists and the Nationalist Aesthetic*. Bloomington: Indiana University Press, 1994.

Edmondson, Belinda. *Making Men: Gender, Literary Authority, and Women's Writing in Caribbean Narrative.* Durham: Duke University Press, 1999.
Edwards, Nadi, "George Lamming's Literary Nationalism: Language Between *The Tempest* and the Tonelle." *Small Axe,* no. 11 (March 2002): 59–76.
Esonwanne, Uzo. "The Madness of Africa(ns): Or, Anthropology's Reason." *Cultural Critique,* no. 17 (Winter 1990–1991): 107–26.
Espinet, Ramabai. "The Invisible Woman in West Indian Fiction." *World Literature Written in English* 29, no. 2 (Fall 1989): 116–26.
Fanon, Frantz. *Black Skin, White Masks.* Translated by Charles Lam Markmann. New York: Grove, 1982.
———. *Studies in a Dying Colonialism.* Translated by Haakin Chevalier. London: Earthscan, 1989.
———. *The Wretched of the Earth.* Translated by Constance Farrington. New York: Grove, 1968.
Fenwick, M. J. "Female Calibans: Contemporary Female Poets of the Caribbean." *Zora Neale Hurston Forum* 4, no. 1 (Fall 1989): 1–8.
Ferguson, Moira. *Subject to Others: British Women Writers and Colonial Slavery, 1670–1834.* London: Routledge, 1992.
Forbes, Curdella. *From Nation to Diaspora: Samuel Selvon, George Lamming, and the Cultural Performance of Gender.* Kingston: University of West Indies Press, 2005.
Foucault, Michel. *The Archeology of Knowledge and the Discourse of Language.* New York: Harper Colophon, 1972.
Franco, Jean. *Plotting Women: Gender and Representation in Mexico.* New York: Columbia University Press, 1989.
Frederick, Rhonda. *"Colón Man a Come:" Mythographies of Panamá Canal Migration.* Lanham, MD: Lexington Books, 2005.
Freud, Sigmund. "The Uncanny (Das Unheimliche)." In *Standard Edition of the Complete Psychological Works of Sigmund Freud,* translated and edited by James Strachey. London: Hogarth Press, 1955.
Gates, Henry Louis, ed. *"Race," Writing, and Difference.* Chicago: University of Chicago Press, 1986.
Gikandi, Simon. *Writing in Limbo: Modernism and Caribbean Literature.* Ithaca: Cornell University Press, 1992.
Gilkes, Michael. "The Madonna Pool: Women as Muse of Identity." *Journal of West Indian Literature* 1, no. 2 (1989): 1–19.
Gilroy, Paul. *Against Race: Imagining Political Culture Beyond the Color Line.* Cambridge, MA: Belknap Press of Harvard University Press, 2000.
———. *The Black Atlantic: Modernity and Double Consciousness.* Cambridge, MA: Harvard University Press, 1993.
———. *There Ain't No Black in the Union Jack: The Cultural Politics of Race and Nation.* London: Hutchinson, 1987.
Glissant, Edouard. *Caribbean Discourse: Selected Essays.* Translated by J. Michael Dash. Charlottesville: University Press of Virginia, 1989.

Godzich, Wlad. *The Culture of Literacy.* Cambridge, MA: Harvard University Press, 1994.

Gomes, Albert Maria. *Through a Maze of Colour.* Port-of-Spain, Trinidad: Key Caribbean Publications, 1972.

Goviea, Elsa. *A Study on the Historiography of the British West Indies to the End of the 19th Century.* Washington, DC: Howard University Press, 1980.

Gumbs, Maurice. "Caribbean Groups: Tribal, Cannibal, Individual, or What?" *New York Carib News,* July 9, 1985, 17.

―――. "Who Speaks for the Caribbean Community?" *New York Carib News,* August 12, 1985, 12.

Harris, Wilson. "Adversarial Contexts and Creativity." *New Left Review,* no. 154 (November–December 1985): 124–28.

―――. *History, Fable, and Myth in the Caribbean and Guianas.* Wellesley, MA: Calaloux Publications, 1995.

―――. *Tradition, the Writer, and Society: Critical Essays.* London: New Beacon Publications, 1967.

Heidegger, Martin. *Being and Time.* Translated by John Macquarrie and Edward Robinson. San Francisco: Harper & Row, 1962.

―――. *Introduction to Metaphysics.* New Haven, CT: Yale University Press, 1986.

―――. *Kant and the Problem of Metaphysics.* Translated by Richard Taft. Bloomington: Indiana University Press, 1997.

Hobsbawm, Eric. *Nations and Nationalism since 1870.* Cambridge: Cambridge University Press, 1990.

Huggan, Graham. "Opting out of the (Critical) Common Market: Creolization and the Post-Colonial Text." *Kunapipi* 11, no. 1 (1989): 27–41.

Hulme, Peter. *Colonial Encounters: Europe and the Native Caribbean 1492–1797.* London: Methuen, 1986.

Hurston, Zora Neale. *Tell My Horse: Voodoo and Life in Haiti and Jamaica.* Foreword by Ishmael Reed. New York: Harper & Row, 1990.

James, C. L. R. *At the Rendezvous of Victory: Selected Writings.* Introduction by Margaret Busby. London: Allison & Busby, 1984.

―――. "Discovering Literature in Trinidad: The Nineteen-Thirties." *Savacou,* no. 2 (September 1970): 54–60.

―――. *Minty Alley.* London: New Beacon Books, 1971.

―――. *Spheres of Existence: Selected Writings.* Introduction by Margaret Busby. London: Allison & Busby, 1980.

―――. "Triumph." *Trinidad* 1, no. 1 (December 1929): 31–33, 35–40.

James, Winston. *Holding Aloft the Banner of Ethiopia: Caribbean Radicalism in the Early Twentieth Century.* London: Verso, 1998.

Jelinek, Hena, ed. *Crisis and Creativity in the New World Literatures in English: Cross/Cultures.* Amsterdam: Rodopi, 1990.

Jeyifo, Biodun. "On Eurocentric Critical Theory: Some Paradigms from the Texts and Sub-texts of Post-Colonial Writing." *Kunapipi* 11, no. 1 (1989): 107–19.

Jha, J. C. "Indian Heritage in Trinidad, West Indies." *Caribbean Quarterly* 19, no. 2 (June 1973): 28–46.

Johnson, Lemuel. "Shoeing the Mule: 'Caliban' as Genderized Response." In *Latin America and the Caribbean Geo-politics, Development and Culture*, edited by Arch R. M. Ritter. Ottawa: CALACS Carleton University, 1984.
Jones, Marion Patrick. *J'ouvert Morning*. Port-of-Spain: Columbus Publishers, 1976.
———. *Pan Beat*. Port-of-Spain: Columbus Publishers, 1973.
Kaminsky, Amy K. *Reading the Body Politic: Feminist Criticism and Latin American Women Writers*. Minneapolis: University of Minnesota Press, 1993.
Kant, Immanuel. *Critique of Judgment*. Translated by Werner S. Pluhar. Indianapolis: Hackett Publishing, 1987.
Kantor, Marissa. "Viewpoint: Katrina's Invisible Victims." *BBC News*, September 22, 2005. http://news.bbc.co.uk/2/hi/americas/4266892.stm (accessed October 21, 2006).
Kasinitz, Philip. *Caribbean New York: Black Immigrants and the Politics of Race*. Ithaca: Cornell University Press, 1992.
Katrak, Ketu H. "Decolonizing Culture: Toward a Theory for Post-Colonial Women's Texts." *Modern Fiction Studies* 35, no. 1 (Spring 1989): 157–79.
Kincaid, Jamaica. *Lucy*. New York: Plume, 1990.
King, Bruce, ed. *West Indian Literature*. London: Macmillan, 1979.
Kirpal, Vingy. "What Is the Modern Third World Novel?" *Journal of Commonwealth Literature* 23, no. 1 (1988): 144–56.
Knight, Franklin. *The Caribbean: The Genesis of a Fragmented Nationalism*. Baltimore: Johns Hopkins University Press, 1978.
Lacan, Jacques. *The Four Fundamental Principles of Psycho-Analysis*. New York: W. W. Norton, 1981.
Lamming, George. *Conversations: George Lamming; Essays, Addresses, and Interviews, 1953–1990*. Edited by Richard Drayton and Andayie. London: Karia Press, 1992.
———. *In the Castle of My Skin*. Foreward by Sandra Pouchet Paquet. Ann Arbor: University of Michigan Press, 1992.
———. *Natives of My Person*. London: Allison & Busby, 1971.
———. *Pleasures of Exile*. Ann Arbor: University of Michigan Press, 1992.
———. "The Sovereignty of the Imagination: An Interview with George Lamming." By David Scott. *Small Axe: A Caribbean Journal of Criticism*, no. 12 (September 2002): 72–200.
———. *Water with Berries*. Port-of-Spain: Longman Caribbean, 1971.
LeSur, Geta. "Wild Women in the Wilderness: Tituba of *I, Tituba, Black Witch of Salem* and Telumee of *Bridge of Beyond* as Maroon Subjects Finding Voice." *MaComère* 1 (1998): 94–100.
Lewis, Gordon K. *Main Currents in Caribbean Thought: The Historical Evolution of Caribbean Society in Its Ideological Aspects, 1492–1900*. Baltimore: Johns Hopkins University Press, 1983.
Lionnet, Françoise. *Autobiographical Voices: Race, Gender, and Self-Portraiture*. Ithaca: Cornell University Press, 1989.

———. "*Logiques métisses*: Cultural Appropriation and Postcolonial Representations." Pp. 1–21 in *Postcolonial Representations: Women, Literature, Identity*. Ithaca: Cornell University Press, 1995.
Lipsitz, George. *Time Passages: Collective Memory and American Popular Culture*. Minneapolis: University of Minnesota Press, 1990.
Lovelace, Earl. *The Dragon Can't Dance*. London: Andre Deutsch, 1979.
Lynn, D. Joanne, Herbert B. Newton, and Alexander D. Rae-Grant. *The 5-Minute Neurology Consult*. Philadelphia: Lippincott, Williams and Wilkins, 2003.
Macauley-Jarrett, Delia. *The Life of Una Marson, 1905–65*. Kingston: Ian Randle Publishers, 1998.
Mannoni, O. *Prospero and Caliban: The Psychology of Colonization*. Translated by Pamela Powesland, 1964. Reprint edition. Ann Arbor: University of Michigan Press, 1990.
Marquez, Roberto. "Nationalism, Nation, and Ideology: Trends in the Emergence of a Caribbean Literature." Pp. 293–340 in *The Modern Caribbean*, edited by Franklin Knight and Colin Palmer. Chapel Hill: University of North Carolina Press, 1989.
Marshall, Paule. *Brown Girl, Brownstones*. New York: Feminist Press at CUNY, 1996.
———. *Praisesong for the Widow*. New York: Plume, 1984.
Marson, Una. "The Age of Woman." *Cosmopolitan* 1, no. 11 (March 1929): 65.
———. "Jamaica's Victory." *Cosmopolitan* 2, no. 2 (June 1929): 66–67.
Maxwell, Anne. "The Debate on Current Theories on Colonial Discourse." *Kunapipi* 12, no. 3 (1991): 70–84.
McClintock, Anne, Aamir Mufti, and Ella Shohat, eds. *Dangerous Liaisons: Gender, Nation Post-Colonial Perspectives*. Minneapolis and London: University of Minnesota Press, 1997.
Mendes, Alfred H. *Black Fauns*. London: New Beacon Books, 1984.
———. "A Commentary." *Trinidad* 1, no. 2 (Easter 1930): 65–67.
———. "Faux Pas." *Trinidad* 1, no. 1 (Christmas 1929): 54.
———. "Five Dollars Worth of Flesh." *Beacon* 1, no. 2 (September 1931): 13–15.
———. "Her Chinaman's Way." *Trinidad* 1, no. 1 (Christmas 1929): 119–26.
———. *Pitch Lake: A Story from Trinidad*. London: New Beacon Books, 1980.
———. "Shop Girls." *Beacon* 1, no. 6 (September 1931): 11.
———. "Sweetman." *Beacon* 1, no. 7 (October 1931): 1–6.
Mohammed, Patricia, ed. *Gendered Identities: Essays in Caribbean Feminist Thought*. Kingston, Jamaica: University of the West Indies Press, 2002.
Mohanty, Chandra Talpade. "Under Western Eyes: Feminist Scholarship and Colonial Discourse." *Boundary 2* 12, no. 1 (Spring/Fall 1984): 333–58.
Moore-Gilbert, Bart. *Postcolonial Theory: Contexts, Practices, Politics*. London: Verso, 1997.
Naipaul, V. S. *The Middle Passage*. Harmondsworth: Penguin, 1969.
Nair, Supriya. *Caliban's Curse: George Lamming and the Revisioning of History*. Ann Arbor: University of Michigan Press, 1996.
Nasta, Susheila, ed. *Motherlands: Black Women's Writing from Africa, the Caribbean, and South Asia*. London: Women's Press, 1991.

Nettleford, Rex. *Mirror Mirror: Identity, Race, and Protest in Jamaica.* Kingston, Jamaica: William Sangster, 1970.
Nixon, Rob. "Caribbean and African Appropriation of *The Tempest.*" *Critical Inquiry* 13, no. 3 (Spring 1987): 557–78.
Nunez, Elizabeth. *Beyond the Limbo Silence.* Reprint edition. New York: One World/Ballentine Books, 2003.
Obeyesekere, Gananath. *The Apotheosis of Captain Cook: European Mythmaking in the Pacific.* Princeton: Princeton University Press, 1992.
O'Callaghan, Evelyn. "*Jane and Louisa Will Soon Come Home*: Rediscovering the Natives of My Person." Presented at the Conference on West Indian Literature, Mona, Jamaica, May 1982.
———. "Journals, Letters, and Stories: Early West Indian Narratives by Women." Presented at the Conference on West Indian Literature, Mona, Jamaica, May 1988.
———. "It's All about Ideology, There's No Discussion about Art: Reluctant Voyages into Theory in Caribbean Women's Writing." *Kunapipi* 14, no. 2 (1992): 35–44.
———. *Woman Version: Some Theoretical Approaches to West Indian Fiction by Women.* Warwick University Caribbean Series. London: Macmillan Caribbean, 1993.
Orgel, Stephen. "Prospero's Wife." *Representations*, no. 8 (Autumn 1984): 1–13.
Oxaal, Ivar. *Black Intellectuals Come to Power: The Rise of Creole Nationalism in Trinidad and Tobago.* Cambridge, MA: Schenkman Publishing, 1968.
Page, Kezia. "'Two places can make children': Erna Brodber's *Louisiana.*" *Journal of West Indian Literature* 13, nos. 1–2 (April 2005): 57–79.
Paquet, Sandra Pouchet. *The Novels of George Lamming.* London: Heinemann, 1982.
Paravisini, Lizabeth, and Barbara Webb. "On the Threshold of Becoming: Caribbean Women Writers." *Cimarron* 1, no. 3 (Spring 1988): 106–31.
Parker, Andrew, Mary Russo, Doris Sommer, and Patricia Yaeger, eds. *Nationalisms and Sexualities.* London: Routledge, 1992.
Parry, Benita. "Problems in Current Theories of Colonial Discourse." *Oxford Literary Review*, no. 9 (1987): 27–58.
Pastor, Robert ed. *Migration and Development in the Caribbean: The Unexplored Connection.* Boulder, CO: Westview, 1985.
Paul, Margaret Joseph. *Caliban in Exile: The Outsider in Caribbean Fiction.* New York: Greenwood Press, 1992.
Peabody, Elizabeth. "Defense of Modern Realism in Fiction." *Beacon* 2, no. 6 (October–November 1932): 6.
Pease, Donald. "Toward a Sociology of Literary Knowledge: Greenblatt, Colonialism, and the New Historicism." Pp. 108–53 in *Consequences of Theory*, edited by Jonathan Arac and Barbara Johnson. Baltimore: Johns Hopkins University Press, 1991.
Philip, M. NourbeSe. *A Genealogy of Resistance and Other Essays.* Toronto: Mercury Press, 1997.

———. *Frontiers: Essays and Writings on Racism and Culture*. Stratford, Ontorio: The Mercury Press, 1992.

———. *She Tries Her Tongue, Her Silence Softly Breaks*. Charlottetown, PE: Ragweed Press, 1989.

Pratt, Mary Louise. *Imperial Eyes: Travel Writing and Transculturation*. New York: Routledge, 1991.

———. "Scratches on the Face of the Country; Or, What Mr. Barrow Saw in the Land of the Bushmen." In "'Race,' Writing, and Difference," ed. Henry Louis Gates, Jr. Special issue, *Critical Inquiry* 12, no. 1 (Autumn 1985): 119–43.

Puri, Shalini. *The Caribbean Post-Colonial: Social Equality, Post-Nationalism, and Cultural Hybridity*. London: Palgrave Macmillan, 2004.

———. "An 'Other' Realism: Erna Brodber's *Myal*." *ARIEL: A Review of International English Literature* 24, no. 3 (July 1993): 95–115.

Rahim, Jennifer. "Rising into Artistry and Personhood: Trinidad and Tobago Women's Literature, 1900–1990." PhD diss., University of the West Indies, 1994.

Ramchand, Kenneth. "The Alfred Mendes Story." *Tapia* 7, no. 23 (May 29, 1977): 6.

———. "West Indian Literary History: Literariness, Orality, and Periodization." *Callaloo* 11, no. 1 (Winter 1988): 95–110.

———. *The West Indian Novel and Its Background*. London: Heinemann, 1983.

Reddock, Rhoda. *Women, Labour, and Politics in Trinidad and Tobago*. Jamaica: Ian Randle Publishers, 1994.

Reid, John T. *Spanish American Images of the United States, 1790–1960*. Gainesville: University Press of Florida, 1977.

Rennie, Bukka. *The History of the Working Class in the 20th Century (1919–1956): The Trinidad and Tobago Experience*. Toronto: New Beginning Movement, 1973.

Retamar, Roberto Fernández. "Caliban: Notes Towards a Discussion of Culture in Our America." *Massachusetts Review* 15 (Winter/Spring 1974): 7–72.

———. *Caliban and Other Essays*. Minnesota: University of Minnesota Press, 1989.

Rodó, José Enrique. *Ariel*. Barcelona: Vosgos, 1979.

Rodrigues, Emilio Jorge. "An Overview of Caribbean Literary Magazine: Its Liberating Function." Paper presented at the Literary Arts Symposia, CARIFESTA (Barbados), 1981.

Rohlehr, Gordon. "Indian-African Relations in Caribbean Fiction." *Wasafari* 1, no. 2 (Spring 1985): 18–23.

———. *My Strangled City and Other Essays*. Port-of-Spain: Longman, 1992.

———. "The Problem of Form: The Idea of an Aesthetic Continuum and Aesthetic Code Switching in West Indian Literature." *Caribbean Quarterly* 31, no.1 (1985): 1–53.

Rowley, Michelle V. "Crafting Maternal Citizens? Public Discourse of the Maternal Scourge in Social Welfare Policies and the Services in Trinidad." *Social and Economic Studies* 52, no. 3 (September 2003): 31–58.

Ryan, Selwyn, ed. *Caribbean Women Writers: Essays From the First International Conference*. Wellesley, MA: Calaloux, 1990.

———. *Race and Nationalism in Trinidad and Tobago.* Toronto: University of Toronto Press, 1972.
Sadock, Benjamin J., and Virginia A. Sadock. *Kaplan and Sadock's Concise Textbook of Clinical Psychiatry.* 9th ed. Philadelphia: Lippincott, Williams & Wilkins, 2002.
Said, Edward W. *Culture and Imperialism.* New York: Knopf, 1993.
———. "Identity, Negation, and Violence." *New Left Review,* no. 177 (September-October 1988): 46–60.
———. *Orientalism.* New York: Vintage, 1979.
Samaroo, Brinsley. "The Trinidad Disturbances of 1917–20: Precursor to 1937." Pp. 21–56 in *The Trinidad Labour Riots of 1937: Perspectives 50 Years Later,* edited by Roy Thomas. (St. Augustine, Trinidad: University of the West Indies Press, 1987).
Sander, Reinhard. *The Trinidad Awakening: West Indian Literature of the Nineteen-Thirties.* New York: Greenwood Press, 1988.
———. "The Turbulent Thirties in Trinidad: An Interview with Alfred Mendes." *World Literature Written in English* 12, no. 1 (April 1973): 66–79.
Savory, Elaine. "En/Gendering Spaces: The Poetry of Marlene Nourbese-Philip and Pamela Mordecai." Pp. 12–27 in *Framing the Word: Gender and Genre in Caribbean Women's Writing.* Edited by Joan Anim-Addo. London: Whiting & Birch, 1996.
Selvon, Samuel. *Moses Ascending.* London: Heinemann International, 1975.
———. *Moses Migrating.* Washington, DC: Three Continents Press, 1992.
Seymour, A. J. "The Novel in the British Caribbean." Pts. 1, 2, & 3. *BIM* 11.42 (January–June 1966): 83–85; 11.43 (July–December 1966): 176–80; 11.44 (January–June 1967):238–42.
Schipper, Mienke, ed. *Unheard Words: Women and Literature in Africa, the Arab World, Asia, the Caribbean, and Latin America.* London: Allison & Busby, 1985.
Shakespeare, William. *The Tempest.* Edited by Peter Holland. New York: Penguin Books, 1999.
Shineborne, Janice. *The Last English Plantation.* Leeds, England: Peepal Tree Press, 1988.
Singh, Vishnudat. "Ralph de Boissière's *Crown Jewel* and Trinidad Society in the Turbulent Thirties." Pp. 18–32 in *West Indian Literature and Its Social Context,* edited by Mark McWatt. Cave Hill, Barbados: University of the West Indies Department of English, 1985.
Slemon, Samuel. "Postcolonial Allegory and the Transformation of History." *Journal of Commonwealth Literature* 23, no. 1 (1988): 157–68.
Sparrow, Jennifer. "Capécia, Condé, and the Antillean Woman's Identity Quest." *MaComère* 1 (1998): 179–87.
Spivak, Gayatri Chakravorty. "Can the Subaltern Speak? Speculations on Widow Sacrifice." Pp. 271–313 in *Marxism and the Interpretation of Culture,* edited by Cary Nelson Lawrence Grossberg. London: Macmillan, 1988.
———. *A Critique of Post-Colonial Reason: Toward a History of the Vanishing Present.* Cambridge, MA: Harvard University Press, 1999.

———. *In Other Worlds: Essays in Cultural Politics*. New York: Routledge, 1987.

———. "Theory in the Margin: Coetzee's *Foe* Reading Defoe's *Crusoe/Roxana*." Pp. 154–80 in *Consequences of Theory*, edited by Jonathan Arac and Barbara Johnson. Baltimore: Johns Hopkins University Press, 1993.

Stanley, Fred L., and Louis Pratt, eds. *Conversations with James Baldwin*. Jackson: University Press of Mississippi, 1989.

Stephens, Michelle Anne. *Black Empire: The Masculine Global Imaginary of Caribbean Intellectuals in the United States, 1914–1962*. Durham: Duke University Press, 2005.

Taylor, Patrick. *Narratives of Liberation: Perspectives on Afro-Caribbean Literature, Popular Culture, and Politics*. Ithaca: Cornell University Press, 1989.

Thomas, Roy, ed. *The Trinidad Labour Riots of 1937: Perspectives 50 Years Later*. St. Augustine, Trinidad: University of the West Indies Press, 1987.

Tiffin, Chris, and Alan Lawson, eds. *De-Scribing Empire: Post-colonialism and Textuality*. London: Routledge Press, 1994.

Tiffin, Helen. "Mirrors and Mask: Colonial Motif in the Novels of Jean Rhys." *World Literature Written in English* 17 (1978): 328–41.

———. "Post-Colonialism, Post-Modernism, and the Rehabilitation of Post-Colonial History." *Journal of Commonwealth Literature* 23, no. 1 (1988): 169–81.

———. "Rights of Resistance: Counter-Discourse and West Indian Autobiography." *Journal of West Indian Literature* 3, no. 1 (January 1989): 28–46.

Tiffin, Helen, and Ian Adam, eds. *Past the Last Post: Theorizing Postcolonialism and Postmodernism*. Calgary: Calgary University Press, 1990.

Trinidad. Editorial. 1, no. 2 (Easter 1930): 57–58.

United Nations Office of the High Commissioner for Human Rights. *Convention Relating to the Status of Refugees*. Geneva: UNOHCHR, 1951. http://web.amnesty.org/pages/refugees-background-eng#refugee (accessed on November 18, 2006).

Vaughn, Alden. "Caliban in the 'Third World': Shakespeare's Savage as Sociopolitical Symbol." *Massachusetts Review* 29 (Summer 1989): 289–313.

Vaughan, Alden T., and Virginia Mason Vaughan. *Shakespeare's Caliban: A Cultural History*. Cambridge: Cambridge University Press, 1993.

wa Thiong'o, Ngugi. *Decolonizing the Mind: The Politics of Language in African Literature*. London: Heinemann, 1986.

Walcott, Derek. "The Caribbean: Culture or Mimicry?" *Journal of Interamerican Studies and World Affairs* 16 (February 1974): 3–13.

Walmsley, Anne. *The Caribbean Artist Movement, 1966–1972: A Literary and Cultural History*. London: New Beacon Books, 1992.

Washington, Mary Helen. Afterword. Pp. 311–24 in *Brown Girl, Brownstones*, by Paule Marshall. New York: Feminist Press, 1981.

Webb, Barbara J. *Myth and History in Caribbean Fiction: Alejo Carpentier, Wilson Harris, and Edouard Glissant*. Amherst: University of Massachusetts Press, 1992.

Williams, Eric. *Capitalism and Slavery*. Chapel Hill: University of North Carolina Press, 1994.

———. *From Columbus to Castro: The History of the Caribbean 1492–1969*. London: Andre Deutsch, 1989.

Wynter, Sylvia. "Afterword: Beyond Miranda's Meanings: Un/silencing the 'Demonic Ground' of Caliban's 'Woman.'" Pp. 355–72 in *Out of the Kumbla: Caribbean Women and Literature*, edited by Carole Boyce Davies and Elaine Savory Fido. Trenton, NJ: Africa World Press, 1990.

———. "Beyond the Word of Man: Glissant and the New Discourse of the Antilles." *World Literature Today* 63, no. 4 (Autumn 1989): 637–47.

———. "The Counter-Doctrine of Jamesian Poesis." Pp. 63–91 in *C. L. R. James' Caribbean*, edited by Paget Henry and Paul Buhle. Durham: Duke University Press, 1992.

———. "We Must Learn to Sit Down Together and Talk a Little Culture: Reflections on West Indian Writing and Criticism." Parts 1 and 2. *Jamaica Journal* 2, no. 4 (March 1968): 23–32; 3, no. 1 (1969): 27–42.

Yelvington, Kevin, ed. *Trinidad Ethnicity*. Knoxville: University of Tennessee Press, 1993.

Young, Robert. *White Mythologies: Writing History and the West*. London: Routledge, 1992.

Zabus, Chantal. "A Calibanic Tempest in Anglophone and Francophone New World Writing." *Canadian Literature*, no. 104 (Spring 1985): 35–50.

Zimra, Clarisse. "W/Righting His/tory: Versions of Things Past in Contemporary Caribbean Women Writers." Pp. 227–52 in *Exploration: Essays in Comparative Literature*, edited by Veda Matoto. Lanham, MD: UPS of America, 1986.

Index

'ab-original,' 6–7
The Absence of Writing. See Philip, M. NourbeSe
acts of fiction, 29–30
aesthetics, 7, 25, 27, 30, 38, 40, 50–51
African diaspora, 4, 7, 15, 19–20, 58, 89, 109, 117, 124–26, 128, 149, 154
Afro-Caribbean, 20, 64, 137, 141. *See also* exile
Against Race: Political Culture Beyond the Color Line. See Gilroy, Paul
Alexander, Jacqui M., 128, 130n30, 157, 159n4
alien, 21, 155, 158,
alienate, 12
alienation, 5, 60, 67, 80, 89, 113–14, 125, 131, 146, 154, 157
alien/nation, 13, 128, 131, 145, 155
alterity, 11–12, 20, 87
alter/native, 5, 8, 26, 29, 58, 89, 116, 154
Anderson, Benedict, 1, 22n1
Anthropology from a Pragmatic Point of View. See Kant, Immanuel
anxiety, 4–5, 71, 78, 106, 113

barrack yard fiction, 45, 54n19, 63, 92
Beacon, 13–14, 26–29, 39, 41, 48–50, 52n1, 53n8, 54n19, 92, 153,
Beacon group, 27
Be(come)ing, 1, 3, 10–12, 22n4, 30, 94, 109, 113, 115, 121, 123, 153, 158

Belmont, James, 38, 53n12; critique of *Trinidad,* 55n27
Beyond the Limbo Silence. See Nunez, Elizabeth
Bhabha, Homi, 114, 128n2
Bim, 26–27
Black: Americans, 133, 135–36, 139, 141, 144, 146, 157; Atlantic, 125; Caribbean subjects, 30; colonial subjects, 25, 29–30, 59; female identity, 92; female subjectivity, 16, 18, 88, 93, 113–14, 126, 128, 130n31, 155; female subjects, 10, 16, 21, 92, 107, 113–15, 132, 153, 155; male subjectivity, 155; subjects, 1, 3, 21, 22n4, 28, 61, 64, 90, 94, 98, 109, 116; women's bodies, 19, 64, 81, 91, 92, 98, 132; women's experiences, 18, 67, 98; West Indians, 26, 47, 52n1, 136
Black Women, Writing and Identity: Migrations of the Subject. See Davies, Carol Boyce
blackness, 13, 19, 42, 62, 138–40, 145
'body politic,' 9, 16, 21, 47, 64
Brand, Dionne, 18
bricolage, 90
Brodber, Erna, 9, 18–19, 22n6, 23n20, 88–89, 114–15, 129n5, 132, 140, 154; *Jane and Louisa Will Soon Come Home,* 116; *Louisiana,* 19, 21, 22n6, 115–18, 122–27, 129n5,

140; *Myal*, 116; *Oral Sources and the Creation of a Social History of the Caribbean*, 9; translation, 118, 122, 154. See also African diaspora; Caribbean: women's literature; Colonial: discourses; displacement; memory; migration; nationalism
Brown Girl, Brownstones. See Marshall, Paule
Busia, Abena, 10
Butler, Tubal Uriah, 47

Caliban, 8, 11, 14, 16, 57–58, 62, 64–67, 71, 75–77, 80, 81n2, 82n8, 83n12, 113
Calibanesque, 8, 26, 58, 63, 81, 84n30
canonical representation, 132
Capildeo, Rudranath, 27
Caribbean: culture(s), 6–7, 13, 96, 148; history, 7, 10, 89; immigrants, 21, 139, 156; intellectual traditions, 17; literature, 3–6, 10, 16–18, 39, 46, 57–59, 80, 82, 87–88, 90, 92, 94, 113, 153, 154, 156; literary traditions, 7, 8, 91, 156; nationalism, 8, 26, 46, 61, 64, 80, 92, 115; subject(s), 6, 30, 40, 96; subjectivity, 58; women writers, 8, 11, 18, 64, 75, 88–89, 93, 109, 114, 123, 140; women's literature, 8, 89; women's writing, 18, 46, 108, 131; writers, 4–13, 28, 51, 59, 61, 88, 95–96, 109n1. See also Black: Caribbean subjects
Carr, Ernest, 27, 52n3
Cipriani, Arthur Andrew, 47
citizenship, 3, 17–18, 21, 64, 132, 134, 157
Class: class lines, 20, 52n1; middle class, 21, 27, 37, 39, 40, 43, 46–49, 51, 54, 125, 145–46, 148–49, 154; working class, 14, 37, 41, 43, 47–51, 53, 54, 141
Cobham, Rhonda, 49. See also Mendes, Alfred
Collymore, Frank, 26. See also Bim

Colonial: culture, 8, 12, 27, 50; discourses, 18, 25, 61, 89, 93, 103; education, 27, 38–39, 59; history, 9, 62; ideologies, 155; institutions, 13, 50; masters, 8; narratives, 10, 30, 68; Other, 8; patriarchal society, 92; subjects, 12–14, 16, 18, 25, 28–30, 50–51, 59–62, 81, 87, 149, 153
colonialism, 4, 5, 62, 74, 77, 90–91, 96, 106, 126, 153
colonialist, 10, 14, 19, 25, 58, 61, 66–67, 69, 75, 88–89, 91, 96, 103
colonized, 7–8, 10, 57, 59, 62–63, 68, 73, 77, 107; subjects, 7–8, 62
'colonizer/native,' 8
Cooper, Carolyn, 3, 22n6. See also transmigration
creolization, 4, 113, 117
Crick, Daisy, 41, 47, 49
Crown Jewel. See de Boissière, Ralph
Cultural: difference, 7, 20; dislocation, 21; ethics, 40; expression(s), 25, 27, 29, 39, 51, 53n8, 64; identity, 11, 114, 123, 129n4, 146

Davies, Carole Boyce, 17–18, 157; *Black Women, Writing and Identity: Migrations of the Subject*, 17
de Boissière, Ralph, 13, 47, 153; *Crown Jewel*, 29, 47–49, 127; *Rum and Coca Cola*, 29, 47, 49. See also Beacon; exile; labor movement; migration; romance novels
de Lauretis, Teresa, 90, 110n4
deep structure, 96, 98
Defence of Modern Realism in Fiction. See Peabody, Elizabeth
demotic variant of English, 95
'deportee,' 21
desire, 3, 13, 18, 28, 38, 43, 45, 60, 63, 68, 71, 74, 76, 89, 105, 127, 135–38, 144, 155, 157
diaspora. See African diaspora
Dis Place—The Space Between. See Philip, M. NourbeSe

Discourse on the Logic of Language. See Philip, M. NourbeSe
(dis)location, 19
displacement, 67, 93–94, 114–15, 125, 156–57
dis/placement, 93, 140, 158
domesticity, 46; cult of, 46
Donnell, Allison, 46; consciousness, 139, 149. *See also* cult of; domesticity

Edmondson, Belinda, 17, 20–21, 84n39, 93, 131–32, 141; *Making Men: Gender, Literary Authority and Women's Writing in Caribbean Narrative*, 20. *See also* Black: women's bodies; exile; migration; nationalism
The Emigrants. See Lamming, George
empire, 8, 15, 17, 25, 28, 34, 37–38, 50–51, 57, 59, 62, 64–65, 114–15, 128n1, 132
Enlightenment, 7–8, 11–12
ethnic identity, 42, 64, 141
exile, 1, 3, 15–18, 20–21, 46, 57, 64, 66–67, 76, 78–79, 88, 92–94, 113–15, 128, 131, 140, 149, 153–54, 156
expatriation, 46, 64; ex/patriation, 154; ex/patri/ation, 93

Fanon, Frantz, 73–74, 84n27; *The Wretched of the Earth*, 73
'father tongues,' 96, 98
'fatherland(s),' 16, 59, 62, 64, 72
Female: bodies, 73; identity, 90, 92; sexuality, 18, 21, 61, 91, 127; subjectivity, 16, 18, 88, 93, 113–14, 126, 128, 130n31, 153, 155
femininity, 46, 90, 137, 144
Foucault, Michel, 85n41, 90
Francois, Elma, 41, 47, 49
Frontiers: Essays and Writings on Race and Culture. See Philip, M. NourbeSe

Garvey, Amy, 41; Garvey Movement, 41. *See also* United Negro Improvement Association
gender: constructions, 21, 48; difference(s), 63–65, 75, 79, 141; politics, 64, 127
Gikandi, Simon, 4–5, 22n8; *Writing in Limbo: Modernism and Caribbean Literature*, 4. *See also* anxiety; modernism
Gilroy, Paul, 12, 50; *Against Race: Political Culture Beyond the Color Line*, 12
Glissant, Edouard, 4–7, 29, 109. *See also* cultural, difference; modernity; native informant
globalization, 21, 96, 154, 156
Gomes, Albert, 13, 27, 52n3, 82n3, 154. *See also* Beacon

Heidegger, Martin, 50
Her Chinaman's Way. See Mendes, Alfred
Holder, Boscoe, 15. *See also* exile
'homelands,' 13–14, 18, 20, 59, 79, 89, 115, 134, 154, 157
Hong Wing, 42–45
Hopkinson, Nalo, 18
Hurricane Katrina, 132–35, 150n4, 157. *See also* Black: Americans; *Brown Girl, Brownstones*; migration; refugees
Hurston, Zora Neale, 116–17, 129n6. *See also* Brodber, Erna

Identity: discourses of, 5, 19, 21, 89, 94, 108, 133, 153, 156. *See also* ethnic identity; National, Identity
immigrant(s), 2, 19–21, 52n4, 63, 84n30, 97, 125–26, 131–37, 139–140, 145, 151n8, 154, 156–57
immigration, 3, 20–21, 115, 125, 128, 131, 132, 135, 148
imperial expansion(ism), 11–12
Indo-Caribbean, 141

James, C. L. R., 13, 28, 30, 51, 52n3, 58, 81n3, 88, 90, 128n4, 137, 153, 156; *Triumph*, 28–31, 33–34, 36–37, 41–42, 44. *See also* barrack yard fiction; *Beacon;* nationalist: narratives; obeah; power relations; productive labor; *Trinidad*; Trinidad Renaissance; utility
Jane and Louisa Will Soon Come Home. See Brodber, Erna.

Kant, Immanuel, 8, 11, 53n8, 56n50, 123, 129n18; *Anthropology from a Pragmatic Point of View*, 11. *See also* acts of fiction
King, Christina, 41, 49
Kyke-over-Al, 26

labor movement, 14, 38, 41, 56n45, 146
Lamming, George, 15–17, 21, 23n30, 26–27, 50–51, 57–63, 65–74, 76, 79–81, 82n3, 93, 129, 131, 153; *The Emigrants*, 16; *Of Age and Innocence*, 16; *The Pleasures of Exile*, 16, 57–59, 61–62, 76, 81, 93; *Season of Adventure*, 16; *Water with Berries*, 16–17, 57–58, 61, 63–69, 71–73, 76, 79, 81, 93. *See also* Caliban; displacement; exile; 'fatherland(s)'; migration; nationalism; Nationalist: narratives; *The Tempest*
Literary: discourses, 11, 156; histories, 46; renaissance, 26–28; representation(s), 14, 29, 41, 45–46, 50, 88, 91, 153
Louisiana. See Brodber, Erna

Making Men: Gender, Literary Authority and Women's Writing in Caribbean Narrative. See Edmondson, Belinda
market value, 38, 42
Marshall, Paule, 19, 21, 134, 154; *Brown Girl, Brownstones*, 19, 21, 134–37, 140, 147–48. *See also* migration; nationalism; s/places

masculinist discourse, 17, 80, 88, 93
masculinity, 17–18, 21, 90, 126, 154–56
McClintock, Anne, 2, 4, 63–64, 73, 75. *See also* gender: difference(s)
memory, 3, 78, 95, 115, 120–23, 127, 139, 149
Mendes, Alfred, 13, 21, 25, 27–28, 41–42, 44; *A Commentary*, 25; *Black Fauns*, 29, 49; *Her Chinaman's Way*, 28–29, 41–42. *See also* barrack yard fiction; ethnic identity; market value
Mentor, Ralph, 27
métissage, 96, 104
metropole(s), 20, 29, 61–62, 82n4, 88, 131–32, 156
'middle minority', 27, 41–44, 52n3
migrating subjects, 18
migration, 3, 14–18, 20–21, 59, 89, 114, 125, 132–35, 149, 154–56; intra-Caribbean, 15
mimic, 74, 113,
Miranda, 16, 58, 61, 64–65, 67–68, 71, 73, 76, 81, 132
mistranslations, 146
modernism, 4–6, 22n8
modernity, 4, 6, 12
Myal. See Brodber, Erna

Naipaul, V. S., 9–10, 46, 50, 131
natio, 78
nation, 1–4, 8, 10, 14, 17, 20–21, 22n1, 29, 37–38, 46–49, 62–65, 70, 71, 73, 75–76, 79, 81, 88, 91, 93, 102, 107, 114–15, 125–28, 131–33, 140, 142, 145, 147, 153, 155–56, 158
National: identity, 2, 4, 11, 16–17, 21, 26, 29, 64, 91–93, 126, 136, 157; imagination, 12, 29, 56; literature, 5, 26, 29, 39–40; locations, 3, 155; resistance, 29, 71
nationalism, 4, 16–18, 20–21, 50, 113, 126, 131–32, 140, 148, 156. *See also* Caribbean: nationalism; West-Indian: nationalism

Nationalist: discourse, 10, 19–20, 47, 49, 75–76, 153, 157; literatures, 9, 18, 29, 40, 51, 113, 132; movement(s), 14, 45–46, 50; narratives, 1, 59, 61, 66, 70–71, 80–81, 88, 91–92, 114
'native informant', 6–7
Negro Welfare Social and Cultural Association (NWSCA), 41. *See also* Crick, Daisy; Francois, Elma; King, Christina
Negro World, 41
neocolonial, 2, 68, 71, 77, 141, 156
non-citizens, 135, 156
Nunez, Elizabeth, 19–20, 140–41, 143, 145, 148–149, 151n29, 154; *Beyond the Limbo Silence,* 21, 140, 147–48. *See also* obeah; s/places
Nurse, Malcolm, 27

obeah, 31–33, 44, 53n11, 145, 149
O'Callaghan, Evelyn, 10; *Woman Version: Critical Approaches to West Indian Fiction by Women,* 10
Of Age and Innocence. See Lamming, George
oral histories, 10
Oral Sources and the Creation of a Social History of the Caribbean. See Brodber, Erna
'Other', 7–8, 12, 29, 62, 67, 79–80, 101, 113, 117, 119–20, 123, 127, 132, 140, 145–46
Other Self, 12, 120, 123
Otherness, 10, 12

patois, 44
Peabody, Elizabeth, 39–40; *Defence of Modern Realism in Fiction,* 39
Philip, M. NourbeSe, 1, 3–4, 19, 87. 89–91, 93–98, 101–9; *The Absence of Writing,* 87, 94; *Discourse on the Logic of Language,* 98, 101, 104; *Dis Place—The Space Between,* 87, 89, 90–91, 124; *Frontiers: Essays and Writings on Race and Culture,* 1; *She Tries Her Tongue, Her Silence Softly Breaks,* 19, 93–94, 109. *See also* Caribbean: nationalism; deep structure; demotic variant of English; exile; father tongues; memory; sexuality; s/places; voiced silence
picong, 32, 53n14, 54n23
Political: consciousness, 48, 51, 128, 130n30; economy, 33–34, 38
polyvocular, 89, 109
Postcolonial: literature(s), 6–7; nationalist narratives, 71; nation states, 70, 81; subjects, 2, 15, 59–60, 113, 132, 153; subjectivity, 12
post-Prospero, 7, 57–58, 71, 73, 75–76
power relations, 37, 69, 77, 104, 107
productive labor, 36–37
Prospero, 8, 16, 65–66, 71, 75, 81, 113
The Pleasures of Exile. See Lamming, George

'Quarrel with History,' 5, 7–8, 58, 62, 113
Queen's Royal College, 27. *See also* Carr, Ernest; James, C. L. R.; Lamming, George; Malcolm Nurse; Rienzi, Adrian Cola; Rudranath Capildeo; Williams, Eric

realism, 39–40
Realist: art, 39; narrative, 39; tradition, 39
Reddock, Rhoda, 41, 55n33, 56n45
refugees, 133–34, 157
re(in)forming, 1, 5, 9, 11
repatriation, 3, 17–18, 21, 57, 79, 131
resistance, 29, 45–46, 49, 58, 60–61, 64–66, 71, 73, 76–77, 91, 102, 138, 147
respectability, 43, 49, 148–49
Rienzi, Adrian Cola, 27, 47
romance novels, 49
Rum and Coca Cola. See de Boissière, Ralph

Sander, Reinhard, 28, 33
Season of Adventure. See Lamming, George
self, 4, 12, 57, 62, 66, 93, 96, 113–15, 120, 122–23, 128, 137, 139, 142, 145, 147–48, 153–55, 158
Selvon, Samuel, 15, 50
Sexual: activity, 36; bodies, 127, 137; consciousness, 127; identity, 18, 127; intercourse, 36; minorities, 157; relationships, 72; roles, 73; transgression, 70, 76
sexuality, 29, 38, 63, 67–68, 71, 76–77, 79–80, 89, 92–93, 98, 101, 125, 132, 137, 153, 154; women's, 29. *See also* barrack yard fiction; Female: sexuality
Seymour, A. J., 26.
See also Kyke-over-Al
Shakespeare, William, 8; *The Tempest*, 16, 57–58, 62, 65, 68, 71, 82n8, 83n12
She Tries Her Tongue, Her Silence Softly Breaks. See Philip, M. NourbeSe
'sons of the nation,' 14, 17, 20, 47–48, 63, 88, 140
Spivak, Gayatri Chakravorty, 6–8, 69, 90, 113–14, 149
s/places, 94, 131, 147, 149, 155
subaltern, 69
Sycorax, 16, 58, 66, 71–72, 76

The Tempest. See Shakespeare, William
translocations, 149
transmigration, 3
transmigratory, 5, 119, 121
Trinidad, 13, 25–26, 28–29, 38–39, 41, 48–50, 52n1, 153
Trinidad Renaissance, 14, 25, 29, 30, 40, 51, 53n8, 61, 63, 88, 90, 93, 115, 127, 154

Triumph. See James, C. L. R.

unhomeliness, 21, 114, 132, 135, 142, 145–46
United Negro Improvement Association (UNIA), 41. *See also Negro World*
utility, 37, 54n25

voiced silence, 87, 89, 94–95
'vrai', 8, 23n18, 80, 85n41

Water with Berries. See Lamming, George
West Indian: identity, 12, 15, 25, 28, 146, 153, 155; literature, 27, 59, 82, 156; musical forms, 10; nationalism, 9; women's writing; 10–11
White: female subjects, 70; political power, 135
whiteness, 62, 67–68, 145, 154
Williams, Eric, 27, 58, 88
Woman Version: Critical Approaches to West Indian Fiction by Women. See O'Callaghan, Evelyn
Works Project Administration, 116
WPA narratives, 116–17, 123, 125. *See also* Black: female subjectivity; Black: male subjectivity; Brodber, Erna
The Wretched of the Earth. See Fanon, Frantz
Writing in Limbo: Modernism and Caribbean Literature. See Gikandi, Simon
Wynter, Sylvia, 36–38, 75–77, 80, 81n2. *See also* James, C. L. R; nationalist narratives; 'vrai'

About the Author

Patricia J. Saunders is an assistant professor of English at the University of Miami, Coral Gables where she co-directs the Caribbean Literary Studies Program. She has held appointments at Bowdoin College and has been a visiting scholar at the University of the West Indies, St. Augustine. She is also the co-editor of Music, Memory, Resistance: Calypso and the Caribbean Literary Imagination (Ian Randle Publishers) and the journal Anthurium. Her current research and scholarship focus on the intersections between sexuality, nationalism and the processes of globalization in Caribbean popular culture.

Printed in Great Britain
by Amazon